HELEN
HUNT
JACKSON

Helen Hunt Jackson

by
Evelyn I. Banning

The Vanguard Press

New York

Library of Congress Catalogue Card Number: 73-83038
ISBN 0-8149-0735-0

Designer: Ernst Reichl

Manufactured in the United States of America

For Gladys Banning Barr

Helen of Troy will die,
but Helen of Colorado, never.
"Dear friend, can you walk"
were the last words I wrote her—
"Dear friend, I can fly"—
her immortal reply.

  —*Emily Dickinson*

Contents

Illustrations

Author's Note

THIS BIOGRAPHY of Helen Fiske Hunt Jackson began quite unexpectedly as the result of a brief account I found of her mother, Deborah Waterman Fiske, who had been a student of Mary Lyon and Eunice Caldwell (see author's *Mary Lyon of Putnam's Hill*) at the Adams Female Seminary in Londonderry, New Hampshire, and had been chosen as the girl most suited to present to General Lafayette a bouquet of flowers on his visit to the school on June 24, 1824. I started my research in Helen Fiske's birthplace, Amherst, Massachusetts, and found myself increasingly interested in this young woman, whose novel *Ramona* I once read with great pleasure in my own school days.

Ruth Odell's biography, *Helen Hunt Jackson, H. H.*, served as the beginning reference, and I am in debt to Miss Odell mainly for the unusually extensive bibliography and list of original correspondence in her book. Since its publication in 1939, however, new material has become available, along with letters in Jay Leyda's *The Years and Hours of Emily Dickinson*, Yale University Press, 1960, which the author used extensively.

The author has thus relied completely on research for the facts; no scenes are invented. Everything in the biography is in chronological order and based on historical events. Conversations and thoughts are conveyed in either the direct words of the speaker as taken from original letters or from articles written by or about Helen Jackson or re-created after comments of the biographee as close to the source as possible.

No attempt was made to evaluate critically the writings of Helen Hunt Jackson, as did Miss Odell, but rather the author has tried to present Mrs. Jackson's works in such a way as to allow the reader to judge for himself the quality of her literary style and effectiveness. The book hopes to show the grave concern Mrs. Jackson developed for the American Indian and the contribution her life made on trying to improve the Indians' condition, first with her *A Century of Dishonor* and *Report on the Conditions and Needs of Mission Indians*, and finally with a fictionalized account in *Ramona*.

To locate firsthand information the author has traveled to the places Helen Jackson lived, from New Haven, Connecticut, and Newport, Rhode Island, to Colorado Springs, Colorado, and San Diego County, California. To verify dates and details, the author also visited Ipswich, Amherst, and Falmouth, Massachusetts, Bethlehem and Wolfeboro, New Hampshire, and West Point, New York.

Evelyn I. Banning

New Haven, Connecticut
October, 1972

AUTHOR'S ACKNOWLEDGMENTS The chief source for this book is Helen Hunt Jackson's own writings—her books, poetry and articles, and, most important, her correspondence. I am indebted to Miss Ruth Odell for the extensive bibliography, including the chronological listing of the letters, and to Jay Leyda for his inclusion of Mrs. Jackson's letters and those of her family in his careful coverage of the life and times of Emily Dickinson.

The poems and excerpts of the poems of Helen Hunt Jackson are taken from Helen Jackson's *Poems* (H.H.), published by Roberts Brothers, 1892. "Spurn the Temerity," a poem by Emily Dickinson from the *Complete Poems of Emily Dickinson*, edited by Thomas H. Johnson, Little, Brown and Company, 1960, has been reprinted with the permission of the Harvard University Press.

The letters of Emily Dickinson, and several of Helen Hunt Jackson to Emily Dickinson, are from the *Letters of Emily Dickinson*, edited by Thomas H. Johnson, 1958 and are used with the permission of the Harvard University Press. Yale University Press granted permission to use excerpts of letters from Jay Leyda's *The Years and Hours of Emily Dickinson*, © 1960 by the Yale University Press. Houghton, Mifflin and Company gave the author the rights to use quotes from the letters of John Muir in Bade's *Life and Letters of John Muir*, 1924, of the Reverend D. M. Conway in his *Autobiography*, 1904, and of Thomas Wentworth Higginson in *Carlyle's Laugh and Other Surprises*, 1909, and *Contemporaries*, 1899.

Original letters were used with the permission of the following libraries: the Samuel Bowles Papers, Yale University Library; the Palmer, Fields, Carr, and Ward letters, the Huntington Library, San Marino, California; the Benham letters, the New Hampshire Society, Concord, New Hampshire; the Morse letters, the San Diego Historical Society, Serra Museum and Library; a letter to Mr. Ward from Mrs. Jackson, The New York Public Library, Astor, Lenox, and Tilden Foundations; and the Warner letters, the Watkinson Library, Trinity College, Hartford, Connecticut.

Through Little, Brown and Company clearance was generously granted for the right to quote from *Ramona*, published originally by Roberts Brothers, 1885. Mrs. Helen Hubbell Alger, who handles the estate of Helen Hunt Jackson, gave the author the necessary permission to reprint excerpts from the letters of Mr. and Mrs. Coronel, of Mr. Teller, and of Mr. Kinney that appear in George W. James's *Through Ramona's Country*, 1909.

My thanks are due the many librarians for their unfailing assistance, especially to Norman T. Allen, Recorder, Falmouth Historical Society, Falmouth, Mass.; to Mrs. Elizabeth H. Newton, Curator, Whipple House, Ipswich, Mass.; to Miss Elinor V. Smith, Hadley Historical Society, Hadley, Mass.; to Hollis Broderick, Curator, Wolfeboro Historical Society, Wolfeboro, N.H.; to Mrs. Harlan Clark, Bethlehem Public Library, Bethlehem, N.H.; to Mrs. Gladys E. Bolhouse, Curator, and to Stanley Ward, Newport Historical Society, Newport, R.I.; to Kenneth H. MacFarland, Albany Institute of History and Art, N.Y.; to Mrs. Johannis de Onis, Reference Librarian, U.S. Military Academy, West Point, N.Y.; to Mrs. Katherine A. DeFries, Librarian, and Miss Brenda G. Hawley, Assistant Librarian, Penrose Public Library, Colorado Springs, Colo.; to Miss Dorothy E. Smith, Curator, Pioneers' Museum, Colorado Springs, Colo.; to Donald A. Silva, Librarian, California Room, San Diego Public Library, San Diego, Calif.; and to Mrs. Sue White Hull, the Henry E. Huntington Library, San Marino, Calif.

The author is particularly appreciative of the source material made available at the New Haven Historical Society and of the references at the Yale University Library, including the Samuel Bowles Papers, authorization for the use of which was granted by Miss Judith A. Schiff, Chief Reference Specialist of Manuscripts and Archives.

I would also like to thank Mrs. Josephine Tootill, Historian of the First Congregational Church of Albany, N.Y., for her kind assistance in tracing the records of the Reverend Ray Palmer and family; Mrs. Hattie W. Taylor of Bethlehem, N.H., who shared her knowledge of the early life in the town; Mr. Richmond Curtiss of Guilford, Conn., who freely offered his records of trains and train travel in early Connecticut; Mrs. Faith C. Scott, Alumni Secretary, Vassar College, for information on the Banfield daughters, all four of whom attended Vassar; Dr. Horace Parker, Balboa, Calif., who lived as a young boy in Temecula and brought to life for me the early days of San Diego County and Ramona country; and Miss Helen Jackson, grandniece of Helen Hunt Jackson and oldest daughter of Helen Banfield Jackson, who guided me through the rebuilt portion of Helen Hunt Jackson's Colorado house in the Pioneers' Museum and took me to the site of the Jackson home.

The help and patience of my friend, Evelyn Rose Robinson, were invaluable to the completion of the biography. She encouraged me, listened to the chapters as they were written, read the final manuscript and galley proof, and went wherever my research took me.

To my dear sister in California, Mrs. Gladys Banning Barr, to whom this book is dedicated, I am truly grateful. Not only did she take me over much of the territory Helen Hunt Jackson had traveled in her Indian research, but she also searched out Mrs. Jackson's writings in bookstores, old and new, collecting for my use most of the biographee's works.

Prologue

The life of Helen Hunt Jackson is the story of courage and deep concern for the American Indian. She lived through three wholly distinct periods: first as an army wife, mother, and woman of society; second, as a literary person, a poet and essayist, writer of travel sketches and short stories; and third, as a "Cause" woman, a woman with a mission, something she had said a thousand times she would never be. At the age of fifty-two, she became absorbed in the generous and unselfish purpose of crusading for the Indians, with all the enthusiasm and strength that characterized everything she did from her childhood in the village of Amherst, Massachusetts, to her death in San Francisco, California.

Helen Maria Fiske was a woman of extremes: while she laughed at the world of fashion, she dressed with elegance and was more than adequate in the social position she held after her marriage at twenty-two to an army officer, Lieutenant Edward B. Hunt. But within less than fifteen years she had lost both her sons, one at a year old and the other, her bright and charming Rennie, at the age of nine, and her husband. As the result of her personal loss, she turned to the relief she gained from poetry and wrote out her sorrow.

In her thirties, Helen Fiske Hunt found a creative ability of expression; she became one of the outstanding female American poets of the century, known both at home and abroad. Ralph Waldo Emerson was said to have carried her poems in his pocket to share with friends. Famous as "H.H.," even after her second marriage to William S. Jackson of Colorado Springs, she continued her literary career, frequently returning east for interviews with publishers and for visits with her many friends. Emily Dickinson, also of Amherst and a warm admirer of Helen's, counted her as a friend. In fact, Emily could not but be aware that Helen Hunt Jackson was the only literary contemporary who believed her to be a great poet.

And how accurate her judgment! Emily Dickinson's poetry has stood the test of time, Helen's has not. Her poems, essays and sketches, and most of her fiction have been relegated to the back bookshelves. Today it is her work for the American Indians that is recognized.

Until she heard in October of 1879 about the cruel plight of the Poncas of Nebraska, no other reform held Helen's attention. She had had no sympathy with women's suffrage nor had she taken a stand on the question of slavery. But the tragedy of the Poncas moved her deeply, and the few remaining years of her life were devoted to Indian problems, especially to those of the Mission Indians of Southern California. Without doubt or misgiving, she believed that her best works were her writings on behalf of the Indians, that *A Century of Dishonor* and *Ramona* would last.

To her credit, *Ramona* became a classic soon after it appeared in 1884. And her impassioned book, *A Century of Dishonor*, the early crusade for Indian reform, has been in paperback for the past six years. It is regarded by students of the American Indian as one of the soundest and most exhaustive works on the subject. Although most of Helen Hunt Jackson's life had been spent in pursuits other than championing Indian rights, her contribution in this field has been a lasting one.

Today, almost a hundred years later, at a time when there is renewed interest in the civil rights of the American Indian, Mrs. Jackson's name ranks high among the crusaders. For in a period of four years before her death in 1885, she had aroused the country to the Indians' plight. About her Allan Nevins wrote, "We can point to her as eloquent evidence that at one period of our history a large body began to be ashamed. And if her writings lacked constructive qualities they were not devoid of vision."

The vision of Helen Hunt Jackson has enriched Americans. She well deserves a place in the annals of American literature of the nineteenth century if for no other reason than for her dedication to the rights of the native American Indian.

Helen
Hunt
Jackson

1

A Madcap

"You ARE TO GO up to the attic right this minute, Helen Maria, and stay there until I come for you."

Stern and uncompromising, her father looked down at her over his glasses, and six-year-old Helen knew tears would be useless. Nor could she explain to him the excitement of her adventure with Mary Snell. For even her mother had scolded her, though she had argued, "Oh, Mother, I've had a perfectly splendid time."

There was nothing to do but leave her father's study; without a word, she stamped out and climbed the attic stairs. How she wished he had given her a spanking, even a hard one, instead of the long lecture that preceded his punishment. She hated the attic where there was nothing but old boxes and trunks and piles of newspapers and magazines. She kicked the stool near the dormer window and then sat down on the floor. For the first time since she had walked into the house at a quarter to ten the night before, she cried.

All the pleasures of the walk through the woods to Hadley, Massachusetts seven miles away, had suddenly faded. She began to wish she had listened to her mother and gone home when the Academy bell rang. But the April morning was bright and seemed to beckon her on. It was spring, and treasures were to be found in Baker's woods, a pine grove with Indian pipes and checkerberries.

But Helen wasn't allowed to sit and cry for long. Her mother arrived almost at once with an armful of cloth. "You can hem these pillowcases and towels," she said. "The money you earn will help pay for the repairs on Mr. Hitchcock's buggy."

In the drive out over the rough muddy roads to look for the two little "lost" girls, Professor Edward Hitchcock's horse had somehow become skittish and in fright had upset the buggy. Luckily no one was injured, but there was some damage to the wagon.

To Helen it hadn't seemed like running away and surely she could have found her way back without all the fuss. And Mary was as much to blame as she was. Now the whole town knew about her escapade. The town bells had been rung, college suspended, and students and professors had gone out searching for her and Mary.

When night came, her father escorted Helen from the attic to her own bedroom, where each night he read to her a passage from the Bible. Then Mother came in to put her to bed. But three-year-old Annie was not permitted to play with her, and her cat Midge was kept in the cellar. It seemed a long three days.

Nathan Welby Fiske, Professor of Languages at Amherst College, had hoped for a son that October of 1830, for the baby boy born the year before had lived but a few weeks. But when he looked down into the cradle at the smiling face and bright eyes of his daughter, he forgot his longing for a son. The next morning, October 15,[1] he wrote his wife's Aunt Martha Vinal that Dr. Isaac G. Cutler had delivered their daughter, Helen Maria, "whose voice was heard last evening about half past eleven. Dr. Cutler . . . and Mrs. Hitchcock were at hand in good season, but we have been taught by severe experience to rejoice with trembling. ...."

The christening was delayed until spring, when the unheated church would be less chilly. Helen was, therefore, not baptized until May 8, 1831, probably the cause of the error in her official birth record. A sturdy and heavy infant, she grew rapidly, laughing easily. Even at Chapel services, she laughed and crowed boisterously at the singing. She seldom cried.

While Deborah Fiske, Helen's mother, had to live carefully within the annual income of eight hundred dollars, the professor's salary in the 1830s, the Fiskes enjoyed their neighbors and were considered a happy and generous couple. With Jacob Abbott, Professor of Mathematics and Natural Philosophy, Professor Fiske was working on a new Bible-class book. The Fiskes worked hard, Nathan getting up at five in the morning for prayers at the College and hearing three recitations daily in addition to his lectures. Deborah took in four boarders to balance the budget. But there was always room for Grandfather Vinal, who arrived often from Boston to visit his only child. He had helped her move from the Thayers' small cottage on Oak Grove to the Tyler home near Lessey Street, where Helen was born. And later, on his return to Boston, he shipped back to Deborah a dining-room set and her "pianoforte" she had longed to have in her own home.

Despite housework and the care of the baby, Mrs. Fiske found time to attend the weekly Sewing Society and prayer meetings. But in August of 1832, seven months pregnant, she left two-year-old Helen in the care of Aunt Maria Fiske of Weston, Massachusetts, and "fled to Cousin Martha Hooker in Lanesboro, to escape the added duties of Commencement."

Two months later, the Fiskes rejoiced in the birth of a son, born October 16. Baby Heman Humphrey, "Humpy" to his doting sister, was soon renamed and christened Humphrey

Washburn Fiske. In contrast to Helen, the baby caused no trouble and was shown off with pride. Deborah insisted on taking sole care of him.

But in early September, both Helen and the baby came down with severe attacks of whooping cough. Even the best efforts of Dr. Timothy J. Gridley failed, and Deborah and Nathan grieved to watch their son slip into unconsciousness. At last Deborah wrote Aunt Martha of her heartache, "I have everything that heart can desire but the lives of my children. I ought to bear it with cheerful submission when God sees fit to take them to Himself...."

But it was a heavy task to accept with submission. Her beloved son died within a few days, less than a year old, on September 19, 1833. And Helen lay in bed with high fever. Throughout the long night her father sat at her bedside, sometimes holding her in his arms to rock and soothe her. When the fever broke in early daylight, he sat with tears streaming down his face, relieved of his worry. Helen would recover.

Though Mrs. Fiske had never wanted anyone else to look after her son, she needed help with Helen. She invited thirteen-year-old Martha Vinal of Boston, Massachusetts, to come in the spring of 1834. She could attend the popular school, Amherst Female Academy, run by Miss Hannah White. Miss White was an intimate friend of Mary Lyon, with whom Deborah had studied at Adams Female Seminary in Londonderry, New Hampshire. And Hannah's school was nearby, in the upper part of Mack's Hall on the corner of Pleasant and Main Streets.

Hannah's younger sister Mary taught "young craft" in a separate room, and there Helen could go. Each morning she would walk to school with Martha, to—it was hoped—"learn her letters." It was such a memorable summer that Helen wrote Martha, after her cousin's return to Boston, sending her a "little bag to keep threads in." She said, "I think you was very good to lead me to school all last summer. . . . I have got through the first part of Mamma's lessons. Papa says I am getting along well, and that Ma had better keep on with her school than to send me to Sarah Baker this winter. . . . You will know that this is not my writing; Ma writes all my letters because I do not know how."

A year after Humpy's death, Mr. Fiske decided to move nearer the College, and located a larger home on South Pleasant Street, one house away from the Hitchcocks. And it was here on a snowy Christmas morning in 1834 that Ann Scholfield Fiske was born, the sister Helen so wanted. It was a difficult birth, and Mrs. Fiske had to remain in bed for a few weeks.

Helen loved her sister dearly and hugged her tightly whenever her mother or father weren't looking. She jumped rope, dressed in any old clothes she could find, and at the most unexpected times would leap out from behind a door. Ann was excited by Helen's "frolics," but they often annoyed her parents—she never seemed to know when to stop. She laughed when scolded, and her favorite answer was, "It's all nonsense," a remark she had heard her father make.

At times she was allowed to go over to the Dickinson Mansion on Main Street to play with Emily. Emily Elizabeth Dickinson, born December 10, 1830, two months before Helen, was a frail girl with bright auburn hair and large dark eyes, a contrast to chubby tow-haired Helen, who was a dynamo of energy, willful and impulsive. But despite their differences, they shared many pleasures and pranks and many a secret. They had happy times together, putting on plays in the old barn and, on hot summer days, lying under the syringa bushes telling each other tales of adventure.

The visits were usually arranged in advance by a note to Mrs. Dickinson from Helen's mother. And her father would take time to drive over in their small buggy and call for her if the Dickinson "family man" was too busy. "If not convenient to send her home," her mother wrote one August day, 1836, "he will call for her in the chaise before nightfall, before the dew falls. . . ."

Under no circumstances could five-and-a-half-year-old Helen be trusted to come right home. There was always too much to explore and enjoy along the way down Pleasant Street. But at home it was Grandfather Vinal who took her side. And it was he who always came to her defense. She was never to forget the Christmas party for cats at the Ferrys. The elderly Ferry sisters had invited Helen to a Christmas Eve party. "You will bring your cat," the invitation read.

For days she had planned for the party, making the paper ruff that had been required for her cat Midge. Now she wondered if she could go. Heavy snow had been falling all morning and by noon the wind had pushed drifts against the stone steps at the front door. Helen could usually see the South Common and the stately tower in College Row from her window, but not today. The back pasture looked like a white carpet.

Hurrying downstairs, she rushed toward her grandfather. "Do you think I can go in this weather?" she asked breathlessly. "Will you take me?"

"Of course I'll take you, my madcap. Midge won't want to miss the fun," he answered, his eyes twinkling.

"Oh, Grandpapa, thank you, thank you." And she threw her arms around his neck, hugging him. Unlike her father, Grandfather couldn't refuse Helen anything she wanted. "She's a real Vinal," he would say to his son-in-law. "She'd charm the birds right out of the sky."

Mr. Fiske didn't agree. "Helen needs a firm hand. She's a madcap, if that is what you mean."

It was not easy for Mr. Fiske to understand his daughter's gaiety and easy laughter, so unlike his younger child, quiet, shy Ann. And Helen, when a grown woman, would find it hard to forget the time her father called her a "stupid child" in front of strangers when she brought him a wrong book from his study. He complained when Grandfather gave Helen a five-dollar gold piece after he had scolded her for not wanting a tooth pulled. And many times he grumbled to his wife that her father used money too freely and loved good brandy better than he ought.

But the summer of 1836 was a memorable one for Helen. For the first time, her father thought her old enough to go with him to visit his family in Weston, Massachusetts. They traveled—just the two of them—the entire distance of ninety miles east, in their own carriage with Charlie harnessed carefully. "If the trip was one of the most pleasant things that ever happened to me," Helen said many years later, "the only drawback was my concern over my best blue dress that had been packed in the little leather valise and hung by straps underneath the carriage. I was sure I would lose it." But the dress withstood the journey and Helen wore it every day during the visit. And every day she had a newsy letter from Midge, dictated by pussy but written by her mother. These she tucked into her apron pocket and these she would keep all her life.

During her absence, Midge—a strange name for a Tomcat—had fallen into a barrel of soft soap and Grandfather had even shared some of his brandy to warm the pussy and had cared for him, placing him in the old cradle. But Midge never quite recovered, losing the sight of one eye. He finally grew so old and slow that even Mrs. Fiske said it would be a mercy to put the cat out of his misery. He no longer followed Helen to school, and she had to carry him upstairs for the night.

And then it happened. Cousin Josiah Stearns, who was living with the Fiskes while attending college, drowned Midge in Mill Valley Pond. Helen was furious. "But we told him he could . . ." her mother tried to explain.

"I don't believe it. I'll never speak to him again as long as I live, so there." And she deliberately ignored Josiah during supper and went upstairs to bed early, without saying good night to anyone. If only Grandfather had come back from his Boston trip!

In the morning she made up her mind. She would speak to Josiah just once more. And running up to him at the breakfast table, she shook her tight fist in his face and cried, "I said I'd never speak to you as long as I live, but I will. You're a murderer, that's what you are. And when you get to be a missionary, I hope the cannibals will eat you—raw—you mean old murderer."

Her father's face red with anger, he shook Helen and said, "Helen Maria, you can leave the room this instant."

She looked over at her mother, apparently too shocked to say anything. And stamping her feet at Josiah, she turned and left the room, muttering to herself all the way upstairs, "He ought to be drowned."

Although her father forced an unwilling apology the next day, she never forgave Josiah and never spoke to him if she could avoid it. Her gentle mother tried in every way to help her strong-willed daughter grow more forgiving. "You will need to try harder," she would insist. "You can't like everyone, but you can be polite."

Often troubled by Helen's strong likes and dislikes, Mrs. Fiske would spend hours talking with Helen about manners and frequently played a game of pretense with her at a make-believe party or tea. Helen loved the games, but she had a "passion for stories," even though she was, according to a neighbor, "an everlasting talker." At night after her mother had told the girls a bedtime story, Helen would beg for more. "Tell that ag'in, Ma," was a frequent request.

Throughout the winter of 1836 and well into the spring, Mrs. Fiske was under almost constant doctor's care. She tired easily, and Dr. Gridley suggested a trip east by herself. Finally realizing that her strength was not equal to the demands of the household, and with her husband's approval, she packed her bags and left to spend a month with the Vinals in Boston. Aunt Martha had been mother to her and the Otis Vinals, who became her family at her mother's death when she was barely two years old. Her father, a lumber merchant and contractor, lived near his business in the city and visited Deborah often; out of his deep love for her he saw that she had everything she needed or wanted. To Helen the absence of her mother seemed long, and she was overjoyed at her return. Again she could study with her at home.

Actually Helen learned more rapidly than her quiet sister, but she was hard to handle and, on occasion, petulant. Though she adored being with her mother, she was an impatient reader, skipping unfamiliar words or substituting for them words she thought must mean the same thing. To Cousin Martha Hooker, her mother wrote in April, "Helen learns very well, but I do not drive her very much to make her very literary—she is quite inclined to question the author of everything; the Bible she says does not feel as if it were true...."

So there came a time when Mrs. Fiske lost patience with Helen and, finding her too energetic and impatient, had to plan for her to study away from home. Most faculty children went to the Nelson's School up the street, and there Helen was eventually sent. The Nelson girls, Emily and Julia, had turned their home, formerly a shoemaker's shop, into a private school for young children. The Snells, the Hitchcocks, as well as the Dickinsons, sent their children there. Edward Hitchcock, Junior, recalled years later that "Annie was a tender little girl, but Helen was tough and hardy, and would wrestle any time or anybody...."

Her mother tried quite unsuccessfully to instill in her a meek and quiet manner. "Ann does not require the vigilance Helen does," she wrote Aunt Martha, "she is honest, artless, and affectionate—telling the whole of everything right out ... while Miss

Helen has no idea of liking 'all those folks' nor of telling the whole of everything . . . ; but I love them alike and quite enough."

A gift a few weeks later from Aunt Martha, a subscription to the *Youth's Companion*, helped 'Miss' Helen forget her disappointment in not studying with her mother. And while Mrs. Fiske looked over the *Boston Recorder*, she had her own magazine to read. In it she discovered a new world beyond home and school, a world of excitement she was never to lose.

2

A Second Home

THAT JULY MORNING of 1840 when Mr. Fiske walked with his nine-year-old daughter up South Pleasant Street to Amity Street and enrolled her at Amherst Academy [1] was a memorable one for Helen. She would no longer have to study Latin with her demanding father, and there would be no more "bad reports" from the Nelsons to upset her mother. How often had she heard her parents complain that she did not study very much and only had "good times" at school!

It would be different at the Academy, and it was. A special student under the supervision of Miss Mary Maynard, she had no time to fool during school hours, and by August had to drop her music lessons because her studying "took nearly all her time."

Helen might have liked to stay on at the Academy, especially since Emily Dickinson and her younger sister Lavinia were going to be there in September—Helen had seen less of Emily since the Dickinson family had moved from the Mansion the year before into a large wooden house on North Pleasant Street. But the Fiskes were dissatisfied with the school, even though Miss Maynard would continue as head of the girls' section. They thought the over-all discipline too lax to risk sending Helen full-time.

Reluctantly she went back to the Nelsons with Annie, and although she promised to apply herself to her studies, the reading lessons bored her and she quickly fell into her old habits of whispering and playing. She simply enjoyed life too much to reform, and her mother finally felt compelled to try teaching her at home again. Helen had clearly outgrown the Nelson's School.

Though Mrs. Fiske still tired easily, she never denied her girls a chance to have their friends to play with. On Saturday afternoons they usually had a party in the Fiske kitchen, with Helen and Annie serving tea in real cups, or at Jane Gridley's house, where lemonade and caraway cookies were served.

When Mr. Fiske was away on college business, the girls had special parties. On November 26, 1840, Thanksgiving Day, the Snell girls were over for tea, which Helen poured from her own tea set. The girls were allowed to wait on themselves, taking turns at the head of the table. And then came the best day of all, Friday, December 4, when Mrs. Fiske opened the parlor for a party. Helen and Annie invited their Sabbath-school class and some neighbors for a two o'clock party. They played checkers, put together paper puzzles, tried their skill at battledore, and, best of all, sat down for supper at the long table in the sitting room, all fourteen of them.

And two days later Mrs. Fiske wrote her husband, "I decided before your letter came not to send Helen to Miss Nelson, partly on account of the Academy vacation, during which some of Mr. Gale's pupils visit Miss Nelson's School and partly because my voice has gained some strength. . . ."

When Mr. Fiske returned home, it was agreed that Helen should be sent to Hopkins Academy in Hadley [2] the following summer.

Though Hadley was only seven miles away, Helen was unhappy at school and her studies showed little progress. Her mother, ill most of the winter, wrote Aunt Martha in a kind of desperation about Helen's schooling. And soon after the term at

Hopkins ended and Helen was home for the holidays, Mrs. Fiske broke the news to her daughter. "Your father and I have made up our minds not to send you back to Hopkins. Instead you are to live with Aunt Martha Vinal in Charlestown and go to Miss Austin's school there." The Vinals had recently moved from their Boston home to one of the new brick houses at 5 Harvard Street in Charlestown across the Charles River.

Mrs. Fiske hesitated a moment and added, "Your cousin Sarah Hooker from Falmouth, Massachusetts will be there, too, and you can go to school with her."

Helen listened with as much patience as she could muster while her father gave her many directives for good and proper behavior. "We are depending on you to do what your aunt asks and not give her any trouble," counseled her father. "And write your mother every day."

Mrs. Fiske's eyes filled with tears, but she knew of no other choice. Her health, instead of improving, was getting worse. "If only Helen were older," she thought, and she worried about her daughter, not quite twelve. "She may be too much for Aunt Martha, but she will love her, I know—as I do." To Helen she said, "You may take along your games to share with Sarah Hooker and the girls and your knitting."

Homesick at first, Helen quickly adjusted to life within the large family. She was all her parents could have wished, even attending Sunday school when her mother wrote that she wanted her to do so. Cousin Sarah from Falmouth, two years older, became Helen's constant companion. They were allowed to take trips after school to Cambridge and at times to Boston.

In Boston, the girls frequently visited Grandfather Vinal on Russell Place and the Scholfields at 47 Pinckney Street near the Common. Mr. Scholfield, formerly a wool manufacturer in England, had married Aunt Martha's sister and had set up a store on Market Street, where fashionable ladies bought imported

British piece goods, fine alpaca and Tibetan merino. Helen delighted in visits to his store. Occasionally they went to see her father's relatives, the Stearns, and when Priscilla and Ellen were home, they would go window-shopping together.

One day Helen went with Sarah to an Indian camp behind Medford Hill in Malden, five miles north of Boston. "I wished very much Ann was there," Helen wrote, describing the scene in complete detail, the four tents, the "baby cradle," and the women strangely dressed with men's hats and a "great deal of red" about their persons. She especially admired the woven baskets the women were making. "They were all as busy as bees making baskets. I had no money with me or I would have bought Ann one. . . ."

Though pleased to receive a box of clothes for her birthday, Helen was disappointed to learn that her father and Annie wouldn't come for a Thanksgiving visit. Her mother was too ill to leave at home alone. Now she could hardly wait for the quarter to end. It was her mother she missed most of all.

Since the doctor required Mrs. Fiske to spend most of the day in bed, or at least upstairs in her room, Helen pressed her father for permission to stay at home to help and not go away again to school. Though he gave in with some reluctance, it was her mother who strongly objected to the loss of schooling for her bright daughter. And on May 3, 1843, she had her registered at the Young Ladies' Seminary in Pittsfield,[3] Massachusetts. It was only fifty miles from Amherst, and her father could go and get her within a day if necessary.

Here she became an outstanding student, and wrote of "a change of heart." She told her mother about her favorite teacher, a Miss Lincoln, with whom she roomed. But on her return home at term's end, Helen could not bring herself to plan for the fall season, even though she had promised Miss Lincoln she would finish the course. One look at her mother and the idea of going back no longer seemed important.

Deborah Fiske now weighed less than ninety pounds and was too frail to carry any of the burden of the home. She spent most of the day either in bed or propped up in a chair by the window, needing more care than Helen and a maid could give her. Finally, Grandfather Vinal was sent for, and Helen turned to him for comfort and advice.

Annie, not quite nine years old, was still attending the Nelson's School. She read her lessons to her mother every afternoon in the quiet house while Helen often went over to have tea with Orra Hitchcock. Concerned about Annie's need to have playmates, Mrs. Fiske arranged for visits to her friends.

With her grandfather's help, Helen looked after her younger sister and on Christmas Day, 1843, delivered a note her mother had asked her to send to Mrs. Dickinson. "If convenient," she wrote, "Ann may visit Emily and Lavinia this afternoon. It is her birthday and I had intended to let her invite your two daughters and two or three other girls, but I am too feeble to bear any noise of playing...."

Ann, nine years old that Christmas, was a "dear friend" of Lavinia Dickinson, "Vinnie," and a birthday without a visit was unthinkable. But Helen at thirteen could not be spared from her mother's bedside. Nor would she have gone, for she knew her mother was dying of consumption—she had nagged Dr. Gridley until he had told her. After that, she was never far away from her mother's room, helping with the letters and greeting visitors her mother had asked to see.

Before another spring, Deborah Fiske had succumbed to the dread disease, now known as tuberculosis. On February 19, 1844, at the age of thirty-eight, Deborah Waterman Vinal Fiske died. Two days later she was buried in the Scholfield plot, Mt. Auburn cemetery, in Cambridge, Massachusetts.

Nathan Fiske in his silent grief did what he thought his wife would have wished. He sent ten-year-old Ann back with her grandfather to live with the Vinals, drove Helen to Pittsfield to finish out the course at the seminary, and stayed alone in the empty house. But Helen missed her "good and wise" mother, and when her father closed the house in Amherst to go east, she felt cut off from everyone she knew and loved.

At the seminary, Helen became so reserved and unresponsive in her classes that her father was notified that she was "quite un-well." And four days later he found her "in a state of unhappy nervous irritation, greatly affecting her mind and spirits." With-out hesitation he withdrew her and on August 1, after two weeks with him in Amherst, he thought her well enough for a trip to Charlestown. There she would stay a month with Annie and then go to live with the Hookers in Falmouth on Cape Cod.

If Helen wanted to stay with Annie and the Vinals, she made no objection to her father's plans for her. He had promised his wife he would board her with the Hookers as soon as she had finished at the seminary. The Hookers had left Lanesboro for the Cape in 1837, when the Reverend Henry B. Hooker ac-cepted a call to the First Church and Society in Falmouth, Mas-sachusetts.

So, when the month was up, Helen rode off contentedly with her grandfather to take the Sandwich-Falmouth coach. She hugged him hard and climbed into the stagecoach. "I'll be back soon, Gramp," she said, wiping away the tears that sprang to her eyes.

As the coach rolled along on that clear September morning, she sat quietly, scarcely aware of the change of scenery. She wouldn't cry. She would take care of herself. Fourteen-year-old Helen had grown up.

And as the weeks went by she grew to think of the Hooker parish home on Palmer Street as her own. She missed Sarah

Hooker, still living with her aunt in Charlestown, but Ann Eliza-beth was a pleasant companion. Though only six months older than Helen, Ann seemed even more grown up than her sister Sarah. With Ann, Helen registered at the Falmouth Academy,[4] May 6, 1845, as a day student. But, unlike Ann, she listed herself as a "resident of Amherst."

Helen wrote to her father, though less often than he wished, and to her Amherst friends, especially to Emily Dickinson, who called her "my prodigal H."[5] It is unfortunate that the corre-spondence between Emily and Helen during these years has never been located. It presumably went the way of most of Emily's letters that her younger sister Lavinia found after her death: they were burned. But the envelopes addressed to Helen make it clear that a correspondence existed between them, and even Lavinia later mentioned that Emily wrote Helen in her up-stairs bedroom by candlelight after the rest of the family had gone to bed.

The days at Falmouth went by too rapidly for many letters, however. With the Hooker family there were trips around the Cape, one to Sandwich, where she saw the famous glassworks. Years later, in Murano, Italy, Helen would be reminded of the glass-blowing in Sandwich, where she had watched the artisans blow glass bottles, drawing out long hollow threads of fiery glass and snapping them off like pipestems.

Berrying on the Quisset Hills and walks in search of wild spring flowers would be long remembered. Helen went at times with the Reverend Mr. Hooker to the Falmouth Landing to watch the Barnstable fishermen as they came ashore with the day's catch. And often she walked across the Green to the Fal-mouth shore, where she wandered along the beach, watching the waves break on the sand. On a clear day she could see across the Sound to Martha's Vineyard and the Elizabeth Islands, and she may well have imagined the joy of taking one of the paddle-wheeled steamers from New Bedford to faraway Nantucket.

On one of his last visits to Falmouth, her father had arranged with the Hookers to send Helen to Ipswich academy as soon as she had completed the course at Falmouth. He had originally talked of sending her to Mount Holyoke, but Helen would have none of it. "Imagine," she wrote her cousin Ann in Boston, "going to learn how to make hasty pudding and clean gridirons. What sort of figure do you think I shall cut washing floors before breakfast and cleaning stew pans after dinner?"

Although Helen had no strong desire to leave her second home, she could not oppose her father. Besides, Ipswich Female Seminary was but half a day's journey by coach from Boston, and the principal, Mrs. Cowles, formerly Eunice Caldwell, had been a classmate of her mother's at the Adams Seminary in New Hampshire. Mr. Fiske felt satisfied to place Helen under the supervision of a woman he could personally trust.

Meanwhile she would spend Commencement Week in Amherst with her sister Annie and her father. Commencement, usually scheduled for the first Thursday in August, was a social event in the village. Actually, it followed four days of celebration attended by all the neighboring clergy, returned missionaries, graduates, and dignitaries. Like all professors and outstanding citizens of Amherst, Mr. Fiske held Open House, and friends and students dropped in to talk and to meet former classmates as well as parents of the graduating class. Supper was "handed about" and Helen and Ann helped with the serving, making their father's home alive for the first time since their mother's long illness and death.

But by the next August, Mr. Fiske was no longer able to hold an Open House. His health had begun to fail over the winter months, and he suffered from a former illness—weakness of the lungs, according to his doctor. A final examination in September of 1846 brought the verdict: no more college teaching for the present and a sea trip for complete relaxation, preferably to a warmer climate. He wasted no time, and on September 26 he taught his last class at Amherst College. Nine days later he sailed from New York Harbor with the Reverend Eli Smith, who was returning to his missionary station in Beirut, Lebanon.

For Helen, although her home was still with the Hookers, she again listed herself as an Amherst resident that November at Ipswich academy. A member of the Middle class, she elected perspective drawing and three languages, Latin, French, and German. "But it is a dull, dull village," she wrote Annie, and told her that the girls were "marched up and down the streets in tiresome procession, with nothing better to do than to flirt with male students."

Helen missed her "Falmouth family," but, most of all, she missed her freedom. She thought, too, of the neat cottages on the Cape and in comparison Ipswich seemed "untidy and huddled. . . . In some of the streets, you see nothing but these gray and brown houses, built with high slanting roofs and the upper storey jutting out over the lower, while as you walk along by these specimens of antiquity you see no one, in, around, or about them but old men, old women, old cats, old dogs . . ." she complained to her cousin Ann.

But to her sister she wrote soon after returning from her April vacation, "I have made up my mind to study and try to enjoy myself here. . . . I now have a friend Lizzie [Ordway], who rooms with me, and together we keep things in some kind of order. . . . My love to you. I'll see you in October between terms. . . ." The letter was signed, as always, "Your naughty sister."

But Helen was called back to Charlestown in early July, for Aunt Martha had received the sad news from the Reverend G. B.

Whiting in Mt. Lebanon: Mr. Nathan Welby Fiske had died in Jerusalem, May 27, 1847.

The loss of her father did not affect Helen so deeply as had that of her mother. She even felt somehow content that he had reached the Holy City he had longed to see. He would be buried at Mt. Zion near the tomb of David.

She took the letter to her room and reread it carefully. She was grateful that Mr. Whiting had been kind enough to describe in detail her father's last days and, in particular, the trip they had made together down the coast of Mt. Carmel to the Plain of Sharon.

Back in Ipswich in October, Helen finally dropped the Amherst address and listed Charlestown as home. She continued in the Middle class for the year and could have stayed on for her third and senior year to earn a diploma had she wanted to, but the lure of New York City proved too enticing. Mr. John Abbott, brother of her father's old friend Jacob, invited her to attend their institute and live with his family on Lafayette Place.

"I'll write you often," Helen promised Lizzie, "and I do hate to leave you, but I'm eighteen this month and Grandfather gave me his permission."

Soon after her father's death, Grandfather Vinal, as expected, assumed the guardianship of his two granddaughters and had a will drawn up on October 4, 1847, to take care of them until his death. He made out a trust fund for them and appointed the Reverend Mr. Julius Palmer of Boston as executor of his will and as trustee and guardian of Helen and Ann.

"I'm really happy for you, Helen,—and I'll write, too," answered Lizzie. Then she added with a smile, "You know you're lucky to have such a wonderful grandfather."

Helen agreed without hesitation. And she boarded the coach out of Ipswich for Boston. Except for a wave to Lizzie, who had come to see her off, Helen never looked back.

From October of 1848 to February, 1849, she stayed with her sister at the Vinals. The days were busy with trips and shopping, and Ann helped in the choice of dress goods: cotton and gingham for school and green silk enough for a best dress for both of them. Then Helen bought a cashmere shawl, dark brown, and matching hat and gloves.

When the silk dresses were finished, Helen and Ann had their pictures taken, daguerreotypes, a gift for Grandfather. While they tried to look alike, both with their hair smoothed down and parted flat and both wearing a velvet ribbon at the throat, the difference was striking. "As unlike as two nations," Mr. Fiske used to say of his daughters, for Annie was always more petite than Helen.

As a last trip together, the girls climbed to the top of Bunker Hill monument as soon as the snow had cleared. There they saw that the *Royal Mail* from England had broken through the ice. It would be safe now for Helen to take the boat out of Boston Harbor. On February 7, 1849, she boarded the schooner *Eastern Light* for New York City.

3

Lafayette Place,
New York City

IT WAS LIKE entering a whole new world. The harbor at New
York was alive with boats. Schooners and sailboats whistled
shrilly as they came into dock, and upriver at Pier 9 was the largest ship Helen had ever seen, the *Atlantis*, just in from Liverpool,
England.

Every kind of carriage rolled along the harborside over the
wide cobblestones: fashionable phaetons, two-wheeled gigs,
hackney cabs. Crossing the main street on foot for a cab was an
adventure for Helen, but she laughed with the excitement of
it all and could hardly wait for the driver to let down the steps
for her.

Mr. Abbott had the cab driven to the Battery so that Helen
might see Castle Garden, the old circular fort where Lafayette's
gala reception had been held in 1824, then up busy Broadway
to Astor Place and south to No. 53 Colonnade Row on Lafayette
Place. The mansions were more strikingly beautiful than she
could have imagined. Ironwork on the steps with the traditional
pineapples of hospitality caught her attention. She would recall
them years later in Newport, Rhode Island.

Colonnade Row—or La Grange Terrace, as it was known
after an estate of the Marquis de Lafayette—was to be Helen's
home for a year at least. Here John and Jane Abbott and their

family, three sons and a daughter, lived, and here they boarded "young ladies." At nearby No. 45, the Abbotts held their school under the direction of Jacob Abbott. All the Abbott brothers, Gorham, Charles, and Samuel, as well as John and Jacob, eventually joined in this educational enterprise. It was indeed an Abbott Institution.

With nineteen-year-old Jennie Abbott to help, Helen unpacked her things and went down to supper with the family, eager to do her share in the large household. It was the year of the Gold Rush, and Helen had heard talk on the boat trip about the gold of California. "Is California part of the country?" she asked Mr. Abbott.

"Yes, indeed. American settlers claimed California as United States territory a few years ago, but it was only last February that Mexico ceded claim to it by treaty," he explained, adding, "And what is your interest in California?"

"I've heard so much talk about the West that I just wondered about it. But I'll not be going tomorrow," she said, tossing her head and breaking into easy laughter. She was at home with the Abbotts.

The New York papers carried long listings of boats headed for the gold regions. Those in a hurry could take passage by ship to Greytown (now San Juan del Norte), Nicaragua, where they would cross the Isthmus jungles by mules, wagon, and boat to San Juan del Sur. On the western side, they would then take another ship up the coast to San Francisco, a journey of a little under four weeks.

Helen was fascinated by the "Ho, California" column in the morning *New York Herald*. First-class packets and schooners would depart daily, each departure offering special advantages, vying for fast sailing time around the Cape. And Californians had arrived in New York in great numbers from the West, exchanging gold for goods to take back or send back by steamer.

Even the advertisement of the Christy's Minstrels advised these Californians to take advantage of their gay performances.

The middle of the nineteenth century in New York City forecast the role of the theater. Every day Helen read of the many plays and programs. In early February, there were the following listed: "Monte Cristo," a smash hit at the Broadway, "Vanity Fair" at Burton's, and "Boadicea" at the Bowery. Helen wondered what it would be like to see a play or even the Christy's Minstrels. But the theater was still frowned upon by many, and Helen dared not ask the Abbotts to take her. With or without permission, however, she and Jennie often went into the shops, walking home through Washington Square and down Broadway.

They looked at the dress goods in Bond's on Sixth Avenue and occasionally went into Stewart's down on the corner of Chambers Street, the most famous dry-goods store in the city. On Broadway they would stop at Dean's, which sold the best molasses candy in town. Once they wandered as far downtown as Arnold and Constable's on Canal Street, an elegant shop with satins, silks, and velvet, patronized by what to Helen seemed the best-dressed women. She admired the bonnets and hats, looking longingly at a gray beaver bonnet faced with cherry-colored satin.

For Helen, the Abbott Institute was "the best and happiest" of her school days. Studying became a pleasure instead of tedious labor. There were no rules except that of quiet during study hours and no punishment for minor infractions; through a system of self-government, the students enforced their own discipline. Helen thrived under this arrangement and earned the reputation of being a "scholar."

Then, too, the Abbotts believed in having outdoor exercises and walked on what Mr. John Abbott called "sprees," often on the spur of the moment, according to the weather. The sprees were usually on Saturday after the midday dinner. In late March, Helen wrote to her sister Annie, telling of their many trips to the Battery, where they enjoyed the water "sparkling in the sun" and where they took a little steamboat and sailed four times across the river.

"We took a roundabout way home, by the wharves where all the steamboats and packets lay, and reached No. 53, our dear pleasant home, at about six o'clock."

Helen was becoming a true New Yorker. She loved her travels with the Abbotts. How exciting to see the operations of a printing press they visited, to walk into the slums of the Five Point Region, or to go to the Tombs, where criminals were tried and confined! They also visited art galleries and museums, including the famous Barnum's American Museum, where she saw the midget, General Tom Thumb, and even the great Chinese Museum on Broadway between Spring and Prince Streets. Thirty years later, when she came back to New York to work in the Astor Library, Helen would be reminded of these days. Opened in 1854, the library would be located opposite the Abbott Institute, and would contain a hundred thousand volumes, the nation's largest collection. (Today it is the home of the New York Shakespeare Theater.)

By the end of March, the Abbott brothers decided to move their school for young ladies to the west side of Union Square, in a building erected for their use by the Spingler estate. Though the girls were to continue living at No. 53, classes would be held at the new location. Their school for boys, located at Bleecker Street under the direction of Jacob Abbott, would remain there. Gorham would take charge of the new school, giving the other brothers a chance to write and to travel.

It had seemed advisable to the Abbotts to move uptown if they were to compete successfully with other schools. The Misses Gibson and Mme. Chegary had located on the east side of

Union Square, and Mme. Okill's school was on Eighth Avenue.
Many socially wealthy families had moved north by this time:
many were now in Washington Place, and Henry Brevoort, a
Dutch merchant, had his mansion at Fifth Avenue and Ninth
Street. Nathaniel P. Willis, editor of the *Home Journal*, explained that society included "those who keep carriages, live
above Bleecker Street . . . have a town house and a country house
and give balls."

Helen had no chance to attend balls, but life in the Abbott
home had its share of gay times. Jacob's son Lyman, a student at
New York University, frequently came in for Sunday-night
song services with his college friends. And on rare occasions
Helen attended a college dance. With her flashing wit and gay
manner, she never lacked an escort.

One of her contemporaries said of her, "She wasn't exactly
beautiful, but she was gracious and vivacious. Her eyes, which
she called 'green,' were more alive than those of anyone else I
knew."

With the opening of Spingler Institute, Helen and Jennie,
along with the rest of the boarders, walked to classes and back, a
trip of about twenty minutes each way. "So far I can make out,
but really I don't have a thing to wear," Helen told Jennie. It was
the walk through Broadway that was her major concern, for by
now her cashmere shawl was looking a trifle dowdy.

She wrote her sister Annie in Charlestown and prevailed upon
her to part with her visite, a plain velvet mantle with bands of
fur, which Helen assured her she would return in July. She
added in her letter, ". . . But I think at any rate I will get along
without a spring garment for church because I shall want more
things when warm weather comes . . . and I had rather have my
money in my *head*, by spending it for traveling and studying,
than on my *back* in clothes which I can do without and be re-

spectable. In May we are going to West Point, and Mr. John [Abbott] is very anxious that you should be here then. . . ."

But the Reverend Julius Palmer, her guardian, considered it unwise for fifteen-year-old Ann to make the trip. So it was not until July that the two girls were together again in Charlestown. And in August they had his permission to go to Amherst for the Commencement program and a chance to visit with the Hitch-cocks. There Helen met Henry Root, a student at Amherst College, and a friend of Austin Dickinson, Emily's brother.

While Ann enjoyed the company of Jane Hitchcock and her many friends, Helen saw much of Henry. But she insisted he was a friend, nothing more, no matter what the neighbors had to say. She knew he had fallen in love with Susan Gilbert, for he talked about her often, even to Helen. She listened to his plans for studying law at Harvard and yet urged him to try teaching for a while, for which she thought him most promising. In a let-ter to her guardian she noted her previous prophecy that he would make "one of the noblest men," or she would "be slow to trust again in the apparent promise of any mind or heart."

The rest of the summer of 1850 passed quickly for Helen, and by the fall she was back at the Abbotts and the Spingler Insti-tute. When the term ended, she received an offer to stay on to teach a section of "young girls." She accepted eagerly, and by early spring wrote her former Ipswich roommate, Lizzie Ord-way, "New York is my Arcadia. I need not tell you that I am perfectly happy. Teaching I enjoy most highly—so much that I can truly say, I was never so happy in my life as at this time. . . ."

But teaching was too soon over, and with a promise to be back at her school desk in the fall, she packed her trunks. She would spend the summer months with the Palmers at 157 Hamil-ton Street in Albany, New York. At her grandfather's request, the Reverend Ray Palmer, pastor of the First Congregational Church, had willingly accepted his share in the guardianship of

his two granddaughters. While his brother, the Reverend Julius
Palmer of Boston, would have the major responsibility and look
after Ann, Helen would have a home with the Albany Palmers
as long as she wanted.

Jennie Abbott drove with Helen to the railroad station at City
Hall to see her off, and watched the train leave as Helen waved
to her from the open coach window. It wouldn't be good-by
this time, she knew, for Helen would return to the classroom in
September. Neither had any way of knowing that it would be
more than ten years before Helen would again make her home
with the Abbotts—and then not in New York, but in New
Haven, Connecticut.

4

A Governor's Reception

"An invitation to the Governor's Reception? I can't believe it," Helen remarked to Lucy Palmer, her eyes bright with excitement. "I wonder who ... ?"

The Reverend Ray Palmer and his wife, Ann Maria, were not the least surprised, but their young twenty-two-year-old niece, Lucy Palmer, who had come for the summer, was ecstatic. She said, "Probably Mr. Clark sent in your name, or any one of the young men who has been calling on you."

Helen Fiske, not quite twenty-one, had no regular beau. Instead, many came to call, to meet the young blonde with the "green" eyes. There had been balls in New York City, but she had been in school or teaching and had not been invited. For the first time she was enjoying social life, and the parsonage at 157 Hamilton Street often opened its doors.

Helen "adopted" the Palmers as her own family. She saw their son Charles, now seventeen, but briefly on a short visit home from New Haven, where he was enrolled at Yale College, preparing to enter the ministry. But there were two daughters at home, Harriet, seven years old, and Maria, three, whom she immediately nicknamed "Bobbie."

Helen looked at the invitation more carefully. She had been to dances and concerts at the Van Vechten Hall, but a gover-

nor's reception at his own mansion! She would tell her special
friends, Hattie Russell and Mary Sprague, who accused her of
"flirting demurely." And, no longer satisfied with a secondhand
coat or shawl of Annie's, she would write Grandfather for an
allowance. Yet shopping was a real problem in Albany, and
Helen complained to Lizzie about "the great lack of facilities for
shopping and the dearth of good dressmakers and milliners,"
that made trips to New York necessary.

Nor was Albany itself the attractive city she had hoped to
find. Though its location on a hill was superb, it was a city "as
dirty as the worst parts of New York." At first she found it difficult to cope with the pigs in the gutters and streets in many
sections, but finally learned how to push them aside with her
"sunshine stick," her name for a fancy parasol.

Even so, it was a gay summer for Helen, that summer of
1851, and she became known as one of the belles of Albany,
noted for her quick laughter and perfect taste in dress.

Inside the festive Governor's mansion, Albany's notables,
dressed in their resplendent best, were assembling that Monday
evening, August 19. Helen joined the members and friends of
the American Association for the Advancement of Science,[1] the
group being honored by the Honorable Governor of New York,
Washington Hunt. The Governor and his attractive wife, Mary
Walbridge Hunt, headed the reception line that formed around
the long entrance hall. With them was a handsome young officer
in uniform.

Lieutenant Edward Bissell Hunt, a brother of the Governor,
was in Albany to attend the association of scientists and would
present three papers during the meetings, in the fields of Geog-
raphy, Physiology, and Mechanics. At his brother's insistence,
he had reluctantly agreed to attend the reception. He cared little for social affairs.

A brilliant scientist, Edward Hunt had graduated from West

Point in 1845, second in the roll of merit, and, after a year of engineering duty in New York City, had returned to West Point as an assistant professor of Engineering. In August of 1849, he had left to become an assistant engineer in the construction of Fort Warren, Boston Harbor, Massachusetts, and two years later went to Washington, D.C. with the Coast Survey, where he served in the Office of Engineering under Alexander Dallas Bache. He was presently on summer assignment in the New York office of Superintending of Engineering.

In his dress uniform—a dark blue coat with brass buttons and a scarlet military cape—he looked most distinguished. And Helen, in a blue velvet gown with matching soft blue hat trimmed wtih yellow plumes, was lovely. During the evening Edward Hunt managed to sit beside Helen at dance [2] intermission, and thereafter danced every waltz with her.

After this meeting, Lieutenant Hunt appeared frequently at the Palmer home, and often unexpectedly. Helen waited eagerly for his visits, and put aside all thoughts of teaching. She would remain with the Palmers, who encouraged her to stay and who, she thought, needed her at least during the winter months.

Though he was eight years older than she, Helen never doubted her love for him. But he made no move to propose or to talk with Mr. Palmer about an engagement. Time seemed endless.

Helen wrote her guardian about him, since she knew when the time came she would need his consent. On April 3, 1852, she compared him to Henry Root, whom she had wished he knew, ". . . And I wish still that you could see Henry Root—ten years older and in some respects of a loftier nature, in the person of no less than 'Lieut. Hunt'. . . ."

In mid-April, still without any proposal from Edward, Helen accepted the invitation of her guardian, the Reverend Julius Palmer, and his oldest daughter Lucy [3] for a two months' trip as far west as St. Louis, Missouri. To her great surprise and utter joy, the first person she saw on board the New York boat out of Albany was Lieutenant Hunt. They went up to "stay in the saloon" then, to her utter amazement, Charles A. Clark, who had been her escort to Albany functions many times, emerged in a few minutes "from quarters unknown."

Helen resisted a strong temptation to plead a headache and escape to her cabin berth, "leaving all candidates to settle their own claims." She had no reason to escape, however, for Mr. Clark made it perfectly clear that he had come aboard merely to "wish her well and bid her goodbye."

Lucy Palmer was equally happy when they landed in New York to be met at the wharf by Mr. Augustus Bachelder, her fiancé. They all went to breakfast at Irving's.

Two events made April 17 an unforgettable day for Helen. In the morning she visited with Edward at the Government lithographing rooms and inspected his work on engravings of charts. Afterwards they loitered about in the warm sunshine, wandering in the regions of New York she had learned to love: Union Square, Fifth Avenue, and the beautiful Colonnade Row.

Mr. Palmer had accepted an invitation to address a church meeting that morning, and Lucy had gone to Brooklyn to call on Julia Cutler and her brother, the Reverend Benjamin Clark Cutler, long-time family friends. That afternoon, Edward took time off from his office duties to accompany Helen and the Palmers on the two-o'clock boat to South Amboy, New Jersey, a sail of an hour and a half. From there he went on to Washington and they took the train to Philadelphia and continued on to Baltimore. It was here that Helen received his letter of proposal and a miniature of himself. She tucked them into her handbag.

"I know now the depth of his interest in me and have not one cloud of anxiety for the future . . ." Helen wrote Mrs. Ray Palmer from Baltimore on April 20. "Don't breathe a . . . syllable outside privacy of home circle at 157, not even to Mrs. Wood. . . . Lucy sends a great deal of love to Mr. Palmer also."

From Baltimore, the party headed for Washington, where they spent a few days in the capital city. It was from Washington, five days later, that Helen changed her tone of secrecy. In her note to the Palmers of Albany, she said, "You may make things without any reserve—for I am wholly, wholly happy!" She even suggested that if the Palmer baby, expected soon, was a boy, Mother Palmer name it "Edward."

Her guardian gave his sanction and approval at once, but insisted that in her answer to Edward's proposal she include his businesslike statement. "Such an arrangement is all right, I suppose, but hardly to my taste," she told Lucy. Your father's prudence has made me look cautious and reserved." But she included the letter with hers.

In a letter to Hannah Terry, she said she had been in "continuous locomotion since the first of April." Though tired, she had enjoyed the trip and confessed she had fallen in love with "mine own sweet, dear Edward."

Glad to be back finally in Albany, she would have liked to stay there with the family, make her plans for the wedding, and enjoy the Palmer girls, especially "dear little Bobbie." But she knew she had a round of visits to make and as soon as Annie's school closed in June, she left for Boston and 11 Pemberton Street. Annie would help with the trousseau, and there Helen would wait more patiently for Edward's infrequent visits.

It was on one of these visits that Emily Dickinson's brother Austin saw Helen with Edward. He was unable to speak to them, for, as he wrote Susan Gilbert, "I was perched on top of an omnibus and she was on the walk with a large, ambling, long-faced, ungraceful, brass-buttoned individual of some forty or fifty years, I should judge, whom from his manner I took to be her lieutenant." Austin said he mused all the way to Cambridge on the "probable bliss of such an assorted couple."

But despite Austin Dickinson's personal opinion, Helen had no awareness of anything but bliss. She spent most of her days in Boston shopping, purchased all the cotton and linen trimmings she needed, and searched out a seamstress. Ann and Lucy both helped her, but Lucy was, she said "a genius at cutting out."

On Wednesday, August 6, Edward again arrived in Boston and spent a day with his sister Fannie in Roxbury, just south of Boston. On his return, Helen went with him to pick out her ring and to purchase a few pieces of furniture she had seen.

Although she had wanted to spend more time with her grandfather and the Vinals, she became absorbed in her preparations. She was somewhat irked that Aunt Martha was disappointed because she didn't get to Charlestown more often. "I went over three or four times and both Sunday afternoons," she told Edward.

She spent one whole morning in Boston shops looking for blue cashmere for her "morning" dress, only to find it ten days later in Amherst, where she and Edward had gone to attend Commencement Week. She soon wrote Mother Palmer that Amherst seemed more pleasant than ever before. Amherst, she told her, "nestled snug in the embrace of a lofty circle of hills and by the side of a river . . . looks more and more lovely, and old associations grow stronger and stronger. . . ."

Such was her pride in her fiancé that she was not even disturbed by Professor Park's unusually long eulogy of the late Professor Edwards—two hours and twenty minutes—at the dedication of the new college library. "It was magnificent," she stated.

Helen introduced Edward to the Hitchcocks, the Snells, and to many of her parents' friends in town. She was especially pleased that her friend, Mary Sprague, came up from Northampton to meet him. And she was pleased, too, to see Henry Root and to hear his "splendid oration" on Speculative Politics at the exercises.

Of the college graduates that Helen knew at all well, Henry had always been the most friendly. When he called Wednesday afternoon to extend his good wishes to both Edward and Helen, she welcomed him warmly. Perhaps now the townspeople would realize that she thought of him only as a brother.

Though more than delighted that Edward and Henry liked each other at first meeting, Helen found it difficult to conceal her disappointment in Edward's plans. Within twenty minutes after Henry's arrival, he was to leave for Washington, D.C. Orders had been received that morning by telegraph, telling him he might have to remain in the capital for a month.

Amherst lost its charms for Helen. The next morning, August 21, she hastily packed her things and drove with Henry to the station, where she took the train for Brunswick, Maine, to spend a few days with Sarah Woolsey at their summer cottage. Afterwards, she would go to New York to purchase the rest of the furniture she wanted for her home.

The wedding, set for late October, was to be a simple ceremony at the home of the Palmers in Albany. But the Palmer baby, a boy just a few months old, became ill, and, in distress, Helen wrote Edward for his decision. He left it up to her, hoping not to postpone the wedding in any case. And though he wouldn't object to having it at the Palmers, his preference under the circumstances would be "elsewhere."

The baby's death two weeks later made impossible any consideration of having the event in the Palmer home. Helen had no choice but to change their plans. They would be married instead in the Mt. Vernon Church in Boston.

On October 28, 1852, Helen Maria Fiske was married to Ed-

ward Bissell Hunt by the Reverend Edward N. Kirk. Helen
asked her Albany guardian to perform the service but he explained that it would be illegal for him to officiate according to
Massachusetts law. But both he and his wife attended the ceremony, along with the Vinals and the Scholfields. Her sister
Annie was the bridesmaid.

5

Army Wife

HELEN LOOKED LOVELY in the soft blue silk taffeta she had chosen to wear for the wedding. A greater contrast can hardly be imagined than that between Edward and Helen. When she stood at his side she could scarcely reach his shoulders, and she was as blond as he was dark. But Grandfather Vinal could not have wished a happier-looking bride. His madcap, his sometimes boisterous and always willful niece, had grown into a most attractive woman.

The honeymoon, planned for Niagara Falls, had to be canceled—Edward developed a severe case of "bilious dyspepsia" that kept them at the Palmers in Albany for several days. When they were able to travel, they stopped off in Rochester, and then went to Hunt's Hollow in upper New York State to be with his family. A snowstorm prevented further travel. Edward wrote the Palmers, expressing his appreciation of their care of him and said, "Fortunately we now find our climate in the head and it is summer there."

In point of heredity, the Hunt family was as old and as completely English as the Fiskes. In the middle of the seventeenth century, Deacon Jonathan Hunt had migrated to Northampton, Massachusetts, from Connecticut and had bought a farm that is now part of the Smith College campus. In 1818, the family

moved again to Portage, New York, and Sanford Hunt became
a farmer in what was soon to be known as Hunt's Hollow in
Livingston County. Edward was the youngest of ten children,
born to Sanford and Fanny Rose Hunt, June 15, 1822.

For Helen, Hunt's Hollow was "one of the wildest places you
can imagine, small, countrified, and lonely," but she knew Niagara Falls was out of the question. "Just imagine a bridal couple, standing under an umbrella with their teeth chattering and
their feet wet, to look at the Falls," she wrote Mother Palmer.
"It would be ludicrous."

Eating apples and popping corn every evening in true country
style had to satisfy them until they were able to leave the Hunt
fireside. She hoped they could get away "without mortifying
Edward or offending the natives. . . ."

In a week's time they were back in Albany at the Palmers, and
by November 12 they reached Washington, D.C., their first
home—rooms in a Mrs. Reed's boardinghouse on F Street between 13th and 14th. A new life began for Helen, a gay and
social one. In Washington she met many friends, some through
her husband's position of engineer with the Coast Survey, and
entered the world of fashion that was the capital, "the city of
politicians." There were dinners and concerts to attend, social
functions of all sorts.

It wasn't long, though, before Helen faced her first heartache
as an army wife. In the early spring, Edward received orders to
report in June to New York City at the Engraving Office. She
was to begin her military widowhood at a time she felt least
ready for it. What should she do? She had no desire to spend
the hot summer alone in the city while most of her friends and
acquaintances would be in their summer cottages on Long Island, the Cape, or Newport.

After much discussion and many days of vacillation, Helen
accepted the invitation of Mrs. Julius Palmer to spend the month

of July with Annie and the Palmer family at their cottage in
Mattapoisett, Massachusetts, on Buzzards Bay near New Bedford. She talked of boarding in Roxbury to be near Aunt Fannie
and her sister in September. But, Dr. Witherspoon advised her
against leaving Washington on her return from the beach in
August.

Murray Hunt was born in Washington on September 30,
1853. "He has blue eyes and knows how to cry already," Edward
wrote the Palmers in his announcement of the baby's arrival.
But he was a good baby, weighing eight and a half pounds at
birth, and Helen was soon up and around. She devoted herself
to his care, not allowing the nurse to take her place. He grew
"fat and solid and strong," she boasted. And although the Hunts
had cards for the homes of the Washington social set, Helen
refused for three months to make calls.

But on New Year's Eve, she followed the custom of the times
and joined Edward and the Preston Blairs (who lived in what is
now Blair House, the home of the Vice-President of the United
States) in calling upon cabinet members and other Washington
dignitaries. At all the houses she found the tables "elegantly set
out with refreshments—huge cakes, fruit, flowers and everywhere a bowl of punch—of eggnog and apple toddy."

The crowds at the White House were so heavy that they decided not to call on President Franklin Pierce. But they did call
on the handsome General Winfield Scott, "a half foot taller
than Edward," and on Mrs. Alexander Hamilton, the ninety-six-
year-old widow of the great Federalist, known as "the oldest
lady in the country." She was the last woman living who had
graced the "republican court" during the Washington adminis-
tration.

"Calling on her was like hearing Ecclesiastes read in the midst
of a forest . . ." Helen said afterwards.

Although Washington was a city of causes, Helen was not a

"cause" woman, taking no definitive stand on slavery or on women's rights. Yet she was intolerant of any unfairness and defended Harriet Beecher Stowe, whose *Uncle Tom's Cabin*, which had already appeared as a serial in the *National Era* in 1850, was now out in book form. Both *Uncle Tom* and Mrs. Stowe were topics of conversation in every social gathering, and when one of her guests called the author, "a talented fiend in human shape," she hotly contradicted him.

With Edward, however, she held her peace in matters controversial. She saw no reason to oppose him and never questioned his opinions when they differed from her own. She well knew he abhorred abolitionsits, and she also knew he disliked arguments and contention of any kind.

When Murray was nine months old, Helen and Edward planned a trip to Boston, but in April she had the sad news of her grandfather's death. He had died in his sleep, the grandfather that had been more of a father to her than her own. "If I ever became angry or upset, he was my comfort. He was the only one who could console me after my mother's death." And, she added, "He could never deny me a thing." She wished he had seen his first great-grandson. She realized only too well that she would always miss him, miss his gruff manner, his laughter, his shrewdness—and his love for her.

By June, summer plans had to be made, for Edward would be in New York City again "on printing duty" and the hot summer season in the capital would be unbearable for her and Murray. At first she thought of going to Williamstown Inn in Western Massachusetts or to Amherst with Annie, but the distance was too far. She finally decided on Tarrytown, New York, about twenty-five miles north of the city, where Edward can reach me in less than a day," she said.

The summer started out happily. Helen took drives on pleasant days with Murray and his nurse, sometimes to Sleepy Hollow, three miles south of Tarrytown. It was here that she first read "The Legend of Sleepy Hollow" and "Rip Van Winkle" in Washington Irving's *Sketch Book*. But what began with such happiness proved to be unexpectedly sorrowful for both Edward and Helen: Murray became ill in August and, despite all the care of nurse and doctor, he died on August 22 from "dropsy of the brain," a little less than a year old.

"I am to blame," Helen repeated over and over. "I should never have brought the baby to such an unwholesome and unhealthy spot."

Nothing Edward said could lessen Helen's grief at the loss of her first-born. For his sake, she held up during the ordeal of the trip up the Hudson to West Point for the burial. But back in Washington, she was overcome with sorrow and shut herself off from her friends. As soon as word reached her sister Annie, she wrote urging Helen to come for a visit. Annie had set her wedding date forward to late October. She was to marry Everett C. Banfield.

Helen couldn't believe the news, since only the previous January Annie had arranged to postpone her plans to marry John Sanford, a student at Harvard Law School whom she had met in Amherst through Jane Hitchcock. They had decided to wait until he graduated and then be married either on Annie's Christmas birthday of 1855 or on his in November. Though Helen had doubted that young John was in any position to support a wife and family, she did not anticipate Annie's breaking off the engagement. But Annie assured her she was in love with Everett Colby Banfield, twenty-six years old and well-established in a law office in Charlestown, Massachusetts.

Originally from Wolfeboro, New Hampshire, Everett Banfield was born September 19, 1828, on a farm just beyond the town, the son of Joseph and Elizabeth Banfield. Unwilling to follow in his father's footsteps and stay on the farm, he had studied law and presently had a successful practice. He had bought a house in West Roxbury, a village a few miles south of Boston.

Ann Scholfield Fiske and Everett Colby Banfield were married October 28, 1854. Two years from the very day Helen had taken her vows, she stood beside her gentle nineteen-year-old sister to witness the simple ceremony performed by the Reverend A. B. Tappan at the Charlestown Congregational Church.

Helen might have hoped to see Henry Root, who had entered Harvard Law that September after a teaching assignment in New Jersey. But in early October the doctors had discovered a "fatal and painless swelling"—he died that same month.

The Sunday after Helen's return to her home in Washington, she persuaded Edward to attend the First Unitarian Church with her to hear the newly installed minister, the Reverend Moncure Daniel Conway. Church attendance was not a regular activity of the Hunts and they had no church membership. "Edward is not a religious man and has never been affiliated with any denomination," she explained to the minister, "but he never retires without reading a chapter of the Bible." Years later, she would tell Mr. George Cullum, historian for the United States Military Academy, "He never did anything which he regarded as wrong."

At the age of thirty-two, Lieutenant Hunt was considered one of the most promising mathematical physicists in the country. He had just published a tract on molecular theory, the *Nature of Forces*. In addition, he wrote extensively for the *American Journal of Science* and prepared papers for the American Association for the Advancement of Science. His biggest project, the *Alphabetical Index* of the annual reports of the Coast Survey, was now under way.

"If Edward seems pre-occupied," Helen tried to explain his indifference to the Reverend Mr. Conway, "he probably is planning his work. Work, either with head or hands, is an absolute necessity for him. Often he loses track of time and may even spend the whole night on his studies without going to bed."

The Reverend Mr. Conway came to know the Hunts well, frequently visiting at their home. A bachelor, he lived by himself in a suite of rooms on 6th Street. After graduation from Dickinson College, he had studied law, but he claimed that the reading of Emerson's works turned his attention away from law to the ministry. At twenty-one, he had entered Harvard University, where he had the pleasure of meeting Emerson in person and through him had become acquainted with the leaders of the Concord and Cambridge intellectual and literary groups.

"The most memorable day of my life," he told Helen with great feeling, "I spent with Emerson." He told her how they had walked around Concord together and had visited Thoreau's hut on Walden Pond. "When we parted," he said, "Emerson gave me a copy of Margaret Fuller's *Woman in the 19th Century,* possibly because I had expressed enthusiasm for this woman journalist."

In his many visits, "Monk," as Helen came to call him, took upon himself the role of her literary mentor. He shared with her his favorite authors, Hawthorne and Emerson among them. Helen knew Hawthorne's works rather well, recently having read his *Snow-Image.*

"Imagine! A guest of ours thought it a fairy tale for children. So I simply adapted my conversation to a gentlemanly blockhead." She laughed in recalling the incident.

But Emerson was not on her reading list and Monk introduced Helen to him by a gift of his poetry. Years later, while traveling on a Boston train, Helen would recognize Emerson and after some hesitation introduce herself to him in Monk's name. A poem to R.W.E. would describe this meeting:

A Tribute

to R. W. E.

Midway in summer, face to face, a king
I met. No king so gentle and so wise.
He calls no man his subject; but his eyes
In midst of benediction, questioning,
Each soul compel. . . .

Monk's interest extended beyond literature. Although a Virginian by birth, he was an anti-slavery man. In his first election sermon at Washington on October 29, 1854, he had spoken about human slavery, calling it "the greatest of all sins."

Though he had read a few chapters of the popular *Uncle Tom's Cabin*, he put it down unfinished, declaring that it was not true of slavery as he had known it in his home state. Monk did not want bloodshed over the issue and regretted the emotional impact of Mrs. Stowe's writings. He finally supported secession as a way to avoid war. But it is doubtful that he ever discussed the question on the Stowe book in Edward Hunt's presence.

In April of 1855, the wandering life of a military household began in earnest for Helen. Edward was assigned to Rhode Island under the Lighthouse Board of the Engineering Department as Superintendent. His major task included charge of repairs on Fort Adams in Warren, Rhode Island. For some ten years he would be stationed at a variety of posts in New England, the first four mainly in Newport, Rhode Island, but occasionally in Bristol and Providence before an assignment in New Haven, Connecticut.

Helen invited Monk to visit them wherever they were "quartered." "I'll see you in Newport sometime during the summer," he promised. And he did, making Newport seem to Helen less a "Sleepy Hollow," her name for the place—a sharp contrast to the gayer and more social life she had known in Washington.

6

Rennie

FROM THE SMALL HOME the Hunts rented on School Street in Newport, Helen sometimes took drives along Bellevue Avenue and out to Easton's Beach, the "Woods," and to Purgatory to look at the remarkable deep chasm in the rocks. But she enjoyed most the days when Edward could go with her, and then they would visit the Warrens, who summered in the Brenton House behind Thames Street. Colonel George Warren was the Engineer Officer in command of all the work on the Atlantic Coast from New London, Connecticut, to Maine. He was Edward's chief superior.

Helen had intended to stay in Newport all summer, but when she learned that the American Association for the Advancement of Science would be held at Brown University, she changed her mind. They left Rebecca, the maid Helen described as her "little sable," to look after the cottage, and sailed for Providence on August 14, 1855. Helen was not only eager to hear Edward read the three papers he had been working on for more than a month, but also looked forward to meeting some of their friends, especially the Horsfords. Professor of Mathematics and Natural Science at Harvard, Mr. Eben Norton Horsford had worked closely with Edward since their first meeetings in Cambridge in 1849.

In Providence, at one of the many social gatherings, Helen

met the Bottas and the Carrs, to form friendships that would last all her life. Mrs. Jeanne Carr was a lady in every sense of the word, her manner both gracious and pleasing. But it was the petite, dark-haired, and dark-eyed Ann Charlotte Botta who charmed Helen at once. Married in March of 1855 to Professor Vincenzo Botta, who had come to America from Italy to study public-school methods, Ann Charlotte had moved with her new husband and her mother to a house at 25 West Thirty-seventh Street in New York City. This home was to be called "the first important salon in the history of American letters."

Ann Charlotte's personal charm and skill at repartee attracted the literary; Ralph Waldo Emerson would always refer to the house as "the home with the Expanding Doors." A roster of visitors to the salon might well have made a *Who's Who* of the day—it included Edgar Allan Poe, found frequently at Ann's home, Margaret Fuller, Parke Godwin, N. P. Willis, the little black sculptress "Estella" Lewis, and even Longfellow when he was in town. Twenty-five West Thirty-seventh became the center for the most brilliant and artistic life of the city.

After the close of the sessions in Providence, Helen accepted Mrs. Botta's invitation to spend a week with her. The delightful circle of "informal and wide-awake people" impressed Helen enormously, and she thoroughly enjoyed the social gatherings. "If I were not so abominably selfish," she wrote Mrs. Botta, October 11, from Newport, "I should add to it—and how I wish you lived in Newport, but I do not wish you lived here, for to exchange such a charming circle . . . would be indeed a misery."

A week later, Helen traveled with Edward to Roxbury. While she stayed with Annie, Edward would spend his time "rummaging libraries in Boston and Cambridge," she told Mrs. Botta. She indicated as well that he might "avail himself of the liberty to run over to New York and do a little work at the Astor Library," assuring her that "in any case you will see his face, of course."

Helen would, however, return to Newport after a "fortnight, to get a little away from people and to be cool and comfortable." In a letter to Mrs. Botta she said, "I have a strong aircastle founded on the rocks down by Purgatory that you will come next year to live in, I trust. . . ."

For the winter, Helen did not anticipate great loneliness, as Edward would be home with her almost constantly, and she was expecting a "little sunbeam (son-beam?) which will make all the days bright." In November, Edward found a more commodious home to rent on Cottage Street near the head of Redwood and just off Bellevue Avenue. Here, on Sunday, December 2, 1855,[1] a baby boy was born at 2:30 in the morning. Rebecca, Helen's "little sable," was the only person with her at the time of childbirth, for Edward had gone in haste for the doctor and a nurse. In all probability, according to Edward's letter to Mother Palmer, the quiet black maid saved the baby's life "by courageously turning him over before the doctor came."

Except in size, he looked to Edward very much like Murray had at the age of six weeks. "[He] in all respects seems wonderfully like him, except in being we hope less nervous, as he cries scarcely at all and sleeps well, sucking his fingers . . ." he told Mrs. Palmer about his "fine son weighing nine and a quarter pounds."

They named the baby Warren Horsford Hunt, after two of Edward's close friends, Colonel George Edward Warren and Dr. E. N. Horsford. Helen quickly nicknamed him Rennie. A bright, healthy child, Rennie filled Helen's life with richness, and she soon forgot the "strange mixture of longing and fear" with which she had awaited his birth. Her joy was increased, too, by the news that her sister Annie also had had a boy, born November 15, whom she had named Richard Banfield.

"And this Newport is a glorious place," she wrote Mrs. Botta, whom she was to call Botany or Bottanie the rest of her life. "I love it better every day—even after terribly warm days we have delicious nights and I am sure you must be half stifled in New York." She told Bottanie of her busy days, "sewing, riding, and walking, with just enough of calling and paying calls or visiting in some shape" to keep her "hurried." She urged Bottanie and her husband to come for the summer or fall and announced that there was a small cottage on School Street available for rent, "only a few steps from our house."

Although it is not clear whether the Bottas ever were able to leave New York and visit the Hunts in 1856, Helen's active life kept her content. And Rennie, who grew like a weed, was a "dear comfort" to her. Each afternoon they drove out in the carriage with the "little gray" Edward had bought for her to Easton's Beach. Helen began to think of Newport as home.

Then came word in the early spring of 1857 of a possible transfer for Edward out of the Rhode Island area. Feeling anxious because he had been ill with his old malady of dyspepsia, he wrote in haste on April 3 to his chief in Washington, Mr. A. D. Bache. "I must rent a house for a year during the coming fortnight or three weeks or give up housekeeping," he explained, for houses had to be rented for a season of four months—from June 1 to October 1—or by the year. "From this you can see," he added, "how important it is for me to know whether I am to change my station...."

In reply, Mr. Bache indicated that General G. Totten was considering an assignment for him at Key West, Florida. The General was the Chief Engineer of the U.S. Army, and his decision could hardly be questioned.

"That tropical bird's nest," Edward complained to Helen. Key West was a little island off the southern tip of Florida, very hot and very muggy. Edward slumped into the desk chair and looked more disturbed than Helen had ever seen him. "You know what that will mean," he said. "Not only loss of health but total suspension of my work on the *Index*, and what I consider to be personal exile."

Troubled for him since he had just recovered from a bout of stomach disorder, Helen urged him to write again to Mr. Bache and in even more detail. Perhaps he could or would assist in postponing the assignment—at least until the *Index* could be completed.

Edward wrote at great length on June 13. He assured Mr. Bache that it would be entirely impossible to finish the *Index* by the due date of November 1858, that his health would be impaired by a Southern station, and that he could not take his wife with him, since she was never well in warm weather. "Thus," he concluded, "an order to the South is to me a virtual decree of divorce. . . . These are certainly very substantial reasons why I should not willingly go to the South. . . ."

But he said he would go "as a soldier" if ordered, and at the same time he threatened to leave the service at the first possible opportunity after the completion of the assignment. In spite of his urgent message, General Totten assigned him to Key West. Life for the lieutenant that summer was a "hammered thing," as he drove himself, trying to complete the *Index*, to finish thirteen lighthouse constructions, and to supervise a good deal of petty detailed work at Fort Adams in Warren, Rhode Island.

Helen worried about him, but was relieved when he talked of attending scientific meetings in Montreal in early August. "I shall take what comes as well as I can," he wrote, "and though my work here is urgent, I mean to go to Montreal."

If only she could go to see her sister and the new baby girl, her first niece, Ann Fiske, born July 8! But Edward had already made preliminary arrangements to move his wife and son to New Haven, Connecticut, on his return from Canada. Besides, she questioned the wisdom of traveling alone with Rennie, only a little more than a year and a half old. She would sort out her linen and prepare for moving day.

On Edward's return from the sessions of the American Association for the Advancement of Science, Helen was amazed to notice that he no longer complained about his Florida assignment. He arranged to keep his six-dollar-a-month office in Newport and there put aside his *Index* notes in a fireproof safe. Then he moved his family to a boardinghouse on Chapel Street in New Haven. For General Totten had finally made a concession —Edward would be reassigned north by the middle of May in 1858.

One early October morning in 1857, a boat southward bound carried Edward away from his family. Helen stood on Steamboat Wharf with Rennie and waved until the boat headed into the harbor. Saddened at Edward's departure, she realized that for the first time since her marriage she would be alone for at least an entire winter—probably longer.

7

Civil War Days

THE LONG AND INEVITABLE separations continued while Edward was south, planning and constructing defenses on the Florida Keys. Except for a few weeks in the summer, he was away on duty all year. But Helen never complained, even when, in the fall of 1858, he left for a two-months engineering assignment to California and Texas to prepare the fortification of Lime Point and Galveston Harbor. She made many friends at Wooster Square and occasionally attended public lectures at Yale College; most of all, she had Rennie. They often rode out by carriage to West Haven, a beautiful village, but most of the time they traveled to Hamilton Park or Westville. She thought the Elm City one of the "handsomest in the country."

Still, Helen and Rennie looked forward to the limited time Edward had at home. Helen might easily have been disturbed by his trip in August 1859, to Springfield, Massachusetts, to attend the meetings of the American Association for the Advancement of Science, but if she did object to his leaving her, she did not let him know.

But she had no intention of letting him go by himself to the August meetings in Newport the following summer, scheduled in time for them to take in the program of Commencement Week at Amherst as well. She would escape some of the heat of

New Haven's humid summer, and she could show off her young son, now four and a half years old.

Young Rennie was sheer delight to his mother, and Helen paid close attention to her growing son. Although he favored his father, with his high forehead and dark eyes, he had his mother's charm. She found it hard to reprimand him—in fact, she would not force him to obey her without a careful explanation of the right and wrong of an act. "They were intimate friends when he was little more than a baby," Sarah Woolsey later recalled in a tribute to Helen. She called the relation between mother and son "the best and happiest" she had ever known.

Sarah Woolsey was a member of a large and sociable family. In 1855, her father, John Woolsey, had moved his family from Ohio to New Haven, a city already full of Woolseys. Her father's brother, Theodore Dwight Woolsey, was then President of Yale College. The oldest of six that included an orphaned cousin, Sarah was uncommonly tall, a vigorous young woman with a sparkling personality, who laughed easily and talked well. She was called by a neighbor one of the "four delightfully brilliant daughters who made New Haven Society interesting." The Woolsey home at 19 Wooster Street, near the corner of Olive Street, was the scene of much activity, and Rennie was one of Sarah's favorite "nephews."

The day after the closing session of the science meetings at Newport, Edward joined Helen and Rennie for the ride to Amherst. And on Wednesday, August 8, Helen and Edward were "part of a delightful reception" at the Dickinson house on Main Street. Emily, according to her younger sister Lavinia, was "charmed with them both."

The Dickinsons had moved back to the Mansion from their North Pleasant Street home in April 1856, now occupying the entire house, only "a hedge away" from the newly built residence of Austin Dickinson and his bride Susan Gilbert. Helen could not but recall happily the days she had played with Emily at this same house when she was younger than Rennie. It was, however, Edward's first meeting with Emily, though he remembered seeing her at a distance eight years before.

Through Emily, Helen had met Samuel Bowles at the reception. Mr. Bowles had come up from Springfield as reporter for the Amherst Commencement for his own paper, the *Springfield Republican*. He was a great favorite of Emily's, but he often called her his "Queen Recluse." He joked with her for not letting him publish her poems and asked for another "valentine."

Actually, Emily had sent the valentine poem to a friend, William Howland, in jest and on February 20, 1852, without a "by-your-leave," it appeared in the *Republican*, with the comment that the "hand that wrote the following amusing medley to a gentleman friend of ours, a 'valentine,' is capable of writing very fine things." Emily easily forgave Mr. Bowles, but denied authorship.

On Sunday, August 12, Helen and Edward went to the First Congregational Church with the entire Dickinson family to hear Professor Warren preach, and called on them that evening. When she wrote her sister about the call, she said nothing about Emily; she did say that "Vinnie had faded," and added, "but her father's hair hasn't." She may have wished not to comment on Emily, for she would have had to admit of a change in her friend. At thirty, Emily was no longer the gay playmate Helen had known and loved as a child.

Edward called Emily "uncanny." He was not impressed with this plain woman with the two smooth braids of reddish hair pulled straight back into a net, and bright searching eyes.

"She has changed," Helen said in an attempt to explain the difference.

"But she has an ally and friend in Carlo," he pointed out.

Carlo was a large shaggy Newfoundland dog that Emily's

father had given her for company and protection on her long walks in wooded areas. "I told her that her dog apparently understood gravitation," said Edward, smiling at his own pun.

According to one account of the Reception Tea on the Dickinson lawn, Edward had watched Carlo rub against the legs of the food-laden tables and snap up a cake knocked accidentally onto the grass.

Ten years later, in a letter to Colonel Higginson,[1] Emily told him about Edward's remark, stating that Major Hunt interested her more than any other man she ever saw. She added that when he said he would come again "in a year," he meant something else. For he added, "If I stay a shorter time it will be longer."

His remark may have amused Emily at the time, and she may have continued to think it interesting, but Emily passed out of his life without a backward glance except to think her odd. To Edward, the possibility of ever seeing Emily again or of attending another Amherst Commencement seemed remote. There had been serious talk of trouble between the North and South. In May of 1859, Abraham Lincoln had been nominated for president by the Republican Party on an anti-slavery platform and many citizens had blamed the party for exasperating the South by the Lincoln nomination. Edward believed war was inevitable.

As a newly commissioned captain, he had received orders to return to Key West to direct the defense of Fort Taylor. By April of 1861, the dreaded fear of secession had materialized, and in early May, Helen watched the first New Haven regiment leave from the depot on Union Street. She held Rennie's hand tight as they stood in the great crowd that gathered.

By the 1860s, New Haven had become a railroad center, with six trains daily between New York and New Haven. Helen could hear the trains arriving at the large depot from which troops left regularly. Occasionally she went with Rennie to the belfry of the Depot Tower, a hundred and forty feet up from the street, to view the city and see "the forest of sailing vessel masts" that crowded the harbor.

Very few people, northern or southern, expected the War to last long, and Helen planned on Edward's return north in the spring.

Edward had directed the defense of Fort Taylor and, although hard-pressed by secessionist sympathizers, he had saved it for the Union. Then, promoted to the rank of major, he was ordered to Virginia as chief officer in the campaign of the Shenandoah Valley.

Helen decided not to wait for him in New Haven any longer. She packed her bags and arranged for a trip to Roxbury and Amherst. She would spend a week at least with her sister in West Roxbury. There were now four cousins for Rennie to enjoy, for, besides Richard and Ann, another daughter, Helen Fiske, had been born May 22, 1859, and a second son, Nathan Fiske, on November 15, 1860. Richie and Rennie, both six years old, were inseparable, Rennie even giving some of his soldier toys to his cousin.

Helen stayed a few days longer than she had anticipated because word had come from a Mrs. Adams, with whom she had planned to room and board in Amherst, that there were several cases of diphtheria in town. Instead, she stopped off in Brattleboro, Vermont, and waited for a message from Amherst. Finally assured that there had been no case of the dreadful disease for a fortnight, Helen and Rennie left Vermont on Wednesday, Christmas Day, for Amherst, where they would spend most of January.

"I should like to live two years in Amherst and lay up a thousand dollars," she wrote her sister, referring to the fact that in Amherst Rennie could wear out his last spring outfit that was "not very nice" in New York or anywhere else. She found the days pleasant, with a chance to see the Hitchcocks and to enjoy

a "little party at the Tylers—all faculty—," and to wait for the
snow to melt before she would "move off."

By July of 1862, the overconfidence of the North was sobered
by the Battle of Bull Run, and the Civil War dragged on. No
one could see the end, and even Edward began to question his
right to remain out of the field of action. "Yet in the field I
would be but one man. If I continue work on the submarine invention of mine, I may do more good for the cause." He convinced himself, and when, during the summer, he was assigned
to New Haven to erect temporary defenses in the harbor, he
felt certain he had made the right decision.

He rented a two-story house at 174 Chapel Street, just beyond
St. Paul's Church, between Olive and Union Streets. Here he
could finish editing the *Index* and continue his research on his
marine invention, a device that would enable a ship of war
to destroy its antagonist at a distance not much less than that of
cannon shot in the air. If he could persuade the army to release
him from active duty within a few months, he would be ready
to try out his experiment at the Brooklyn Navy Yard.

The War absorbed everyone's energies, and Helen agreed in
the spring of 1863 to give some volunteer time at the army hospital on Cedar Street, to the injured and sick soldiers being
treated there.

But Helen hated the War and the continual talk of battles and
the count of young men dead and wounded. Local papers even
carried war songs and announcements of committees being
formed, mainly women's societies for sewing and preparing
bandages. Women organized the New Haven Soldiers' Aid Society, using rooms in the Connecticult State House, where they
made garments to send to hospitals. To the United States Sani-
tary Commission (the modern Red Cross) they sent everything
from dried apples to knitted socks.

Helen probably wouldn't have decided to join Sarah Woolsey, Hattie Russell, and others in volunteer work at the Knight United States General Hospital if Edward hadn't been encouraging.

"I'm not very good at nursing," Sarah confessed, "but I could read to the soldiers."

Helen agreed. "And I guess we could write letters for them and do a little sewing. Perhaps we could be of some help."

They helped, spending most of their time sitting on two hard wooden chairs, "mending, mending, mending," giving out socks, shirts, and shoes in the linen room, and sometimes assisting the nurses.

Even though her Albany friend, Hattie Russell, was the superintendent of the diet kitchen, Helen thought the discipline lax; but she tried to keep a happy disposition and sense of humor. Soon she and Sarah were placed in charge of the linen room "in a fit of mingled patriotism and romance," according to Helen.

Years later, Helen gave a faithful picture of her hospital experience in a short story, "Joe Hale's Red Stockings," only slightly disguising the names of her friends and co-workers. "Not to be sacrificing one's self in some way to the shrine of the country's need seemed to prove one to be next door to a traitor—in fact, worse," she commented.

When time permitted, Helen dropped in to see the Abbotts at 150 College Street. Mr. John had accepted the pastorate of the Howe Street Church the fall of 1861. He and she often talked together about the War and the question of slavery. Mr. John made his position clear. "I am an abolitionist, Helen," he volunteered one day. "I have tried as many others have to persuade the President to free the slaves now and prevent further bloodshed."

Despite the insistence of the abolitionists, President Lincoln failed to issue an edict of freedom for slaves, lest it alienate the loyal border states. Only after the successful Antietam cam-

paign did there come, on January 1, 1863, a formal Emancipa-
tion Proclamation. But it wasn't until the victories of Gettysburg
and Vicksburg that it was evident the War would soon end. All
over the North, as news of victory spread, there was rejoicing,
the firing of guns, and the ringing of bells. August 6, 1863, was
proclaimed by the President a Day of Thanksgiving.

The time seemed ripe for the transfer of Major Hunt from
his army assignment to special duty in the Navy Department.
Edward's request to test the practicability of his submarine invention was granted, and the Hunts left for New York City.

8

"Lifted Over"

I⊤ WAS ONE OF New York's hottest summers and in "stifling quarters" on Beekman Street, Helen suffered some of the most uncomfortable weeks she had ever known. Near her rooms were blocks of buildings with shops on the flrst floor and tenements above. "I can hardly stand the cries of the children," she said in desperation at the "shrieks and cries . . . and the angry words from tired, overworked mothers."

Nights, when every window had to be thrown open and the noise of quarreling parents and screaming children could be heard distinctly through the hot still air, were no better than the days. And she worried about the effect on Rennie's health.

Meanwhile, Edward was across the East River at the Brooklyn Navy Yard, making tests on the "sea-miner," as he now called his invention. For this device he had used a partially floating and watertight box covered with a deck, with a manhole in the top for entrance into it by a ladder. At the expulsion of the gun or projectile from the chamber, the gases would escape through the manhole.

Confident that all was in order, Edward set September 30 for a trial run. But through some oversight, according to the writer of his *Memoirs*, the usual provision for opening the manhole was not made, thus filling the chamber with deadly gaseous poison.

Edward went down the ladder, unaware of what had taken place, since he was not in the chamber at the time. Although he returned directly to the ladder as soon as he smelled the fumes, he fell heavily to the bottom. Several men sprang to his aid, but each man was in turn prostrated. Water was thrown on them and all were resuscitated—except Major Hunt, who was rushed at once to the Brooklyn Naval Hospital. Unconscious for forty-eight hours, Edward Bissell Hunt died October 2, 1863, shortly before Helen could reach him.

Stunned when the news of the accident arrived, she felt certain she could have prevented his death if she had been able to reach him earlier. But the doctors at the hospital assured her that Edward's concussion had been fatal and that he had never regained consciousness.

For a second time Helen stood beside the grave of her first-born son, for Edward was buried at West Point with a military funeral befitting an Army major. She looked down at her seven-year-old son Rennie and grasped his hand tightly.

Returning to New Haven, she went directly to the Abbott's home. "I must keep cheerful for Rennie's sake," she told them.

"Stay with us, Helen—for a while at least," Mr. John urged. And his wife added, "We should so love to have you. It would be like the old days at Lafayette Place."

"I should like to, but I have a house to look after—and Rennie. . . . I'll come back on Sunday for services though."

Neighbors and friends called on Helen and tried to make the adjustment easier for her.

"I could send Rennie to boarding school, but I would like to have him study at home with me," she told Sarah.

"Why not open a school for a few other children his age?" Sarah questioned Helen.

"Yes, why not?" thought Helen. She recalled how much she

had enjoyed her teaching at the Spingler Institute. She would teach Rennie and at the same time he would have other children for company. He needed that, she knew. So the first lonely months went by quite rapidly.

Not only did Helen devote herself to Rennie, but she also gave attention to the perfection of Edward's sea-miner. She was assisted in her efforts by Professor Alexander C. Twining of New Haven, an inventor and engineer, and by Professor W. P. Trowbridge of the Engineer Agency in Washington, D.C. They both believed in the invention and considered it important enough to try to complete it. Helen supported the effort in every way she could.

But when spring came and school days were over, Helen sold the house on Chapel Street and moved into a suite of rooms at the New Haven House on the corner of Chapel and College Streets. She would spend the summer with friends and relatives, perhaps even taking Rennie on a train trip to Albany. The Palmers had often invited the Hunts, but Helen had hesitated to take the trains, so often tied up by the military. She settled instead for a short train ride to Leete's Island, Guilford, Connecticut, on the New Haven and New London Railroad line. There they could picnic on the beach and Rennie could play in the sand.

From New Haven they took carriage drives or horse-car expeditions to Hamilton Park, to Wintergreen Falls, and the village of Whitneyville. Picnics became part of their summer days; sometimes "Aunt" Sarah or Jennie Abbott went with them.

One day came the long-awaited news of victory for the North —the end of the Civil War! On Palm Sunday, April 9, 1865, Lee surrendered at Appomattox Courthouse, and this time it was no false alarm. The dark days of war were over. Helen and Rennie would journey to West Roxbury for a long visit with Aunt

Annie and her family. Rennie packed his favorite toys to share with Richie.

Spring had come to West Roxbury. Everywhere there was a sense of relief from war. But inside the Banfield home was no joy or concern for the nation: Helen and Rennie lay sick with fever.

The day before, Helen had taken Rennie and Richie out for a walk and shortly after they left the house she noticed that she had forgotten to put on Rennie's scarf and gaiters. Surely, she thought, it was spring, and the day was clear and sunny. No need to go back for them.

The next morning Rennie had a slight temperature and seemed sluggish. The doctor said it was croup and Annie brought out the Byronia-Bella Donna. But Rennie's temperature mounted and his breathing became difficult. Richie and little Annie developed the same symptoms. Helen tried to take care of the children but soon became ill herself. They had all come down with diphtheria, and although Helen couldn't know it at the time, there was never any hope for nine-year-old Rennie. He died April 13, 1865, the son whom Helen loved and around whose life her own was centered.

The following day, funeral services were held at four o'clock at the Banfield home, near Highland Station. The *Boston Evening Transcript* that day carried on its front page:

SHOCKING TRAGEDIES
PRESIDENT LINCOLN SHOT AND KILLED
ATTEMPTED ASSASSINATION OF SENATOR SEWARD AND HIS SON
ESCAPE OF THE MURDERERS

It was a sad day for the nation, but for Helen her personal loss was greater. Stunned and numb with shock, she could shed no tears. Her second son would be buried later at West Point beside his brother and father. "And I alone," she grieved bitterly, "am left, who avail nothing."

As soon as Annie and Richie had recovered and Helen was able to travel, she left her sister's home for New Haven and the Abbotts, where she shut herself up in her room. "I can see no one at all—no one but the family," she told Jennie Abbott, whom she would always refer to after this as "that saint in New Haven."

Night after night she dreamed Rennie was alive again, smiling and cheerful. She even waited awake for long hours into the early morning for him to come back from the other world to speak to her. She had talked with Rennie of this possibility just before his death, and now she waited, but no sound came. Any belief she may have had in spiritualism she lost. Her precocious son had not been able to return to her.

The days were also painful, for whenever she got up, she expected to see him at her side, ready to hug her.

For a long time it seemed to Jennie as though she would never come out of the shadows. "She has been able to write some letters though," Jennie whispered to Sarah Woolsey, who had called daily to inquire about her friend. "Perhaps this will help her express her grief, and recover."

"I do hope so," Sarah agreed, still looking worried. The usual talkative Sarah could find few words to console the Abbotts.

But the writing eventually helped Helen—not the letters so much as the poems she wrote and sent to Parke Godwin, a friend she had met at the Botta salon in New York, assistant publisher of the *New York Evening Post*. On June 9, his newspaper carried the first poem Helen had written in her sorrow. Dated May 27, she had signed it Marah and titled it "The Key to the Casket." Marah undoubtedly was a shortened form for "*Ma* of *R*ennie *H*unt."

Pouring out her grief, she blamed herself for her "cold re-
membrance and mere form of "thanks" she had given God for
the precious gift of her son. With Mr. Godwin's encouragement, she continued to write, finding relief for the heartache she
could not otherwise express. "It Is Not All of Life to Live"
appeared in the June 30 issue:

It Is Not All of Life to Live

God help me! What a thing this life of ours can be
Deep sorrow of another day, black-robed and pitiless
And night like Judas, treacherous and soft of foot.

Oh, God forgive us that our life should ever be
Such utter emptiness!
Anoint our eyes, so each day we can drink in
Patience, and with prayer, the bitter draught.

And patience began to come back to Helen, patience and acceptance. A month later, at Mr. Godwin's suggestion, Helen
submitted a sonnet to the *Nation*, a weekly journal devoted to
politics, literature, science, and art. The sonnet, "Lifted Over,"
accepted by the editor, Mr. S. L. Godkin, closed with the reso-
lution of her despair, "Shall I not then be glad, and, thanking
God, press on to overtake?"

"Lifted Over" brought Helen recognition and praise. "Written straight from her own bereavement," Sarah wrote, "it went
straight to the hearts of other bereaved ones." For this reason,
many refer to the poem as Helen's first publication.

Lifted Over

As tender mothers guiding baby steps,
When places come at which the tiny feet
Would trip, lift up the little ones in arms
Of love, and set them down beyond the harm,
So did Our Father watch the precious boy....
He saw the sweet limbs faltering, and saw

Rough ways before us, where my arms would fail;
So reached from heaven, and lifting the dear child.
Who smiled in leaving me, He put him down
Beyond all hurt, beyond my sight, and bade
Him, wait for me! Shall I not then be glad,
And, thanking God, press on to overtake?

One of her last Marah poems, "Summer Rain," she wrote in July. In it she cried, "Oh, iron-handed grief, which holds my soul in searing grief . . . and will he give to me . . . at last, as unto His Beloved, sleep?"

Helen cried out her sorrow, and sleep came at last. The days of dark despair were over, and one warm July morning, after months alone in her room, she appeared downstairs, dry-eyed and content, with her old vitality and charm.

"I know I'm escaping," she told Jennie, "and I'm not ungrateful for all you have done for me. You have been angels, but I need to flee. . . ."

She talked of traveling through New England, and said, "First I must return to West Roxbury to comfort my dear sister Annie and to see the new baby, Mary Chapman."

"And then what are your plans?" asked Mr. John, hoping against hope that she would want to make New Haven her home.

"I don't have anything definite in mind as yet. I may go to Boston for the winter months. I'm just not sure." She tried to explain her need to leave the city, where memories of Rennie were everywhere, and urged Sarah to travel with her.

"You know you're a real New Englander, Sarah," she teased her friend. "Why not see some of the countryside?"

"I should love that—maybe later, Helen." Helen knew that Sarah had her father's care in mind. He had been unwell for some time.

So Helen traveled alone most of the summer. Among her many jaunts, she went to Princeton, Massachusetts, where she

spent a month at the Inn, delighting in the walks through the up-
lands and amazed at the unusual variety of trees. Later she would
write about this town, calling it the "Hide and Seek Town,"
since, she said, "it dodged in and out of view while it was yet
miles away."

There were shorter trips as well, to Dorchester, Hingham,
Boston, and to Brattleboro, Vermont. But the one to Bethlehem,
New Hampshire, satisfied her the most, and there she would
stay until the snows came. The invigorating mountain air and
the agreeable temperature of this small and little-known mountain village cured her usual summer bout of hay fever.

On one of her walks up Strawberry Hill, Helen took along
her black morocco writing case and sat down under the pines on
a "fine rocky seat," to try her hand at an account of her "mountain life." Comparing the town of New Hampshire's Bethlehem
with the ancient city, she described its location and told "all
about it." Though it was not ready for tourists, she predicted it
soon would be and would even have a growth greater than that
of Conway, south of Mt. Washington.

Then, on impulse, she sent the article to Mr. Godwin, who, to
her amazement, published it a month later. This time she used
her initials, H. H. Marah, she thought, with its sorrowful con-
notation, no longer suited her. She couldn't or she wouldn't use
her full signature, for women rarely identified themselves as
writers. Many readers in the 1860s were hostile to women writing seriously, sometimes referring to as "ink-stained women."
Pseudonyms were common.

The good response to her Marah poems and now the publication of her first prose article, for which she was actually paid,
stimulated Helen to consider writing as a career. She asked Mr.
Godwin for his honest opinion. He encouraged her, suggesting
she first try "some pleasant gossipy letters on the very unpleas-
ant subject of Boston." She did.

9

Newport, Rhode Island

AFTER RENNIE'S DEATH, Helen had no desire to have a permanent home, but Newport, of all her army-life "homes," seemed
the most promising place for a writer. If she were to enter a circle of literary people and make her way into the publishing field,
she thought Newport had more to offer than any other eastern
city, even New York.

For Newport in the 1860s was a center of literary and artistic
groups. According to Colonel Thomas Wentworth Higginson,
"There were more authors in that city than any other in America." Unlike Saratoga, New York, the city was not a "fast" place,
and for those who lived there the year round, the summer season was one of picnics, sailing parties, and home soirees. Tourists
received little, if any, attention, and it was a delight when they
left the island and Newport resumed its normal way of life, with
no four-or-six hands dashing along Bellevue Avenue, no fashion
shops open, or Turkish vendors from Constantinople. Sarah
Woolsey would write of her winters in Aquidneck (Newport),
"That isle of Peace, . . . with time to study, to be lazy, and to
form friendships."

If Helen were to write for publication, she knew she would
need a literary adviser, someone whose opinion she could trust,
and Colonel Thomas Higginson might be just the one. She had

met the Colonel ten years before at a scientific gathering in Providence, and since then had frequently read his articles and stories in the *Atlantic Monthly*. She had greatly admired his *Outdoor Papers* and thought the book a perfect specimen of literary composition. The Colonel had moved to Newport in 1864.

When Helen learned that the Higginsons were boarding at the Dames' home on the main street, she made a firm resolve to board there too. A man who could write as well as the Colonel might help her in her writing. Hadn't he printed "Letter to a Young Contributor," in the April, 1862, *Atlantic*, full of advice for the inexperienced?

Early in January, Helen began her arrangements and, still dressed in deep mourning, arrived at the Dames on February 10, where two upstairs rooms were assigned her. She was satisfied with the clean and comfortable furnishings and grateful that her windows, in the large gambrel-roofed house, looked out onto the main thoroughfare, then known as Broad Street. Lined with stately elms, the street was not far from the City Hall Square and the wharf.

At first she wondered if she had been wise in returning to the town where Rennie had been born, and she avoided both Cottage and School Streets in her daily walks. Loneliness was never far away, and every time she opened a door she would have the queer feeling that Rennie would come running to meet her and throw his arms around her neck. A brief visit to West Point to inspect the graves of her husband and sons and a poem, "Burial Service," offered relief and hope of "resurrection":

A Burial Service

> To Christ's protection
> Now let us leave it,—the tomb and the key! He
> Will remember us, if there may ever be
> Resurrection!

She soon felt at home with the Dame family; her early doubts were gradually dispelled. If all went well, she might even stay until fall.

Mrs. Hannah Dame, a small Quaker lady and widow of Jonathan Dame, and her two daughters, Elma, a schoolteacher, and a younger girl Mary, made her most welcome. Meals around the large table brought out Helen's talent for telling stories, and Colonel Higginson began to have some difficulty in outwitting her. "She seems very bright and sociable," he told his wife, Mary Channing, "and may prove an accession."

Evenings, Helen often visited with the Higignsons in their rooms across the hallway. Although Mrs. Higginson was crippled with chronic rheumatism and spent most of her time in a wheelchair, she went out driving on good days. Her husband had purchased a cab and had one side removed so that her chair could be wheeled directly into the carriage.

Through the Colonel, Helen gained entree at once into a circle made up largely of artists, and met many authors and painters. She formed a strong friendship with Sarah Clarke, sister of the Reverend James Freeman Clarke of Boston, and an artist of merit who often spent weeks on the beach at her painting. Although Helen was some twenty years younger than Sarah, she enjoyed the artist's great charm, and it was in Sarah's home that she first met socially Mr. and Mrs. Ralph Waldo Emerson of Concord, who were spending a week with the Clarkes in Newport.

On clear days the Colonel often went out in his dory to sail about Narragansett Bay; sometimes he was off horseback riding, and on occasion he rode out to Lawton's Valley with Helen to see the Howes. Helen could not help but recall the gay time she and Edward had been entertained there along with the members of the Association for the Advancement of Science in 1860. But only since her return to Newport six years later had she realized the role Julia Ward Howe played in the life of the town. "Queen of the literary group," the Colonel called her. She was now nationally known for her "Battle Hymn of the Republic," published in the November, 1861, *Atlantic Monthly* and had brought distinction to Newport.

In early March, Helen finally got up courage to show Colonel Higginson a few of her verses, and asked him about the prospects of writing professionally. Would she be able, she wanted to know, to earn a living with her writings?

The Colonel encouraged her, saying he would be glad to help her as much as he could. And as he promised Mrs. Hunt, he was reminded of Emily Dickinson, who four years earlier had asked for his criticism. "Are you too deeply occupied to say if my verse is alive?" she asked in a letter of April 15, 1862. She told him she had been moved by his "Letter to a Young Contributor" —and by his forthrightness. For in his comments he had cautioned the beginning writer, remarking, "The majority are too bad for blessing and too good for banning."

"Did you know Miss Dickinson of Amherst?" he asked, knowing Helen had lived in western Massachusetts as a child.

"Yes, slightly," she answered, hesitating briefly. "I grew up in Amherst, but left when I was thirteen after my dear mother died."

"She writes poetry," he commented.

"I didn't know," she said, "though I knew her at school. I haven't seen her for some time. . . ."

Then the Colonel [1] told Helen the little he knew of Miss Dickinson, whom he corresponded with but had never seen, how she sent him her poems, which he described as "rather idealistic" and "strange."

"Actually, she has never published—or wanted to publish—her verses, her only wish being to know 'if they breathe,'" he told Helen.

Of Emily's poems the Colonel shared with her, Helen most liked the simplicity of her nature poetry. "I hope to go to Amherst this coming August for Commencement," Helen said, thinking to herself that she might see Emily again. And she wondered if she could persuade her to publish.

Meanwhile Helen turned much of her attention to her own writing. The two poems she had first shown the Colonel, "March" and "An Alcove to the East," were accepted by the *New York Evening Post*. And on April 12 there appeared in the *Nation* her poem "Tryst," which the Colonel had edited.

She used her initials again as her signature. Alliterative as it was, she thought it better than using her full name. "Helen Hunt" sounded too much like the pseudonyms Fanny Fern or Grace Greenwood, which she couldn't abide. In any case, if she couldn't make her initials a marketable signature, the full name would not help much.

Under the Colonel's schooling, she set herself to learn her craft. She studied and wrote and then rewrote, going over every word, line, and sentence. She followed as carefully as she could her adviser's basic principles: "Never use an obscure phrase or an unusual word when direct language or a single term will express your meaning," and "Be neither too lax nor too precise in your use of language."

With the approval of her adviser she sent more poems to the *Nation* and to the *New York Evening Post*, some of which were printed. Then, encouraged to continue, she suggested he let her try the *New York Independent*, a paper under the editorship of Theodore Tilton. The paper was a liberal weekly, called "an infidel sheet" by some critics because many Unitarians wrote for it.

"Almost all the writers of the day are included in it, even you," she remarked, smiling across the desk at the Colonel, "and I may be able to have some of my poems and articles published there, ones that the *Nation* refuses to accept."

Someday she would like to publish in the *Atlantic Monthly*, but she agreed that her work wasn't yet of the high standard of that magazine. She needed time. "I hope you approve."

He did, and suggested instead that she try the *Independent*, submitting her first Biblical poem "Hagar"—he thought the Biblical title might help insure acceptance. Not only did Mr. Tilton accept "Hagar," but he also asked for others. Helen was delighted with his response and immediately sent "Bread on the Waters." She would write during her lifetime three hundred and seventy-one poems and prose pieces for the *Independent*.

If it hadn't been for the influx of summer visitors, that great "army of occupation," Helen would probably have stayed in Newport. The "Sleepy Hollow" had become for her almost "home," a pleasant place to live and work. And she began to find acceptance in literary circles, especially enjoying the one that met at Colonel Warings.

At times she still went with the Colonel to the cottage of Julia Ward Howe, who held receptions in a "world of her own." While many came to Newport in the summer from Boston and New York to escape the heat and "to take possession of the Island for a few months," Helen packed her trunks and fled the arrival of those who came, as she said, "to show off their fine clothes, handsome horses and carriages."

"I'll see you soon," she wrote her sister. For Helen was on her way to New Hampshire with cousin Priscilla Stearns of Boston, who had agreed to climb Mt. Washington with her.

"I wish you might come with me, Annie," she wrote, although she knew well that Annie's hands were busy with her large family, two boys and three girls.

Winters in Newport became more and more active for Helen. While she spent much of her energy writing, she began to enter more fully into the life of the town, and even attended some of the lectures at the Redwood Library. Occasionally she still drove out with the Higginsons and, to brighten the dull days of February a ball was held in Mrs. Dame's back parlor.

"There's to be no gorgeous apparel," the invitation read, stating that the guests were not expected to take off their cloaks or bonnets. Helen took charge of the arrangements of the parlor. "She draped two American flags over the doors, and all the rest of the decorations were green boughs and hanging baskets," reported the Colonel in his *Oldport Days*. The party was held in broad daylight while "all the world sat on sixty chairs." Actually, it was a musicale with works played by the Mendelssohn Quintette Club.

That spring of 1867, Helen was finally encouraged by the Colonel to send several of her poems to Mr. James T. Fields, the distinguished editor of the *Atlantic*, including a new one, the "Zone of Calms." They were mailed on May 11 and signed Mrs. Edward Hunt, Box 224, with stamps enclosed. Helen took no chance of either losing her poetry or of not having it returned for publication elsewhere. The poem was rejected as were all the others; she would hesitate a long time before she tried the *Atlantic* again. "I'll wait until I have written something of which I can be sure," she told Colonel Higginson.

When June came, she began to plan for another trip to New Hampshire, but this time she put off her departure date to go with Sarah Clarke and her young niece Lilian to Nova Scotia. The Clarkes were to take the boat from Lewis Wharf in Boston at 1:00 P.M., June 10, for Halifax. "I can never resist a boat trip," Helen declared when Sarah first asked her. In fact, Helen could never resist any trip, boat, train, or stagecoach. She was a traveler with trunks and valises ready at almost a moment's notice.

Out of her two-week experience in Nova Scotia, into Evangeline country to see the places about which Longfellow had written, Helen was to publish two travel articles, signed Rip Van

Winkle. She liked to use this pseudonym as indicative of her life in Newport. While she used it only for the articles in the *Evening Post*, she would drop it even there in a few years in favor of her usual H. H.

In July, as she had promised Priscilla Stearns, she traveled with her through Vermont and New Hampshire, spending a month in Brattleboro, Vermont, and several weeks in Bethlehem, New Hampshire, where she found to her surprise that the mountain village was crowded and her old rooms occupied. "It is a bad plan to tell the other boys where the bird's nest is," she laughed.

Each fall after her travels in the mountains, Helen sent back to Newport trunks full of pressed ferns and leaves. The Colonel reported in his journals that she sent "half the Brattleboro woods, gentians and a mammoth basket of moss and climbing ferns, leaves, and vines." And with her she also brought new manuscripts for his advice and editing.

Her account of the trip up Mt. Washington with Priscilla in the summer of 1866 had resulted in her second published prose article, "In the Mountains." She had become an accepted writer for the *Post* and the *Independent*.

Her literary output continued to increase, and as her interests grew and her horizons broadened, she experimented with different forms of writing and on different topics. It was only natural she should try her hand at writing for children: many women writers of the day were turning out poems and stories to meet the growing demand for juvenile literature. She was sure she could do better than the *Dolly Dimples* of Sophia May.

Her first attempt was a translation from the French of Florians's "Tale of Bathmendi," a poem telling how the genie Alzin gave money and help freely, but couldn't give life. Despite the Colonel's dislike of the translation, Aaron K. Loring of Boston published it. Helen had heard of this bookseller and publisher of the Up-Town Bookstore, who had already published Louisa

May Alcott's *Moods* and Horatio Alger's books for boys, and she thought he might be interested in adding a juvenile poem to his listings. He was, and, pleased with its publication, Helen started to write stories based on events from her own childhood. Mr. Horace E. Scudder accepted "A Christmas Tree for Cats'" in his *Riverside Magazine*, and after that, many of her childhood pranks appeared in this magazine. Helen was said to have gloated that their only moral was that they were true.

Eager as always to see new places, Helen explored Block Island for an article for the *Post* in the summer of 1868. The trip to this isolated island some twenty-five miles southeast of Newport took seven sailing hours. Helen traveled about the island by oxcart over rough roads, passing on the east side of the Great Pond and visiting the cottage of Mrs. Bell, "almost lost in mist and flowers." But she found no evidence of ghosts, as indicated in Whittier's "The Wreck of the Palatine," a legend of the phantom Dutch ship; all she found was a graveyard with stones dating back to the seventeenth century and a pond filled with large white and yellow lilies.

"The island was really primitive," she reported in the *Post*, "yet perfectly safe. I didn't get even a twinge of fright on the island, but the boat ride back was a bit 'shoddy'. . . ."

She would have gone directly to Bethlehem on her return but for an unexpected assignment from Mr. Tilton of the *Independent*. "Could she report on the annual meeting of the National Academy of Sciences [2] that was to be held from August 20th to the 25th in Northampton, Massachusetts?" She could stay at the Round Hill House with Mrs. Lucia Calhoun.

She could, and she would, especially since Mrs. Calhoun had promised to spend a month of "mountaineering" with her after the meetings. She had met the widow earlier on one of her visits to New York through Mr. Tilton, who called her his "favorite woman editorial writer" of the *New York Tribune*.

The days at the White Mountains ended far too soon for

Helen. But Bertie, as Helen nicknamed Mrs. Calhoun, had to be back in New York to prepare for her coming wedding to a young lawyer, a Dr. C. A. Runkle.

In October, Helen returned to Newport and to her writing. Each year since she had started her professional career she had added more publication outlets to her list of magazines and newspapers. At the age of thirty-eight, Helen Hunt had made her name.

The Colonel wanted to include her in an article he was writing for the *Independent*, titled "The Female Poets of America." For some reason of her own, she objected, telling him she preferred to keep out of "this sort of mention." Instead, she gave him more of her poems, a few of which she had earlier sent in manuscript to admirers and friends. One of them, "Tribute," she undoubtedly had sent to Ralph Waldo Emerson during the winter of 1867–68 and probably, if the inference is correct, had asked for his criticism of it.

To Bottanie, to whom she often sent a poem with her greetings, she wrote on February 24, "Here is the little sonnet, completed by unworthy. One man says he loves it, but I think it is because he loves me, and is waiting to love you. . . ." The month before, Helen had published in the *Post* a poem to Bottanie, titled "A.C.L.B." It was, Helen thought, a long-overdue tribute to Bottanie's "royal welcome to the friends who reach her threshold."

It may have been that Helen hesitated to have the Colonel write about her because he had been her literary adviser, but he was right in his estimate of her accomplishments. Whether or not Helen was listed among the female poets of America in 1868, she was in a class with Harriet Beecher Stowe and Louisa May Alcott. She had become a recognized poet who had "struck her stride."

10

"Coronation"

IT WAS THE CUSTOM of the day for American men and women
of letters to take the "grand tour." Helen, too, was ready to extend her travels to include England and the Continent. "I can
record my journey in poems and sketches," she told the Colonel,
fully aware of the competition she would face if she planned to
publish travel notes: the "gossip of the grand tour" made up
part of the literature of the time.

Several such travel records were already in print. Julia Ward
Howe had just published her account of European travels in
*From the Oaks to the Olive: a Plain Record of a Pleasant Jour-
ney*. And Grace Greenwood's *Haps and Mishaps of a Tour of
Europe*, published in 1854, remained popular reading, as had the
travel experiences written by William Dean Howells, Harriet
Beecher Stowe, and others. Helen's plan was different.

She outlined for the Colonel her idea of writing a monthly
round-robin letter that would go to sixteen of her closest friends,
first to her sister Annie. These letters would be known as "encyclicals" because they would find their way to "the faithful."
Would the Colonel act as her adviser and "broker" while she
was away for at least a year?

With his promise of assistance, Helen set sail with the Stearns
sisters, Priscilla and Ellen, on November 5, 1868, out of Boston

on the S.S. *China* for Liverpool, England. From Liverpool to London, Paris, and finally Rome in December, Helen would jot down her notes for letters to go back home. The list would include Molly Hunt, her sister-in-law, then on to a larger circle in Newport, to Jennie Abbott in New Haven, to Bottanie in New York, and finally to the Colonel for safekeeping.

The seven days' crossing of the Atlantic was more of a lark than Helen had supposed it would be. To begin with, the voyage was so smooth that she could sit out on deck every day although hot-water jugs were needed at her feet each night. She discovered that she ate more and oftener than she should, even though she tried to avoid the midmorning bouillon.

In fact, the time passed so swiftly for Helen and the Stearns girls that it was a surprise to be told one late afternoon that the ship would soon dock at Queenstown (Cohn, Cork Harbor), Ireland. After rushing to post her letters for home, she stood on deck and watched the eighty-seven bags of mail put ashore.

By the next morning the S.S. *China* was sailing on the Irish Sea between the coasts of Ireland and Wales into Liverpool. The S.S. *Russia* passed them on its way out and Helen wouldn't know until much later that she had missed Professor and Mrs. Botta on their way home.

Unexpectedly for Helen, Liverpool seemed old and musty with its great Norman houses; she expressed a "vagabond indifference" to the place and was delighted to board the train to London. Train travel in England was fast and at nine that evening she was settled into Batt's Hotel on 41 Dover Street, Piccadilly, London. But London's smoke and lack of sun distressed her. It was as cold as Boston in March. She could scarcely wait to leave for Paris and 9 Rue Castiglione, where the Clarkes were staying.

She would stay the two days in London as planned, however, and she did, attending with Priscilla the South Chapel Place

Church services in Finsbury to see and hear her old friend of Washington days, the Reverend Mr. Conway. She thought Monk looked a "bit seedy and down at the heels"; the church appeared equally shabby, with a small and poor congregation. But Monk's talk was "alive" and Helen was glad to have seen him, if only for a few minutes after the service. She had long wanted to express to him her sympathy in his Washington experience. In 1856, he had had to quit the pulpit because he refused to soften his attacks on the slavery question.

On Monday she shopped for a waterproof cloak, looked for a copy of Christina Rossetti in the bookstores on Paternoster Row, visited Westminster Abbey, and dined with the Stearns at Blanchard's Inn. Off to Paris in the morning!

She packed with anticipation of the trip across the Channel. From Folkestone it was a two-hour sail and more uncomfortable than she had imagined. But she refused to stay in the cabin where the stuffiness and smells made her feel sick. Instead, she spent the crossing on deck, clinging to the settee while the boat pitched and rolled.

Strangely, she heartily disliked Paris and not even a French gown made by the famous Hillé could appease her. She preferred her daytime walking dress of black silk and her gray poplin skirt without a hoop. Paris was simply "New York grown up, graduated, and with a diploma," she told Sarah and Lilian Clarke, when she met them there. With a brief stopover in Nice, France, "the noisiest, coldest, and muddiest garden," and after two days in Genoa, Italy, they reached Rome on December 14. There Helen unpacked "her pin cushions and slippers as if meant to stay a week. . . ."

The ancient city captivated her. Rome made December seem like spring. She realized that it would be hard to leave and decided to stay until April—if they could locate an apartment. They were in the midst of the winter tourist season and there were six of them to be satisfied. For besides the Stearns sisters, Sarah and Lilian Clarke had joined them with a friend, Margaret Foley, a young New Hampshire girl, who had studied sculpture for seven years in Boston before going to Rome.

A "small pension" on the Via Quattro Fontano, near the Barberini Palace, with four "faultless rooms," was perfect, from a kitchen gleaming with sunlight on copper to the beautiful Marianina, "maid of all work." With the *Murray* guidebook in hand, Helen put on her black traveling dress and large white straw hat and went sight-seeing. On January 3, 1869, she sent the first of the encyclical letters to the Colonel.

Though social life in Rome was "anathema" to Helen, friends often came to lunch at the pension, and she relented enough to attend a Charity Ball, staying until five in the morning to let the girls dance as long as they liked. It is very likely that it was at this time that Helen first met Charlotte Cushman,[1] an American actress. Tall and deep-voiced, Miss Cushman was famous for her readings as well as for her acting. She had crossed the Atlantic many times and, after two farewell performances in America in 1865, had returned to her Roman villa.

The weekly Open House at the Cushman villa was one of the highlights of a visit to Rome, and it is probable that Helen met her there. If not at the villa, she certainly met her during the Rome visit—long enough to arrange a meeting in July in Munich.

Early in February, Sarah Clarke presented Helen one day with a snowdrop she had picked on her early-morning stroll. Enchanted with its delicate beauty, Helen wrote a sonnet, "Snowdrops in Italy," and sent it directly to the *Nation*. Most of her poems, however, she continued to mail to the Colonel. He had her permission to submit them to whatever magazine or newspaper he thought best suited.

That month the *Independent* carried "Spinning," and "Coronation" appeared in the *Atlantic Monthly*. Of "Spinning," Helen wrote the Colonel, "I am glad you like it. I didn't know it was good." But it was the poem "Coronation" that brought her the greatest satisfaction. It marked her entry into the *Atlantic* columns and recognition by its editor, Mr. Fields, who called it "devilish good"—for him, a compliment indeed!

Coronation

At the king's gate the subtle noon
  Wove filmy yellow nets of sun;
Into the drowsy snare too soon
  The guards fell one by one.

Through the king's gate, unquestioned then,
  A beggar went, and laughed, "This brings
Me chance at last, to see if men
  Fare better, being kings."

The king sat bowed beneath his crown,
  Propping his face with listless hand;
Watching the hour-glass sifting down
  Too slow its shining sand.

"Poor man, what wouldst thou have of me?"
  The beggar turned, and pitying,
Replied, like one in dream, "Of thee,
  Nothing. I want the king."

Up rose the king, and from his head
  Shook off the crown and threw it by,
"O man, thou must have known," he said,
  "A greater king than I."

Her only disappointment was in the signature. "By what right?" she immediately asked the editor, "I want to know by what right did you substitute Helen Hunt for the H.H. I sent in?"

Disturbed, she made no pretense of her feelings. It was bad enough with a Mrs. prefixed, but without it she sounded like Minnie Myrtle.

Travel in a group had become unwieldy, so she decided to strike out on her own. At Berchtesgaden in Bavaria, she searched until she found a "hill study" outside the village. "I am leading the life of a hermit," she wrote Sarah Clarke from the cottage high on a mountain trail, so steep, she said, it caused "even the hen to slip."

The trail reminded her of Brattleboro paths, and the mountains were like Mt. Washington in its best October days, purple or gray, with dazzling white snow on the peaks. Writing, taking long walks, reading Emerson and Henry Morris, Helen was for the first time in her journey "absolutely and entirely alone."

It wasn't easy for her to leave her "beloved studio," but she had promised to join the Stearns girls for Gastein. It was a "wrench" to leave the mountains she had grown to love but, she said later, "It seemed foolish to lose Gastein because I was in love with a hillside."

Gastein was so crowded that even Helen was ready to give up the struggle for rooms, but she had developed a sore throat and was too ill to leave with Priscilla and Ellen for Salzburg.

If Helen missed her studio, she was rewarded at Gastein with her attic room in the quaint hillside home of Dr. Gustave Proell, her doctor. "I don't know if he has a strawberry mark on his left arm, but [he] is surely my long lost brother," Helen assured the Colonel. She told him about the doctor's faith in the curative waters of Gastein and his ability to spin out the tales of the villagers.

From the front window of her room she could see the three-hundred-foot-high waterfall in the center of town. For Helen, Gastein was "Brattleboro and Bethlehem married and come to spend a honeymoon in the Alps." She picked heath along the ra-

vines, admired the hollyhocks and bluebells, but she would have
given a basket of Alpine strawberries for one saucer of berries
from New Hampshire.

In contrast, Munich was a disaster. Charlotte Cushman wrote
from Great Malvern, England, at Gully's water cure, "I can not
join you. If I am not soon better of an inducated gland in my
left breast, I shall go to Coblenz for special treatment."

It was days before Helen could bring herself to answer the
sad note. "How dreadful," she thought, "for one so alive and energetic." She didn't know that Miss Cushman had been suffering
from cancer for months, and had left Rome for England to con-
sult an expert, Sir James Paget.

Back in London, even with visits from Monk and his wife and
an evening with Sarah Clarke, she grew restless. Annoyed at the
cold days and the fog, she decided to try the water cure at Malvern. "Perhaps it would help rejuvenate me," she thought.

But somehow the magic of Gastein and Dr. Proell was lacking
and Helen was disappointed in the methods for a cure. Possibly
it was all an anticlimax. In any case, she made plans to leave
England, and on January 22, 1870, sailed alone from Liverpool
on the S.S. *Russia*. "*Coming Across*," a poem writen in passage,
told of her eagerness to be back in Newport:

> Ah! my darlings, you never will know
> How I pined in the loss
> Of you all, and how breathless and glad
> I am coming across.

While in Europe, Helen had sent many of her manuscripts to
the Colonel, but not all of them. Some she had sent for comment to Sarah Woolsey and other close friends. From Munich,
she had sent on her own two "Rip Van Winkle" articles to the
Post, but they were rejected. And the two prose essays she had

forwarded to *Hearth and Home*, a weekly magazine for the "farm, garden, and fireside," were refused.

"I am dumb with astonishment," she told the Colonel. Yet the editor had tried to explain that he no longer wanted the European travel letters, since they had become a "drug on the market."

To Helen, however, it was financially necessary that she have her writings published and paid for. She submitted the rejects to Mr. Richard Watson Gilder, editor of *Hours at Home*. She had heard he paid ten dollars a page, and although she didn't know him and thought little of the magazine, she would settle for the added income. "The man who writes, if he needs pay for his work, must write what the man who prints will buy," she stated firmly.

After her return from Europe, she went almost immediately to Bethlehem, New Hampshire. There she set to work writing up her travel notes and editing the "encyclicals," the letters that had traveled round robin from West Roxbury to New Haven, New York, Washington, D.C., and back to the Colonel in Newport. By early May, she was ready to leave New Hampshire and she had encouraged Sarah Woolsey to join her in Bethlehem in the late summer. First she would stop over in Boston and then go on to Amherst, where she hoped to talk with Emily Dickinson about her writings. Helen had begun to think of writing stories with an Amherst background; perhaps Emily would help.

It may well be that Helen talked briefly with Emily about such writings, but, in the light of later correspondence, it seems doubtful that Helen spent more than a few minutes with her. Yet after Emily's death, Lavinia spread the story that the widow Helen Hunt stayed two weeks with her sister and sent off several manuscripts under the pen name, H. H. She also stated that Helen had urged Emily to help her write a short story with Amherst background and that, piqued by Emily's refusal, had later worked her into a novel as a character. Perhaps Vinnie, who labored diligently to secure recognition for Emily, came to believe the event actually had occurred.

But one thing is clear. Helen had the courage lacking in Emily's other literary advisers—she urged Emily to publish.

Dr. Holland, who had been an assistant to Samuel Bowles on the *Springfield Republican*,[2] had known Emily since her teens. Though he thought her poems "too ethereal" and insisted on making editorial changes in meter and rhyme, he printed several unsigned ones in the columns of the paper's Cultural Department. The Colonel, on the other hand, made no effort to have her submit her poetry, for he thought it "remarkable, though odd," "too delicate," and not strong enough for publication.

Although Sam Bowles wanted to print some of her work, Emily would have none of it. She sent her poems to him to read —"not to print," she told him. And when he printed her poem on the snake that had apparently come to him through her sister-in-law Sue, in the issue of February 14, 1866, she keenly felt it a betrayal and wrote, "I was robbed of it." Altered possibly by Dr. Holland, the poem would be the last one to appear in the *Republican*. Already sensitive to editorial corrections, Emily was torn between a desire to share and the knowledge that it could not be on her terms. She felt helpless in the matter of publication; when she wrote "publication is the auction of the mind of man," she was no doubt writing an apology for the isolation she would endure because she had no other choice.

But Helen believed in her and in her work, thinking it "marvelous." By 1870, she had read many of the poems sent by Emily to her "safe" friend and mentor, Colonel Higginson; she was the only literary contemporary who spoke their unqualified praise. She may have asked Emily's permission to use some of them or she may have wanted Emily to refresh her memory of Amherst people and places; whatever took place in this "assault on the ivory tower," surely a bond was established that would not be broken.

Ah-Wah-Ne

IT WAS IN Bethlehem, New Hampshire, that Sarah Woolsey wrote the poem.

> Each day is a fresh beginning
> Every morn is the world made new,

and each day she and Helen walked in the woods and hills. "To walk by her side as she threaded the Bethlehem woods, with quick and unerring steps . . . was a revelation," Sarah wrote of her friend this summer in the New Hampshire town.

As Sarah watched Helen, she noted the blond hair braided around her head and the strong chin and winning smile that was ever a part of her. Of Sarah, Helen could have made the same comment, for Sarah loved the walks and strode with equal energy, collecting the ferns and flowers she would later sketch or paint. For Sarah, the fall months of 1870 were the beginning of her writing career. She had written stories and poems for children, but it was in the mountain town that she outlined her first book.

One day, wandering off from the Barrett boardinghouse and the long veranda with the row of rocking chairs, she went up under the pines. And there, sitting on a log, she jotted down an outline for the *New Year's Bargain*, a Christmas story for children—a series of twelve stories, told by each of the months to make good a promise to a little boy.

"I'll sign myself Susan Coolidge," she told Helen.

"Instead of S. W.?" Helen questioned.

"Yes, Helen. My sister Jane has already used the pen name of Margaret Coolidge.[1] Somehow I think it might be fun to be a sister of the famous Margaret."

Later in the month, well after the manuscript was all but completed, Sarah agreed to let Helen send one of her short stories to Mr. Fields. Helen wanted to assist new authors as she herself had been helped. "I could never have become a writer without the Colonel's help," she told Sarah, noticing her reluctance to try the *Atlantic*.

But Helen not only sent Sarah's story, explaining that Miss Woolsey had been writing for two years for *Harper's Magazine*, a widely read "quality monthly"; she also enclosed a poem of her own. She wasn't sure she should have dared, but nonetheless was annoyed at the rejection of them both. But Sarah finished her book and sent the manuscript to Thomas Niles, editor of Roberts Brothers of Boston. To her joy, it was accepted. It would be published in the spring of 1871.

When the autumn colors began to appear and the days grew colder, Helen tried to prevail upon Mr. Fields to bring or send Tom Hughes, "the rare soul" from England, up to see the "woods ablaze from Lowell to Littleton," and she told him of the insulated cable that would soon be laid up Mt. Washington for a railroad.

"Professor Hitchcock has promised to take Miss Woolsey and myself to see it done," she wrote. Perhaps he could use a sketch of the ceremonial for the laying of the cable.

Mr. Fields disappointed her on both counts. He failed to arrange for a visit from Tom Hughes, author of *Tom Brown's School Days*, and he rejected as well her account of the ceremony. Undismayed, Helen sent the manuscript to the *Independent*, and a year later would send a second article describing her ride up the mountain in the cog railroad, feeling, she said, "like an eagle" as she sat on the edge of the tender.

Although her travel letters [2] had been accepted, she bargained with Mr. Fields most of the summer months as to price and content. Finally he said he would accept the letters if combined into one long article. And, much as she wanted the *Atlantic* to publish them, she refused his first offer of sixty dollars for the Gastein letters, which she thought her best—she held out for seventy-five. "I am writing (I mean printing) for money to pay for publishing my verses," she declared. She was determined to earn enough with her letters for the expenses of the stereotype plates for a "little volume of verses."

It was not until the "first feathery snow" in November that Helen and Sarah left their mountain home for Boston, where Helen called on Mr. Fields with the *Encyclicals* in hand. "I can present my case more easily in person than by letter," she told Sarah. The end proved her means correct, for the *Valley of Gastein* was accepted. Mr. Fields also agreed to publish two articles she was working on about New Hampshire scenes. And to cap the gains, the *Atlantic* would carry in their June, August, and September issues her "Encyclicals of a Traveller."

From Newport, she wrote Mr. Fields on December 26, "I never write for money, I write for love, then after it is written, I *print* for money."

She asked a hundred dollars for the "Ampezzo" article, explaining that, though cash was a vile thing," one thing viler is a purse without any cash in it." She added that Mr. Gilder had paid her friend Sarah Woolsey fifteen dollars a month for a page and a half on home topics. But even so, she wanted him to know that the four articles published in the *Atlantic* had helped her "more than years of work anywhere else."

Then, just before the new year, Fields, Osgood, and Company of Boston put out her *Verses*. The reviews were gratifying. *Scribner's Monthly* had one that eclipsed all the others, stating, "This little volume of *Verses* with its red edges, and old-style lettering and crisp leaves . . . what blue summer sky it brings to us here by the winter fireside. . . ." Dr. Holland, editor of this new magazine, also approved of it. Helen was delighted.

She was equally pleased when Dr. Holland asked her for some fiction. In the five years Helen had written professionally, she had been successful with prose articles and poetry, but she had never tried fiction. Though she had once considered the possibility of writing stories of Amherst life, making use of characters, settings, and circumstances drawn from her own experiences as a child, she wondered if she could handle pure fiction.

What harm was there in trying? But she would keep authorship a secret, just in case the stories didn't sell. A new signature would be essential—she would take no chances on losing her reputation as a poet. For reasons known only to herself, she chose the pseudonym Saxe Holm, possibly reminiscent of her days in Gastein and of the tales Dr. Proell had told her there. Smiling to herself as she signed her first story, "Whose Wife Was She?", she said aloud, "No one will be able to identify Helen Hunt or H. H. as the author."

She told Dr. Holland of her wish to remain anonymous and shared her secret with the Colonel. She would tell no one else for a while, not even Sarah Woolsey.

During the winter months, she continued with her writing, publishing a few items in newspapers and magazines. It was still the *Independent*, however, that took the great bulk of her work. She also reviewed books at a price, preferring to leave most of them unsigned, as was the usual practice at the time. Although many of them cannot now be identified with certainty, the glowing comments on Anna Leonowens's "An English Governess at the Siamese Court" in the *Atlantic* was clearly hers.

She also reviewed Charles Dudley Warner's [3] *My Summer in a Garden* for *Scribner's*, a book she so thoroughly enjoyed that she took the liberty of writing the unknown author. "It will seem odd, no doubt, to have a stranger write to thank you for being alive. . . ." Mr. Warner didn't find it odd at all and corresponded with Helen the rest of her life. Pleased with his quick response and his open invitation to visit him and his wife at Nook Farm in Hartford, Connecticut, she wrote him from Newport, "I should like of all things to come to your house some day, perhaps before the end of next summer I will. . . ."

But next summer she and Sarah Woolsey would be on their way to California. She had sent a Saxe Holm story from Bethlehem, where they were spending another summer together and planning to go West the one thereafter. Helen had longed for such a trip ever since Mrs. Runkle had chosen to visit Yosemite instead of joining her in the Tyrol, but travel was expensive. Round-trip tickets to San Francisco over the Union and Central Pacific were just under three hundred dollars. And everything else would be extra: the drawing rooms and berths, meals, hotels, horses and guides. The trip would cost each of them seven or eight hundred dollars.

Of course, she could have asked her former guardian and banker, Mr. Julius Palmer, for financial help—"he being the man who supplies me with my money," she told Sarah. But money was no problem the spring of 1872 for either Helen or Sarah. Their writings had been sufficiently profitable.

Sarah's *New Year's Bargain* had made a "pretty penny." The book was not only well-received in America but it successfully went overseas. Among other reviewers, Jean Bigelow and Christina Rossetti had sent "cordial congratulations on the originality and beauty of the story." Sarah could celebrate her first book royalties. And if Helen had any doubts about being able to finance such a trip, the success of her European travels dispelled her doubts. For James R. Osgood and Company, successors of Fields, Osgood and Company, published her first prose volume, *Bits of Travel.*

Most critics called the small book, made up of her best European sketches, "the work of genius," and *Scribner's* gave it high praise, stating that "no woman in America showed so much promise as H. H." True, the *Nation* thought it was spoiled by "too much vivacity," but the general response was complimentary.

In her publications to date, Helen had earned more than an adequate living with her poetry, prose essays, and sketches. Now it was her fiction that brought her the highest financial returns —and the highest prase. She wrote the Saxe Holm stories, she confessed, to please Dr. Holland and his assistant, Mr. Gilder, depicting her characters in a way that would not offend "the moral scruples of an idealist."

As usual, Helen made several trips to Boston and to New York to see her publishers and to visit friends. Her stay of four days in Boston at the Parker House proved rewarding—she heard Miss Cushman read twice. "I suppose I shall never feel again, in my life, as I did while hearing her read my 'Funeral March,'" she wrote Bottanie from Newport. She thought Miss Cushman's readings even "grander than her acting." "Boston audiences," she said, "were fairly electrified and applauded as I have never heard them before."

In New York she spent a few weeks with Bottanie. It was there she first met Mrs. Anna Leonowens, whose intriguing book on her life in Siam she had reviewed two years earlier. Charmed by Mrs. Leonowens's gay and easy manner and the excitement of her foreign experiences, Helen could not resist asking her to Newport to lecture about them.

When Helen told Sarah of the accepted invitation, Sarah could hardly believe her ears: she knew Helen did not approve of women taking the lecture platform. She had openly expressed her dislike of Kate Field,[4] who had not only irritated Helen with her stand on women's rights but had also offended her by charging that she had been a "spendthrift of brains" in writing the *Encyclicals*. But Helen didn't stop to rationalize her championship of Anna Leonowens. She only realized that Anna had a message, and she threw herself into the planning of the event. She put Kate Field out of her mind—there was no comparison.

Where would Anna give the lecture? Helen suggested the Redwood Library, which would hold about a hundred and seventy people. "It costs nothing," she told Anna. On the other hand, if the audience was larger, she could use the Opera House for a rental fee of forty-five dollars. "I dare not decide for her," she notified Bottanie, "and I shall write her tomorrow and make her decide."

The Opera House was rented at Anna's wish, and Helen sent advance notices to the *Newport Mercury*, sold tickets, and got her friends to do the same. She even persuaded Bottanie to help "shape Anna's lecture." Helen was so caught up in the excitement of the programing that not even the Colonel's lukewarm support troubled her. After the successful lecture, she continued to disregard his criticism. "I find her statistics do not tally with the information I found in the encyclopedia," he reported. "And I don't think she showed good taste in the talk." He had objected, even though he was willing to write his publishers on Anna's behalf.

"What did you find most disturbing?" Helen finally asked him, hoping he had forgotten his first reaction.

"The love story of the slave girl Boon," he said sternly. "It's made-up nonsense."

But Helen as firmly disagreed, and a few years later she would make the story into a long poem, "The Story of Boon." Neither, of course, could know that Margaret D. Landon would rewrite and modernize Anna's book in 1944 under the title of *Anna and the King of Siam*, and that it would eventually appear on Broadway as a musical, *The King and I*.

A month after Anna's talk, Helen and Sarah were packed, ready for the trip west to California. On May 9, 1872, they left from the Erie Railroad Station in New York for a two months' journey to the West, boarding the train with parcels of "life preservers"—baskets containing orange marmalade, chicken, crackers, and Albert biscuits. The drawing room was comfortable, with space enough for the bags, bundles, and baskets, and they settled in happily, hanging up their cologne bottles.

It was normally a ten-day trip from New York to San Francisco, but they had decided to take a side trip from Ogden to Salt Lake City. From Ogden west, there was no longer drawing-room service and they had to be content with a Pullman on the Silver Palace cars. For Helen, the first night, trying to undress in the small berth by the dim light of a kerosene lamp, was a nightmare. "I dislike the sleeping car sections more than I have disliked . . . anything in the world," was Helen's final judgment. But the discomfort was soon forgotten in the beauty of the Sierras the next morning and of the valleys with their masses of blue lupine and yellow poppies and "mustard by the acre."

"It seems as if California's hidden gold had grown impatient of darkness and burst into flower!" Helen remarked as they left Sacramento for San Francisco. But the train did not enter the city—they were deposited in Oakland for the ferry. "Half an hour on a steam tug!" Odd, thought Helen, to cross a continent —prairies, deserts, mountains—and then be ferried to its far western side.

San Francisco, with its 150,000 population on streets steep as those in an Alpine town, looked to Helen like a "toppling

town . . . hopelessly crowded." In her disappointment, she
complained, "There is nothing in the City to detain the traveler
many days." But once out of the city, Helen found that California far surpassed her expectations. She was enchanted with
the colors at sunset, with Mt. Tamalpais yellow with mist, and
with Mt. Diablo purple as they traveled from Vallejo to Calis-
toga Springs.

On a trip south from "Frisco," as the miners called it, through
the Santa Clara valley, she admired the waving sea of yellow
mustard and the little village of Santa Cruz. She learned of the
old padres who had built the mission there. The adobe buildings
had long crumbled, but she noted that the "communion of saints
is never banished from the air it once has filled."

Best of all in their travels through California was their trip
into Yosemite on the western slope of the Sierra Nevada range,
about a hundred and fifty miles east of Oakland. Helen insisted
on calling it Ah-Wah-Ne, the old Indian name for the valley.
This trip had all the adventure of the pioneering West: horseback riding over precipitous trails, accommodations that were
quite primitive, and food that tested the hardiest stomach.

Yet Helen and Sarah couldn't complain. They couldn't have
had a better guide than John Murphy, who knew every inch
of the valley. Nor could they ever forget the grandeur of the
mountain walls, Sentinel Rock and El Capitan, and the Falls. The
tremendous roar of the great Ah-Wah-Ne Falls moved Helen
deeply, as did the first sight of Pohono (Indian for "Bridal
Veil") Falls—how wonderful its "fine-spun gossamer fleeciness
with one broad brilliant rainbow in a perfect circle"!

Setting out at half-past six one morning, they reached Glacier
Point at noon, where they "crouched between high rocks . . .
peering over the edge, drinking in the loveliness of this marvelous miniature picture of Ah-Wah-Ne." But grander than the
view and more awesome than the other mountain walls was the

South Dome. The Sierra Nevada lay three miles away in "its immortal beauty."

Helen was breathless at this scene in the intense blue of a cloudless sky and wrote in an article, "Patillima and Loya"—Indian names for Glacier Point and the South Dome—"Little Ah-Wah-Ne was an emerald spot, walled by bare granite masses. Mountains seemed piled on mountains, and yet, beyond them and between them we could see the great valley stretches of the San Joaquin and the Sacramento, and to the west a dim blue line, which marked the Golden Gate."

The visit to the Big Trees of Calaveras and a final stop at Lake Tahoe seemed to Helen "less enticing" after the wilderness of Yosemite, and she objected to the socially late dinner hour of the Pacific Coast. "I verily believe," she said to Sarah, "if we went down far enough, we should find the California moles taking their worms at six p.m."

For Helen, dining at six meant losing the best part of the afternoon, and she always asked the landlord for an open carriage "to be at the door at six."

And when the host commented, as he invariably did, "But we dine at six, Madam," her reply was always the same: "I never dine at six."

And she never did, according to Sarah's account of the trip —she dined at five. But when she was ready to leave San Francisco in July, she assured Sarah she would return, she hoped next summer.

"I want to study the old missions," she told her. She had no way of knowing it would be more nearly ten years before she would again see the City on the Bay—and never again with Sarah.

12

In the
Shadow of Pike's Peak

THROUGHOUT THE LATE SUMMER and fall of 1872, most of which Helen spent alone in the White Mountains, she thought, talked, and wrote of little else than California. Though disappointed to learn that Sarah couldn't go with her again—she had made reservations to tour Europe with her sister and widowed mother—Helen was still determined to return to the West in the spring.

So she set to work in Bethlehem on the articles she had promised William Ward for the *Independent* and on October 18 told him she was really sorry to bring her California essays to completion. "Next year, I do hope to go again," she explained to him, "make studies of the old mission towns, stay three months in the Yosemite and go up to Oregon and come home by the Isthmus—that is an air-castle. . . ." Air castle or not, she continued her plans on such a trip after she returned to the Dames' boardinghouse in Newport despite a sore throat that "tortured" her off and on well into January.

On the fourteenth of the month, she interrupted her activities long enough to send a hurried note to Charles Dudley Warner about Mark Twain's attack on Sarah Woolsey, asking him to clear up the charge and tell Mark Twain that Sarah had not plagiarized from his *Innocents Abroad*. Helen could assure him that Dorry's journal in *What Katy Did* had been copied ver-

batim from a diary kept by her own son Rennie. Helen had
shared with Sarah the diary she had urged Rennie to begin on his
sixth birthday ten years before. It had been an ordeal for her
son who, after writing "forgit what did" for a few times, gave
up the whole idea on April 1, recording, "Have dissided not to
kepe a jurnal enny more."

The last of the month an attack of bronchial catarrh put
Helen to bed. She called it diphtheria, for when all but well she
had a relapse that she described as "far worse than the first."
"I do not feel as if I should ever be well again," she wrote a Boston friend,[1] but I am slowly gaining strength."

Bundled up like a mummy, on sunny days she would take an
hour's drive with her nurse and maid, Emma. "You can go to the
bottom of the class," she wrote Mr. Warner. "I've had diphtheria. What's quinsy [sore throat] to that? . . ."

But she kept on as much as possible with her writing and correspondence. She sent Mr. Warner advance sheets of *Bits of Talk
about Home Matters* and asked him to do anything he could to
copy "Wanted—A Home" in his newspaper, the *Hartford
Courant*.

With so much talk about women's rights and the movement
for women to gain them, Helen had finally felt compelled to face
up to her own opinion on the subject. She had stood Kate
Field's cries for the downtrodden female as long as she could
without an answer. "Wanted—A Home" she claimed as her protest "against the wrong side of the Women's Right Movement."
She hoped, she told Mr. Warner, that the whole book was sig-
nificant of views of life incompatible with the movement and
that it would go into the homes of the common people.

"There is an evil fashion of speech which says it is narrowing
and narrow life that a woman leads who cares only for her husband and children; that a higher, more imperative thing is that
she herself be developed to her utmost. . . ." Helen made it pain-

fully clear that she believed otherwise, that a woman "who cre-
ates and sustains a home, and under whose hands children grow
up to be strong and pure men and women, is a creator, second
only to God." If there had been any doubt about Helen's refusal
to join the "cause," there was none now.

By March, she was well enough to resume her planning for a
trip West. With Sarah's assistance, she discovered that Louisa
May Alcott's youngest sister—also named May—author of the
Concord Sketches, was interested in the journey. After a tour of
Europe with Louisa that had to be cut short for family reasons,
May hoped the West might be a good source of inspiration for
her art sketches and painting.

So Helen tried to get railroad passes for herself and May from
Mr. Ward, with promises of future articles, but she was unsuccessful. Then she turned to Oliver Johnson of the *Christian
Union*, but he, too, rejected her offer. A month later May wrote
she had changed her mind and was going back to London at the
end of April. Her sister Louisa had been able to give her, out of
her royalties, a thousand dolllars, and May could continue her
art studies in the galleries there. All Helen's plans were shattered.

What could she do? Time was running out. Perhaps she should
look for a companion for a trip to Colorado instead, for her doctor had suggested that, with its clear dry air, it was a good place
to recuperate from bronchial and lung trouble. Her friends ral-
lied around to advise and assist.

Charlotte Cushman, now living with Emma Stebbins in her
Newport villa, advised her to go alone if necessary, but to go.
Sam Bowles wrote to his friend William Bross, Lieutenant Gov-
ernor of Illinois. Mr. Bross and his family had traveled with
Bowles to the Pacific Coast in 1868, and his daughter Jessie was
intrigued with the prospect of repeating the trip. With her fa-
ther's help, she secured two cross-country round-trip passes to
San Francisco, one for Helen and the other for any friend Helen

wished to take. Jessie may have hoped Helen would ask her, but Mrs. Bross insisted the friend should not be her daughter.

Helen even asked the Warners to go. On March 23, she wrote at length, "Don't you want to go to California? That is the goal to which my longing eyes turn, but there is nobody to go with me, or rather there are very few people with whom one could go—I mean would go...."

Of all the friends she approached that spring, it was a Mrs. Edward Guild [2] who finally took up her invitation to use the second pass. The Guilds of Boston had summered many times in Newport and Helen admired Mrs. Guild's sculpture, especially her "heads." Later Helen would write a poem suggested by the head of David, one of Mrs. Guild's best-known pieces. "Just be sure the Indians don't cut off your hair," the Reverend Mr. Guild said. He had questioned her safety in traveling out West with all the talk of Indian troubles and train robberies, but Mrs. Guild smiled at her husband's grave concern for her long auburn tresses, the ends of which could touch her shoes. She agreed to accompany Helen to Colorado at least, and as soon as she wished.

The May 31 issue of the *Republican* carried the news of departure. "Mrs. Helen Hunt and her friend Mrs. Charles Guild of Boston start today for a six-weeks' visit in Colorado."

But if Mr. Guild still had qualms about his wife's hair or the tales of Indian raids, he had no reason to worry further. For Helen had to postpone the trip. She was too ill to travel, and on June 19 the paper stated in its column of Eastern Massachusetts items that "Mrs. Helen Hunt was overtaken by serious illness on her way to Colorado and had to return. She will spend the summer at the White Mountains and Princeton, and try the Rocky Mountains in the early fall."

It was a long month before Helen could travel again, but finally, with the help of Emma, she went to Bethlehem. Too uncomfortable to write or even enjoy sitting on the veranda at the

Sinclair House, she had Emma repack her things, and they left the next day for the Inn at Princeton. There her oldest niece, sixteen-year-old Ann Fiske Banfield, came up from Wolfeboro to be "helpful."

Ann, whom Helen had nicknamed "Nannie," was her favorite niece. Soon after Rennie's death, she had begged her sister and brother-in-law to let her adopt Nannie as her own. "You have another daughter and two sons and I have none," she had said. But Annie could not part with any of her children, much as she loved her sister.

Despite all Nannie's help and Emma's care, Helen still complained that she could not get much writing done. "I try to work lying on my back," she remarked. But it was obvious she was in pain.

No more comfortable at Princeton than she had been in Bethlehem, she began to wonder if she shouldn't leave the cool and sometimes moist air of the hills. She thought of her childhood home and wrote Emily Dickinson to ask about a boardinghouse in Amherst that would be "dry and clean." Emily told her of a house where two of her cousins were staying, promising there was "no dampness," and stating that her cousins were "very timid themselves."

Within the week Nannie left for home, and Helen went on to Amherst with Emma. But it was a mistake to have made the trip so soon after traveling from New Hampshire to Massachusetts. Exhausted on arrival, she was "prostrated in twelve hours" and had what she called a "most disastrous week." She found the boardinghouse rooms not only damp but very close and stifling, and was sure she would never have got out alive but for the good fortune of finding there a fine homeopathic doctor to help her, Dr. Hamilton J. Cate.

Homeopathy had been the rage for some time in both England and America. It had to do with giving patients pills containing toxins that would counteract the germs which bothered them.

Helen believed in no other kind of medicine. In this she was joined by the Colonel, the Hawthornes, and Harriet Beecher Stowe.

Dr. Cate thought it best for her to return to Princeton and arranged to see her there in a few days. On August 22, she wrote Nannie from her rooms at the Inn, "I am lying in bed just where you saw me three weeks ago—thankful to get back. . . . If anybody ever jumped from the frying pan into the fire I did in going from here to Amherst. . . ."

But she soon was out of bed and had gained back enough strength so that she was given permission in October by Dr. Cate to spend a few days in Boston. She could then go back to Amherst, where she would be able to stay with the Reverend and Mrs. L. S. Potwin until she was ready to leave. At Dr. Cate's advice, Helen had reluctantly agreed to go to Denver for the winter months. "If you don't," Dr. Cate insisted, "you may not be well for a long time."

The memory of her own mother's illness and wasting away with consumption frightened her. Could it be possible she had the same dread disease? She would make the trip if Dr. Cate would go with her.

Before leaving Amherst, Helen donated copies of all the books she had written and several other books of poetry and travel to the library. She left the East with Emma and the good doctor "for the benefit of her health" on November 17. The *Amherst Record* was kind in not mentioning her illness, stating simply that Dr. H. J. Cate had left Monday for a two-week trip to Colorado.

But Denver was "horrible," and Helen doubted that Colorado was any better for her than Boston. Her first sight of the Colorado plains terrified her—"blank, bald, a pitiless gray, under a gray November sky"—and to compound her problems she developed a "rose cold." She would have taken the next available train back had not the doctor advised her to try at least a few weeks in Colorado Springs, a new town some seventy miles south of Denver.

He arranged for temporary quarters on the north side of Kiowa Street in one of the connected portable houses from Chicago, unfortunately called "Dead Man's Row" in recognition of the invalid population. At first the Springs seemed no improvement over Denver. Even the move into the comfortably furnished rooms of the Colorado Springs Hotel, billed as the "most elegant hostelry between Chicago and San Francisco," did not allay her actual terror of the dusty, treeless, and bare settlement. "One might die of such a place alone," she said bitterly. "Death by disease would be more natural."

She had crossed the country, ill and disheartened, to find "a climate which would not kill," and instead she had a feeling of "hopeless disappointment" in the town she described as "small, straight, new, treeless." It lay between a "dark range of mountains, snow-topped, rocky-walled, stern, cruel, relentless and a bleak, bare, unrelieved desolate plain."

The dust that sifted in through the windows and settled everywhere was almost unbearable. But soon after her arrival at the hotel snow fell, and the "delicious winter weather" cleared the air. Helen could now open her windows at night and look out at the mountain range and at Pike's Peak nearly fifteen thousand feet high. And on a clear day, she could see the Spanish peaks, Sangre di Cristo, a hundred miles away—"two blue pyramids."

She and Emma would stay in the Springs, since her throat was improving and she had recovered from the rose cold. Emma could cook the oatmeal gruel and bake gem cakes Helen so enjoyed with her morning coffee. Thus Dr. Cate was able to return to Amherst at the end of two weeks as planned, satisfied that the diet and the climate would restore his patient to good health.

13

Colorado Springs

THE WINTER DAYS proved exhilarating, and Helen was soon well enough to go to the dining room for her meals with the other guests although she lived, she said, largely on the "gruel and the iron pills" the doctor had prescribed. She considered herself fortunate to have at the table seven "agreeable talkers," and overlooked what she called the "poor fare" because they laughed so much, she wrote Bottanie. They were Walter Ferris, an English artist "who does the loveliest water colors and plays like an angel on the violin"; another young Englishman, waiting for the building of a home for an aunt; "a very clever young man from Canada, who came for his throat"; an English physician, Dr. S. E. Solly, who was there "for his lungs"; two nice ladies from Philadelphia, "not bright especially, but well-bred and chatty"; and a "Colorado banker, born a Pennsylvania Friend."

Helen was placed opposite the banker, a Mr. William Sharpless Jackson, who paid little attention to the chatter around him. A tall and large man with deep-set eyes, he smiled easily but talked less than the others at the table, answering any questions with a simple "yes" or "no." Helen had wondered about him since the day she saw him drive up to the hotel in an open carriage with two of the finest-looking white horses she had seen in Colorado country. His heavy beard and whiskers had a touch of gray, but he had zestful energy and a joy in the West that matched his sparkling brown eyes.

William S. Jackson was a Quaker from Kennett Square, Chester County, Pennsylvania, thirty miles west of Philadelphia. Born January 16, 1836, he was educated at Greenwood Dell and Eaton Academies and had, in compliance with his father's wishes, served as an apprentice, learning the trade of an agricultural machinist. After his schooling, he worked for two years as a confidential clerk for the man from whom he had learned his trade. When free at last to go out on his own, he first accepted a job in the lumber- and car-building industry at Latrobe, forty miles west of Pittsburgh, but had soon after gone to St. Paul as treasurer of the Superior and Mississippi Railroad.

Intrigued by an opportunity to go even farther west, Mr. Jackson accepted, in the fall of 1870, a similar position with the newly organized Denver and Rio Grande Railroad and moved out to Denver, Colorado, where he stayed until the line was extended to Colorado Springs on October 26, 1871. He went to the top quickly and was elected vice-president of the company. He had ridden the narrow-gauge line from Denver on the Montezuma that puffed its way into town bearing two passenger cars named Denver and El Paso on the first run.

Mr. Jackson watched as the new streets were being laid out at right angles, alternating between a hundred and a hundred and fifty feet wide, with narrow streams of water running along the curb. In a tract of about ten thousand acres, a hundred and fifty to two hundred portable houses shipped from Chicago were put up in a matter of hours until permanent ones could be built.

Known originally as the Fountain Colony, Colorado Springs was, in 1873 when Helen arrived, fulfilling the dream of its founder, General William Jackson Palmer, who had formed the Colorado Springs Company for the purpose of establishing a city on the mesa. The money derived from the sale of two-

Helen Fiske Hunt,
at about the
age of twenty-five.
Courtesy Miss Helen Jackson

Lieutenant Edward
Bissell Hunt, soon
after his marriage
to Helen Maria Fiske.
*Courtesy Miss
Helen Jackson*

Warren Horsford
("Rennie") Hunt,
about six.
*Courtesy Miss
Helen Jackson*

William Sharpless
Jackson,
in a portrait
of the 1890's.
*Courtesy Miss
Helen Jackson*

Birthplace of Helen
Maria Fiske in Amherst,
Massachusetts.
*Courtesy The
Jones Library*

Home of Emily Dickinson, near
Helen Fiske's birthplace,
Amherst, Massachusetts.
Courtesy The Jones Library

Emily Dickinson, poet and lifelong
friend of Helen Fiske, from a
portrait (1848) when she
was seventeen.
*Courtesy Amherst
College*

Don Antonio de Coronel and his wife, Dona Mariana, friends of Helen Hunt Jackson, at their ranch in Los Angeles in the 1880's. *From a photograph of a painting by A. F. Harmer; Courtesy Los Angeles County Museum of Natural History*

"El Recreo," the Coronel home in Los Angeles, where Helen Hunt Jackson was often a welcome guest.

The home of William and Helen Hunt Jackson in Colorado Springs, Colorado. (1876-1885). *Courtesy Pioneers Museum, Colorado Springs*

San Diego Mission, California: Padre Junipero Serra's first mission, "now . . . a pile of crumbling ruins."
(*From* Ramona, *by Helen Hunt Jackson*)

The bell tower of the Pala Mission
From a photograph by the author

San Luis Rey Mission, California: "Nothing but the garden and orchard left."
(*From* Ramona, *by Helen Hunt Jackson*)

thirds of the property at a dollar an acre was being used in the construction of canals, parks, roads, schools, and the planting of trees. General Palmer appointed a forester to protect the trees along Fountain Creek and in the Garden of the Gods. He hired William Lennox to plant trees in the town as well for fifty cents a tree, he sank wells, and he set aside land for a college.

"My theory for this place," the General wrote a friend, "is that it should be made the most attractive place for homes in the West, a place for schools, colleges, science, first-class newspapers. . . ."

News of the town, five miles from the foot of Pike's Peak in El Paso County, spread across the country. Almost as soon as the first stake had been driven, July 31, 1870, at the corner of what is now Pike's Peak and Cascade Avenue, people were attracted to the territory. Many came from England and the Eastern seaboard, alone or in couples, suffering from asthma or consumption, hoping to regain their health from the soda springs of Manitou.

Only two or three hundred people lived in the new town at first, but when Helen reached Colorado Springs, in the register in General Palmer's Colorado Springs Hotel that had opened January 1, 1871, were the names of more than three thousand tourists—largely from England. No wonder the Springs became known as "little London"! The residents lived on hope and scenery, or, as Miss Isabella L. Bird, an English writer, expressed in her *A Lady's Life in the Rocky Mountains*, the Springs was a "splendid life for health and enjoyment."

The national panic of 1873 caused some concern for the General and his supporters. William B. Young's bank failed, but Mr. Jackson, a staunch Republican, bought its furniture and started the El Paso County Bank. And as the panic and the depression deepened almost everywhere in the United States, Colorado Springs "flourished like a weed patch."

Helen's first description of the Springs would not hold for
long. The town that lay bare with never a tree was fast becoming a fine city. Major Henry McAllister, a friend of Palmer's, another Pennsylvania Quaker, had planted five thousand cotton-
woods along the ditches lining the main streets. Helen told "how
property had trebled in value in six months."

"You might like Colorado even better," Mr. Jackson said to
Helen one Saturday morning, smiling at her across the breakfast
table, "if you could see more of the beauty of its mountains and
valleys." Then he asked quickly, "Would you like to go out for
a drive tomorrow morning, Mrs. Hunt?"

Helen needed no urging. Hadn't she thought of hiring a
driver! She was already well enough to walk out in the sun with
Emma for about a half a mile daily and she had driven to the
Garden of the Gods quite often, but how much more pleasant
to go with someone who knew and loved the country.

By the calendar it was winter, December 14, 1873, but, as
she wrote later in "A Winter Morning at Colorado Springs,"
winter that "woos and warms like June." The mercury registered only fourteen degrees at six o'clock in the morning when,
wrapped in furs, she climbed into Mr. Jackson's open carriage.
The horses, she said later, bounded "like frolicsome kittens,"
only settling down to a steady trot after they had crossed the
foothills and reached Colorado City. They climbed gently up
the slopes to Fountain Creek and into Manitou Springs," a glen
. . . a little fairy canyon."

Here Grace Greenwood [1] had built a dainty cottage "in a
clematis tangle," and here Dr. William A. Bell had his home. Dr.
Bell, an Englishman who had joined General Palmer's surveying
party in 1867, had never returned to St. Louis to study further
the homeopathic medicine he had come to America to learn
about. He gave up his medicine forever when the General asked
him to help build Colorado Springs.

From Manitou, Mr. Jackson drove through the Ute Pass,

"walled in on either side," where the road seemed to Helen to lead straight into a mountain of rock. After following the creek part way into the pass, they left the carriage and walked to the main waterfall of the creek while the horses toiled up the steep road.

The beauty of the creek amazed Helen: "Ice bridges; ice arches; ice veils over little falls." But she would never forget the ice canopy hanging over the main fall. In the center, reaching almost to the rushing water, hung "one pendant globule, pear-shaped, flashing like a diamond in the sun."

"The solitare of all the world," said Helen, "and presently it shall be dissolved and swallowed in a foaming draught."

"And who sits at the banquet?" William asked.

"The name of the Queen is Nature, and he who loves is emperor always," was Helen's quick reply.

Then Mr. Jackson took her hand and together they crept out to the edge of a sharp rock and sat in the warm noon sun. As she looked down "into the huge crystal bowl—solid white snow at the bottom and frost-work up the sides," Helen felt a peace she had not known for many years. Later she would write that they rode home over the plains "seven miles to the hour," the sun, like June, burning their faces and the December snow dazzling their eyes. And this was midwinter in Colorado!

January 28, Helen wrote Bottanie to come to Colorado: "Sell your lot in Newport and buy one in Manitou, where Grace Greenwood has built her little cottage. . . . Fancy being six thousand feet above the sea—high as the top of Mt. Washington and yet never having a day when you cannot drive or walk with comfort."

But New England was still home to her, and she added in her letter, "Oh, do write me . . . for spite of the air and spite of the grand and glorious scenery and spite of getting well—I am as homesick as a cat."

14

Our Garden,
Cheyenne Mountain

By the first of the year, Helen started to write steadily again. "I am beginning very cautiously," she told Bottanie in her letter of January 8, 1874.

Helen had added to her list of journals the *Christian Union*, which Henry Ward Beecher was now editing, and the *St. Nicholas* under the editorship of a Newport friend, Mary Mapes Dodge. She also continued her work on the Saxe Holm stories, six of which had already appeared in *Scribner's*. She would finish the "Four-Leaved Clover" for a June publication date.

She was amazed that her Saxe Holm stories had become popular reading, bringing her more income than any of her other writings, but she was also annoyed at the attention they attracted in attempts to identify the author. Writing fiction had been a gamble for Helen, and she knew that few women were successful in this field. She preferred to be known as a poet and essayist.

At first she was amused at the speculations, and not at all surprised when Sam Bowles stated in the *Republican* of December 30, 1873, "The latest conundrum who is Saxe Holm? The latest answer Helen Hunt." He was sure he had discovered the answer in the slightly veiled allusions to Amherst.

But while it seemed "fun" to Helen when either she or some of her friends were the target—the guesses ranged from Mary

Mapes Dodge to Sarah Woolsey—it was quite another thing when total strangers made claim to authorship. For Helen was nothing if not honest. She might indirectly deceive her readers by anonymity but she would never think of claiming an honor that was not hers.

Despite the fact that she denied authorship in an issue of the *Woman's Journal*, she was absolutely furious when Celia Burleigh assured her readers that a friend of hers was the author. Helen insisted that Mr. Holland write a private note of denial to Mrs. Burleigh, guaranteeing that her friend was an imposter. And in April, Helen had a second denial printed, entitled "Saxe Holm Rises to Explain," by Saxe Holm. She would not even tell Mr. Warner of her authorship although he asked her outright if she was the author of "Four-Leaved Clover."

Besides working on her stories, Helen took drives almost daily, going to the mountains on picnic luncheons with friends she had made in the town "where everybody knew everybody." She avoided the large parties that sometimes went on camping trips on horseback. When her dislike of such social gatherings was questioned, she said crowds gave her "tangled vibrations."

Colorado Springs had become more than a temporary home for her. She sent back east for her trunks and in April wrote Mr. Bowles from the hotel, "We are likely to spend the summer in this state. . . . Come and bring Mrs. Bowles."

When she learned of Mr. Warner's proposed trip to Egypt, she told him that the Springs was "worth all the ashes of the Pharaohs, ten times over." And in her prose articles for the *Independent* she wrote about the Springs: "Today that plain and those mountains are to me well-nigh the fairest spot on earth."

Her favorite companions that first year were Queen Mellen Palmer and Rose Kingsley, and for quite different reasons, although they all enjoyed spending afternoons reading Shakespeare, Milton, Byron, Victor Hugo, and even Zola. Queen

Palmer, the General's lovely and sensitive wife, came from
Flushing, Long Island, New York, and had just returned to the
Springs with her two-year-old daughter, Elsie. In no sense a
pioneer, Queen, who loved the theater, symphony concerts, and
the opera, herself a mezzo-soprano, had been unable to accept
the limited and crude living conditions. The plain clapboard
house of Glen Eyrie at the mouth of the canyon her husband
had named after her, five miles from town, was hardly an improvement over the one-story single-board shed in Manitou.

When Queen's husband and Rose and Maurice Kingsley, assistant treasurer of the colony, went on railroad business to
Mexico City, Queen refused to stay behind and left instead in
early March of 1872 for New York. She wanted "proper medical care and all eastern conveniences" while she awaited the
birth of her first child. It was doubtful that she would spend
many months more at Glen Eyrie. The General was utterly
absorbed in the business affairs of the Springs and of Mexico, and
was often away from home many days and nights.

Meanwhile Queen relieved her unhappiness and boredom
with the picnics and the drives. She liked the company of well-
bred people like Helen and Rose Kingsley, daughter of the great
clergyman and novelist Charles Kingsley, whom she had known
in London in the days of her honeymoon in 1870. Unlike Queen,
Rose was far more strenuous, and liked to scramble over the
foothills, armed with a trusty pickax, which she used to search
out rare stones.

Sometimes she went with the DeCoursey twins, Gerald and
Marcellin, Springs pioneers whom the General had recruited
for his Fifteenth Pennsylvania regiment during the Civil War.
But she could never persuade Queen to go with her. "I prefer
the lower meadows of the canyons," Queen would say.

A tall and angular spinster, Rose was all British, wearing the
same heavy tweeds, the same floppy hat day in and day out, wool

stockings, and stout coarse shoes. But Queen and Helen admired Rose's plucky nature and were delighted when she found time to leave the office above Field and Hill's Dry Goods store where she wrote out agreements for lots and membership for her brother Maurice, to accompany them on a morning drive.

Rose knew the flora of the region well and brought Helen her first Colorado flower when snow was still on the ground in late April. Only half open, the blue windflower looked to Helen "like a Maltese kitten's head."

"A crocus, out in chinchilla fur!" she exclaimed.

"Not a crocus at all, an anemone," Rose answered in her crisp manner. She promised to show Helen a carpet of them, and later they drove to the foothills to the west of the Springs where ridges were already blue with them. As often as possible, Helen took "botanical trips" with Rose to see the low white daisies that Helen called incorrectly "the harbinger of spring," the mountain hyacinth with its star-shaped blossom that was really a lily but had the odor of the hyacinth.

By the middle of June there was "a mosaic of color" around her, flowers of all kinds, vetches and lupines, white, yellow, and purple, blue and yellow columbine, red lilies, white violets, and the common red lily of New England. Never did they return to the hotel without a carriage filled with flowers, the top thrown back and every available space in the wagon as well as their laps and baskets "filled with the more delicate blooms."

There was one spot in the Cheyenne Mountain that was the best part of the "procession of flowers." Helen called it "Our Garden," and talked of working it out on "shares." Later she wrote in the "Procession of Flowers in Colorado": "We look as if we were on our way to the ceremonies of Decoration Day. So we are . . . but it is the sacred joy of living that we decorate. . . ."

In the early days of Helen's convalescence, she had found the interest and sympathy of neighbors charming, but local gossip began to disturb her. Though she recognized that everyone knew her business, sometimes even before she did, she called it "an offense or a pleasure according to the measures of good will in the curiosity and familiarity."

When she rode out with Gerald DeCoursey,[1] she learned to her great dismay that she had been criticized for going out with a married man. It didn't matter that his wife had urged her husband to take Helen on buggy rides to Cheyenne Mountain for reasons of his own health—no one cared about this. When he died of a lung hemorrhage in July, Helen wrote a poem to him, "Flowers on a Grave," and spoke of his gentleness and loyalty:

> Our ruder lives, for years to come, will miss
> His sweet serenity, which daily shed
> A grace we scarcely felt, so deep inbred
> Of nature was it . . . Alas, dear friend, we knew not how
> Our hearts were won to love thee, until now. . . .

If there were rumors about her friendship with Mr. Jackson, Helen paid no attention to them. She had been a widow for ten years and Mr. Jackson was six years younger than she, an eligible and popular bachelor. She gaily accepted his invitations and they would drive out often, sometimes going across the railroad tracks south of town, over Fountain Creek and up the long flat valley to Cheyenne Canyon, where they tied the reins to a pine tree and walked into it. At times they went on a Sunday picnic to Blair Athol, a park about six miles north of the Springs, an exquisite cuplike park, described by Helen as "no spot more beautiful."

When the *Rocky Mountain News*, a Denver paper, linked her name with "one well-known in the Territory," Helen called it an "impudent paragraph," but Mr. Jackson disagreed. On the following Sunday, he proposed. Helen didn't know what to say —she had not planned to remarry, not to anyone and certainly not to Mr. Jackson. It wasn't because as a young man he had been indentured for four years with no further schooling or because she was recognized as a literary woman. It was merely that marriage had been furthest from her mind.

Besides, she explained, she had made commitments to her publishers and a book was under way, as well as some articles she had promised and two unfinished Saxe Holm stories. But Mr. Jackson was persistent. "I'll wait, then," he said.

As the summer months passed, he waited. Helen realized that no amount of talking or rationalizing would convince him. It would be better, she decided, not to see him too often and she took long trips away from the Springs, including one to Denver on the narrow-gauge line, where she met the Bottas on their way to California. In July she took a one-week trip into South Park with three tourists from the East who wanted to see the mining country of Fair Play, a town at the foot of the mountains on the Platte River. And when August came, she packed her trunks and left for Bethlehem, New Hampshire. "Being slowly grilled with the heat," was her excuse.

There she finished editing "My Tourmaline," for which *Scribner's* paid her the largest amount she had ever received for a Saxe Holm story—four hundred dollars. But the days dragged by for her despite the comfortable coolness of the mountain village, and she grew lonesome for Colorado Springs and the Rockies. She wrote not of the East, but of her Colorado jaunts.

By early November she had convinced herself and her friends that she could write better in the high, dry air of the Springs. The *Republican*, under "Gleanings and Gossip," indicated that her health was greatly improved by the "marvelous sunshine" of Colorado Springs. She said it was "enough, almost, to raise the dead."

Within a few days after her arrival at the Colorado Springs Hotel, Mr. Jackson called on her. He wanted her to drive with him to see a house he had bought on the corner of Weber and Kiowa Streets. It was a large house built by Joseph Dozier and Winfield Scott Stratton on the "old red lot" purchased by Stratton's partner, Mr. R. W. Grannis.[2] Mr. Grannis had bought the lot on condition he put up at once a first-class residence. And first-class it was, a two-story house with tall shuttered windows and two large chimneys, a house "superior to any in town."

"I bought it for us," Mr. Jackson said simply. "I am asking you again to marry me, Helen."

"But I thought you understood—I never meant . . ." Helen looked at him, unbelieving. The same excuses remained, but they seemed less important to her after the months away from the Springs. "Maybe," she said to his second proposal, "but I need a little longer to be sure it is what we should do."

Helen missed Queen Palmer, who had returned to New York, but her writing kept her busy and she accepted few social invitations. Mr. Jackson called regularly and even when she refused a Sunday drive, he gave no indication of withdrawing. He was persistent and determined. It was stated years afterward that long afternoons of buggy drives in the Colorado sun to Manitou and to Mount Cheyenne canyons helped the romance to "bud."

Mr. Jackson promised he would never interfere with Helen's writing. And if she didn't like the arrangement of the rooms in the house, she could change them in any way she wanted. It didn't matter, he assured her over and over again, that she was forty-four and probably could not bear him children. He loved her; that was all that mattered.

By the end of January, 1875, Helen had no more doubts. But she asked that the wedding plans be kept a secret from the Colorado Springs "busy-bodies." She set October as the wedding month and they decided to be married in the Quaker faith in Wolfeboro, New Hampshire, at her sister's summer home. The

Banfield's had moved from Roxbury to Washington, D.C. in 1869 when Everett had received his appointment as solicitor of the Treasury Department. He opened the family home in New Hampshire each June to escape the heat of the Capital.

From January to midsummer Helen continued her travels in Colorado, sometimes with Will, but more frequently alone with her own driver. For she no longer drove out merely for pleasure; she was under contract for articles about the Territory in eastern magazines.

Her poems for children were sent to *St. Nicholas*, but others went to Oliver Johnson of the *Christian Union*. Two years earlier he had taken as his second wife Jennie Abbott, and because of Helen's friendship with Jennie, she had gained easy access to the columns of the *Union*. In 1874 alone, Mr. Johnson had accepted eighteen poems and two prose articles, only one of which ever appeared in her later collections.

A Quaker Wedding

MONK LOOKED ACROSS at Helen in Bottanie's New York home, thinking her even more attractive than in her Washington days. She wore a deep blue silk that made her eyes look less gray. Although he knew she now avoided the "world of fashion," she had a charm that gave her an air of elegance. He could not but notice that she sparkled as she talked of her wedding plans and he was pleased that she had lost the shift of moods that had plagued her since Rennie's death.

"And you will come to Colorado Springs to stay for a while with Mr. Jackson and me," she insisted. "We'll be married this October in my sister's house and then back to 'the fairest spot on earth.'" She chuckled as she added, "My Unitarian friend won't object, I hope, to joining a Quaker household."

Monk had been a good friend to Helen and though she seldom saw him, she kept up a regular correspondence. Calling him her second "literary adviser," she confessed her authorship of the Saxe Holm stories when the *First Series* was published. But she begged him not to betray her secret until after her death. "Then I wish it be known," she told him.

Her visit with Bottanie was a short one. She stayed only long enough for a shopping tour to purchase a new traveling dress and bonnet and a light summer dress of green voile for the wedding. Then, escaping the intense Indian-summer heat of New York City, she left for Newport for a few weeks with Sarah Woolsey and her mother at their new home on Rhode Island Avenue. The *Newport Mercury* announced on Saturday, October 9, that "Mrs. Helen Hunt of this city, the poetess, is to be married this month," and the *Daily News* added the information that it would be "to a Mr. Jackson, a well-known banker of Colorado."

With the news out in the press, it was time, Helen decided, to leave for Wolfeboro. She would make but one stop en route, and that to Roberts Brothers of Boston, who had asked to see her since they were preparing a collection of her verse and prose for young readers. They wanted to know what items to include.

On this visit she had the pleasure of meeting for the first time Thomas Niles, partner and manager of the company. Mr. Niles had, she knew, discovered Louisa May Alcott. It was he who proposed that she publish her hospital sketches of the Civil War and, after looking over the manuscript had said, "I think, Miss Alcott, that you should write for girls. I should like to see you try."

But at first he saw little value in the story she finally wrote for girls and doubted that *Little Women* would have a market. As for Helen, he made no such suggestion, but shared a new idea he thought promising. "I plan to publish a series of stories by famous authors," he remarked, speaking in his odd, slow manner, "with authorship a secret, letting the reader guess the name of the writer of each article."

Publishing was Mr. Niles's prime interest, and he lost no time in small talk. His excitement about the proposal was indeed catching. "What will you call your . . ." Helen interrupted.

"They would be called *No Name Stories*," he replied quickly, explaining in detail an idea that his assistant, Mr. Starke, had identified as his "twelve-months' brain child."

If the idea worked, as Mr. Niles felt sure it would, he expected to publish as well an anonymous collection of poetry. Although Helen was intrigued, she hesitated to offer a story. She was satisfied with *Scribner's* and had no desire to complicate her Saxe Holm secret. Still, the scheme was an unusual one, and she promised some poems.

To Will, Helen wrote from Wolfeboro listing the route she knew so well. "You can get the Boston and Maine train from the Northern Union Station in Boston that leaves at eight-thirty in the morning. It takes less than four hours and comes right up to the wharf." She suggested he buy the cheaper five-dollar excursion ticket and he could take a boat ride on Lake Winnipesaukee with the Banfield children whenever he wanted to.

The children were indeed happy to take "Uncle Will" anywhere he wanted to go. Nathan, fifteen and a student at Wolfeboro Academy preparing for Phillips Academy, and the two little girls, Mary and Edith, ten and five years old respectively, took turns driving out with Mr. Jackson and had more boat rides and picnics than usual. Unlike Nathan, the older son Richard had defied his father's wishes and gone to sea on a merchant ship out of Boston. Annie and Helen were both at Vassar College, Annie a sophomore and Helen a freshman. College had opened on September 24, but they would both be home for their aunt's wedding.

In the evenings, Mr. Jackson told the children stories of the West. October 1875 was a month to remember. Helen immortalized it with "October's Bright Blue Weather." The poem closed with the stanza she most loved:

October's Bright Blue Weather

O sun and skies and flowers of June,
    Count all your boasts together,
Love loveth best of all the year
    October's bright blue weather.

For it was on a bright blue October 22 that Helen Maria Fiske Hunt and William Sharpless Jackson were married in a ceremony of the Society of Friends in the Banfield garden. If daughter Annie [1] recalled correctly years later, the service took place under a "beautiful scarlet maple" in the yard, and Helen and Will exchanged vows in the presence of the family and Friends from the Meeting House nearby.

Eight days later, the *Colorado Springs Gazette* reported matter-of-factly, "Mr. and Mrs. William Jackson came to us from the East today. We welcome them and offer our congratulations."

But it would be many months before they could move into the house Mr. Jackson had bought the year before. Helen was not satisfied to live in it until it had been made to front on Kiowa, instead of Weber, Street, with the windows facing Cheyenne Mountain. "I must be able to see the snow-clad mountains from the front of the house, not from the kitchen," she told Will, who was perfectly content to let her have her way.

She hired Mr. Stratton, master carpenter, who had helped in the building, to remodel it for her and, with his assistant, Mr. Ege, to fashion pieces of furniture to her taste—corner bookcases, alcoves, fireplace mantels, and tables and chairs. And she had a front stairway built, designed after one she had admired in Newport, Rhode Island, with a border of stars cut into the richly finished siding, and thickly carpeted.

Daily she trailed the carpenters, determined that the remodeling suit her demands. Most of the shelves and cupboards were built by Mr. Ege, but she looked to Mr. Stratton for her best pieces. She rearranged the downstairs completely, changing the kitchen into a large living room with a fireplace. An ell was added onto the back of the house for a kitchen and separated from the main house by a narrow passageway. A back stairway led into the kitchen, modernized with a sink and drainboards, but Will objected to an upstairs bathroom. Helen had to be content with a water closet inside the woodshed that offered semi-indoor plumbing.

She had the little New England entry walled up on the outside so that the carpenters could make a tiny alcove off the parlor, with the shelves from floor to ceiling. This cozy room with the odd-shaped shelves she would always call "flirtation corner."

The back porch became an open living room and from the porch she would be able to see the great bald summit of Pike's Peak and her beloved Cheyenne Mountain. As soon as the rest of her trunks could be unpacked, Helen hung the walls with her prints and etchings by French and English masters. The bas-relief, a life-sized head of Rennie, was placed on the wall over the door, and the della Robbia group of singing children decorated the fireplace mantel.

Then she filled all her vases with Colorado flowers. "I cannot stand artificial flowers anywhere," she once told a guest, "not even on embroidery or crewel work." Her books and magazines were placed on large revolving tables and on corner bookshelves throughout the house, and wherever space permitted, she used the three-cornered buffets for her china.

To her many friends in the East, Helen wrote of her great happiness in being once more in a home of her own. She started a Quaker novel, which would be called *Elspeth Dynor*, possibly to use the initials of her Amherst friend. All winter and well into the spring, she worked on a new short novel for *Scribner's*. The title? *Mercy Philbrick's Choice*, or the *Lady of Ensworth County*. It would be a Saxe Holm story, but longer than usual.

In a letter from Monk, November 16, 1875, she learned of another Saxe Holm claimant, a rumor she thought had already been squelched. The Lowries, with whom Monk was staying in Chicago, claimed a friend of theirs as the rightful author. Colonel Higginson had told Helen she would get into trouble someday, but she still felt the secret safe. She answered Monk with assurance.

"The Colonel is the only one man who can swear that I wrote them. He read the first three or four, page by page, as I wrote them. Mr. Jackson can swear to "Four-Leaved Clover" and "Tourmaline" for I read them to him, page by page as I wrote them." She urged Monk not to be concerned and to come instead to the Springs. "Give your lecture in Denver and come and visit us," she pleaded.

The one sad note of the winter was word from Emma Stebbins of the death of Charlotte Cushman on February 17, 1876, at the Parker House in Boston. In a poem published in the *Independent*, Helen expressed again the greatness of her actress friend, "beloved woman," and spoke in her poem of Charlotte's "great soul, still glowing pure and white."

Soon after moving into her home, Helen received from Emily Dickinson wedding congratulations:

> Have I a word but Joy?
> E. Dickinson
> Who fleeing from the Spring
> The Spring avenging fling
> To Dooms of Balm—

In her usual impetuous manner, Helen sent the poem back, asking for an explanation, but Emily never explained and unfortunately the letter in which Helen sent it back is missing.

On March 20, 1876, Helen wrote Emily, "But you did not send it back. . . . Thank you for not being angry with my impudent request for interpretations. I do wish I knew just what "dooms" you meant, though. . . . I wish very much that you would write to me now and then, when it did not bore you. . . . I have a little manuscript volume with a few of your verses in it —and I read them very often—You are a great poet and it is wrong to the day you live in, that you will not sing aloud. . . ."

By late June, the Saxe Holm novel, *Mercy Philbrick's Choice*, had been finished. It ran to some eighty pages, but Helen thought it ready to mail to *Scribner's*. She sent a hasty note to Dr. Holland, "I have sent the next Saxe Holm story to you. . . . Please send me at once eight hundred dollars of the ten hundred and eight that it is worth. . . ."

Dr. Holland was stunned. Helen had never before made quite so heavy a demand. And financial question to the contrary, however, neither Dr. Holland nor his assistant, Mr. R. W. Gilder, liked it. They questioned its value for the market and agreed that her handling of the main character, Parson Dorrance, might offend some of their readers. It was refused.

But Helen did not give up easily. She set to work expanding the novel. She would send it to Mr. Niles for his consideration as a *No Name* story.

Meanwhile she could join Will on some of his trips for the Denver and Rio Grande Railroad. The line was hoping to push its way south to El Paso, Texas, and into the silver mine of the San Juan region to Leadville. The Atchison, Topeka, and the Santa Fe had already entered Colorado in the summer of 1873 and a continual "battle" was on for the rights of passage.

On one trip they made to Walensberg, south of Pueblo, they drove six miles from Cucharas in a springless wagon with "unmated horses" over the Cucharas meadows. Helen had her first look at the mud huts of the Mexicans, not more than six or seven feet high and flat-roofed. "Surely," she gasped, "the native Mexicans must be first cousins to a mud-sparrow."

But Will had little to say; the problems of the Mexicans were not his. After he had located the engineers at a place called Early's, a store and log cabin some twenty miles from Walsenburg, and had transacted his business with the men on the surveying of a route across the mountains into San Juan country, he headed back. To Helen's delight, they saw on the way one of the caravans "bound on the pilgrimage to that shrine of silver —eleven white-topped wagons, with ten mules to each wagon." She regretted that in a few weeks the steam engine would replace these colorful wagon trains.

As they returned to Walsenburg at sunset, graders arrived, and the place that had been sleepy when they first entered was now alive with wagons, horses, men, stacks of equipment. Tents and shanties were going up "like magic." Helen marveled as she saw the cutting of the first furrow. In a moment the plowshares had turned the rich brown earth; as she watched with Will, the plower walked westward, rod after rod.

"A town will grow up here and replace this Mexican trading post," Will said with assurance. "The trains are bringing life to the Territory." In fact, in time the wilderness would indeed surrender to the railroads. Will firmly believed in the railroad expansion. He supported the Denver and Rio Grande's rights to the land, insisting that the Santa Fe didn't belong in Colorado since it was not a Colorado line. No trackage concessions should be granted.

June of 1876 had been a beautiful month in Colorado. Helen had enjoyed her travels with Will, even recording notes for later articles. And by July she received word from Mr. Niles that he would accept *Mercy Philbrick's Choice* as his first *No Name* story.

Would she be able to come East in the late summer to oversee its publication for an early September release? he wanted to know. She would, and she persuaded Will to meet her in Princeton, Massachusetts, where she would plan to work at any editing there might be. "I'll meet you as soon as I can," he said. "And I'll want to go to Philadelphia to the Centennial Exposition—this time we can stay with my family."

Helen smiled at Will. She had tried to understand his manner, his direct and often unexpected comments. She overlooked any slight irritability, realizing he had been a bachelor for a long time before she married him. She never asked him any longer for an explanation of his absences and instructed her housemaid Effie to keep dinner waiting for him whenever he was late. But his excessive thrift occasionally bothered her.

"And we might stop over in Washington to see my sister and the family," she stated with a questioning tone in her voice.

"Wish we might bring young Helen back with us," was his quick response. "The climate might be good for her."

Helen Banfield, seventeen years old, had just finished her freshman year at Vassar and had been ill since the close of the spring semester. Neither the doctor nor her mother could determine the cause of her illness.

It would be five weeks before Will could reach Princeton. He had expected to be there earlier, but business kept him in New York City. He wrote that he was unable to leave until August 5, and that they should go on to the Centennial Exposition the second week in September.

16

Helen of Colorado

WHILE HELEN WAITED in Princeton, Massachusetts, she edited the *No Name* story for Mr. Niles and started another novel. Intrigued with his idea of publishing an anonymous collection of poems as one of the series, she went to work composing a few.

To Emily Dickinson she sent a circular of the proposed anthology. She had promised, she told Emily, to make a contribution, as had Ralph Waldo Emerson and Louisa May Alcott. And she wanted Emily to contribute. "I enclose to you a circular which may interest you. When the volume of Verse is published in this series, I shall contribute to it, and I want to persuade you to. . . ." She continued, "Unless you forbid it, I will send some that I have. May I?"

But Emily delayed replying to the request, probably trying to decide how best to withhold her consent without hurting Helen's feelings, but she did send poems for Helen to read. Receiving no immediate answer from Helen, Emily wrote again to ask if H. H. was offended. The answer was a definite "No." "My dear Miss Dickinson, how could you possibly have offended me? . . ." Helen would try again.

After Will arrived from New York on the eighth, Helen answered Mr. Warner's invitation to visit at Nook Farm. She wrote, "Mr. Jackson is a 'man of reason.' " She could, she thought, persuade him to go to Hartford with her for at least a night and a day on their way south. She still had not given up the idea of visiting the Farm.

To Sam Bowles she sent off a hasty note, asking him to come and spend a day or two at the Inn. "We have a guest chamber which is empty now, but it has held a succession of friends whom I much enjoyed.... We both want to see you...."

Unfortunately, Bowles was not able to make the trip, and Helen and Will left Princeton, stopping off in Hartford on August 20, 1876. Nook Farm, on the western edge of Hartford, was a cultural center, a mecca for distinguished literary visitors attracted by Mark Twain and Harriet Beecher Stowe as well as by the Warners. Annie Fields called it "a halfway land between New York and Boston," and William Dean Howells wrote of the Farm residents, "They go in and out of each other's houses without ringing and nobody gets more than the first syllable of the first name...."

Charles Dudley Warner and his lovely wife, Susan Lee, welcomed the Jacksons warmly to their home on Hawthorn Street, a charming house with beautiful chestnut trees around it. Helen regretted that Harriet Beecher Stowe and Mark Twain and his family had left for the summer months, but she most regretted the fact that Will did not wish to stay any longer. "We have," she wrote Emily, "that great chore of the Exposition to do." And she included her forwarding address: "Roberts Brothers, Boston, will always find me, wherever I am—and I am always glad to get a line from you."

But the Centennial was more fun than Helen had anticipated and the eight days they spent there passed quickly. The Exposition featured everything from the greatest steam engine ever built to the first public demonstration of Alexander Graham Bell's telephone. One of the places that particularly impressed Helen was the Woman's Pavilion, with a woman operating a six-horsepower steam engine. But the State buildings were the most appealing.

In her usual style, Helen sent off two articles about the Centennial, one for children to *St. Nicholas* and the other about the Kansas and Colorado buildings to the *Independent*. A converted Westerner, in spirit at least, Helen described the attractive display of the products of the two states. Though she mentioned Colorado's claim to being "one of the great treasure-houses of silver and gold," she thought the state should also have shown its success in raising sheep and cattle, the beauty of its mountains and parks, and the "priceless elixir of its air." "Bless her," was Helen's closing comment.

"I'm sorry you need to leave so soon," Helen said to Will as he prepared to pack for his return to the Springs. They had spent more time at the Exposition and with his family in Kennett Square than she had originally planned. There would be no Washington trip and they didn't have time to go back to New York for another visit. She was disappointed, even though she knew he was running for the office of senator from Colorado and that his further absences might lessen his chance of election.

"If I can come East again in November, I shall, otherwise you can come home as soon as you are through here," Will told her.

"You'll let me know?" Helen pressed her face against his and he kissed her lightly, saying, "Take care of yourself, and I shall telegraph you in Ashfield when I arrive."

Helen watched as the trained pulled out of the Philadelphia station and for a short time felt concerned that she hadn't gone back to the Springs with him. But he knew of her desire to spend the month of October in New England. She had arranged to stay for a while with Mary Warner,[1] the recent widow of former Professor Aaron Warner, at the Inn in Ashfield, Massachusetts, twenty-two miles west of Amherst across the Connecticut River.

It was, according to Helen, "the greatest find" she had had for many a day, "thirteen hundred feet above the sea and nestled among the billows on billows of hills." She thought the air the best she had ever breathed outside of Colorado and decided to stay two weeks longer than she had planned and finish the Colorado papers.

To Sam Bowles, she wrote on October 8 to express her unhappiness in not being able to accept his invitation to visit his family in Springfield. "At present I am unable to make any plans, for I am simply 'waiting orders' as the Army people say. Whether Mr. Jackson will return to the East, or send for me to join him in Colorado is uncertain. . . . If he comes East again, we will try once more to show ourselves to you. . . ."

Two days later she drove Mrs. Warner back to Amherst, where Helen called on Emily Dickinson. The visit was a short one, for Helen had only one idea in mind—to secure a promise of a poem for the *No Name* anthology. Emily had already declined to contribute, but Helen was undeterred. She came to plead her case in person, asking Emily not to decide for a few days and giving her another circular to look over.

As soon as Helen had left, Emily sent the circular to the Colonel, saying, "Mrs. Jackson of Colorado was with me a few moments this week, and wished me to write for this—I said I was unwilling, and she asked why?—I told her I was incapable and she seemed not to believe me and asked me not to decide for a few days—meantime she would write—She was so sweetly noble, I would regret to estrange her and if you would be willing to give me a note saying you disapprove and thought me unfit, she would believe you—I am sorry to flee so often to my safest friend. . . ."

Her "safest friend" furnished no guidance on the question of how to deal with the persistent Mrs. Jackson and, through some misunderstanding, he judged Emily was talking about stories.

Helen never gave up hope. However, soon after this visit she became a trifle remorseful when she thought back on her comments to Emily, who had appeared suddenly and silently in the doorway of the library, dressed in white pique with a soft blue worsted shawl over her shoulders.

". . . truly," she apologized, "you seemed so white and moth-like and your hand felt like such a wisp in mine that you frightened me. . . . I felt like a great ox, talking to a white moth and begging it to come and eat grass with me to see if it could not turn itself into beef! How stupid. . . ."

But Emily had resolved not to publish then or ever, and the subject of a contribution to the anthology lapsed, although Emily still sent Helen poems. Helen reassured her of their greatness. "I like your simplest and most direct lines best. . . . You say you find great pleasure in reading my verses. Let somebody somewhere whom you do not know, have the same pleasure in reading yours. . . ."

During the fall, one of Emily's letters to Helen went unanswered for so long that Emily wrote again asking if her face was "averted"; instead of a poem, she enclosed a picture of her two-year-old nephew, her brother Austin's only son Gilbert, whom she adored. Apparently the letter and perhaps the picture, reminiscent of her loved Rennie, disturbed Helen somewhat, for she answered the note promptly.

"My face was not averted in the least," she said. Then she chatted on in a friendly manner and asked the question uppermost in her mind: "Would it be of any use to ask you once more for one or two poems, to come out in the volume of *No Name* poetry which is to be published before long. . . ."

Helen promised to send them in her own handwriting and to tell no one whose poems they were, not even Roberts Brothers. "Only you and I would recognize the poems," she stated, hoping that Emily would be willing to bear this limited publicity. She would wait for weeks before she had an answer.

It was early in November before Helen returned to Colorado Springs. Will had telegraphed her at the Parker House in Boston, stating that he could not get back East to meet her. She left almost immediately for home, somewhat concerned that he might be elected senator and be sent to Washington, D.C., a city she now "abhorred and loathed." In her letter of October 25 to Mr. Ward, she had said, "Mr. Jackson thinks there is little chance he will be elected. Votes are bought and sold in Colorado and he will not buy a vote, so I trust and hope he will be defeated."

He lost the election. She was glad for herself. She had no desire to live in Washington again, but she had tried not to betray her feelings during the campaign. Still, Will had enough to do in his many activities in the affairs of the Springs. He served on the Board of Trustees of Colorado College, contributing to its growth, and was a member of the town's school board.

She was satisfied that the months away from the Springs had been worth the separation. Indeed, the summer and fall of 1876 had been fruitful. *Mercy Philbrick's Choice* had gone to press, and *Hetty's Strange History*, her second *No Name* story, was under way. And Dr. Holland was ready to publish another "Saxe Holm."

Besides preparing a collection of travel articles on California, Colorado, and New England, Helen had outlined her first novel for children. Out of the experiences she and Sarah Woolsey had had in crossing the country and from her own first reactions to Colorado country, she would write *Nelly's Silver Mine*. In it she would be young Nelly March, daughter of a New England minister quite like her own father.

If Helen had wanted to stay East longer, she gave no indication; she was happy to be home again. There were more trips

with Will, one to Denver in January, another back to Walsenburg through the Cucharas meadows, this time looking out of a
train window at the thriving town marked only by the cut of a
furrow a year before.

Often she traveled about the Springs and neighboring areas
with only her own paid driver, John. She kept a burro with a
rancher near Seven Falls, and rode this sure-footed animal up
and down the canyons. But on Sundays she and Will frequently
took a picnic lunch of chicken, fruit, coffee, and claret wine to
their favorite spot on Cheyenne Mountain, a spot crowned with
flowers from early spring to late autumn. "In the great cathedral
of the Canyon we worship God," she told Sarah.

Friends from the East came to visit, including the Bottas and
Monk and his wife. They were warmly welcomed by Will,
who enjoyed having his home filled with guests, both his own
and his wife's. Sarah Woolsey, "Sally" to Helen, told how Helen
prided herself on her housekeeping and that "the spell of her
enthusiasm affected her very servants." Her dinners proved particularly pleasant, and her ideas in arranging flowers at the table
were original. "I remember," Sally recorded in a short biography
of Helen, "a wreath of pansies of all colors, arranged in narrow
tins half an inch high and curving in shape, so as to form a gar-
land round the whole table, and her saying that it took exactly
four hundred and sixty-three pansies to fill them."

Up at sunrise every morning, Helen, now grown stout, with
hair quite gray around the temples, walked down to the market
to shop for fruit and vegetables. Her New England habits were
noticed by her neighbors. "She gets up too early to enjoy her
home," they said, complaining that she bought all the best things
before they were awake.

"I like the early morning," was her answer to the criticism.
"And 'first come, first served,' I always say."

To some of the townspeople Helen was a "snob" from the

East. Unwilling to associate with members of the community in whom she was not interested, she did not fit in perfectly with the socialites. Yet she was never lonely. Aware of what it meant to be a stranger, she repaid kindnesses lavishly and helped out anyone who was an invalid or alone. She was adored by her servants, and by miners and ranchers and their wives.

"I live in a palace," she told her friends, "and by palace I mean any house, however small, in which love dwells, and one on which the sun can shine."

She wreathed her writing desk with the kinnikinnick vine [2] and there, on her return from marketing, she sat at work through most of the morning.

"Success"

"I AM QUITE at sea about the book," Helen confessed to Monk in a letter on January 14, 1877. "I honestly tried my best to write a good story—and I honestly thought it was a fairly good work, but *Saturday Review*, the *Literary World* and the *Nation* all abuse it. . . ."

For the very first time in her writing career, Helen had to face several harsh reviews. "Perhaps I can't write a long story," she added in her letter to Monk, "but I mean to try once more."

The *Nation* compared her story of Parson Dorrance to a Sunday-school tract, and the *Saturday Review* found it an "elaborate mistake," while at the same time acknowledging the good and painstaking work that had gone into it.

The Colonel thought it good. "It is much stronger than any of the Saxe Holm and far better written," he maintained, praising her work in his reviews. Though somewhat relieved by his comments, Helen still worried about the criticism of others. For, after all, the Colonel was not only her adviser but also her friend, and she thought she probably should discount his praise.

But she was deeply hurt. "What utter trash!" was the remark of an intimate Colorado friend. And when she turned to Will, all he said was, "I'm not qualified to give any suggestions. You're the literary one in this house, Helen."

His remarks made her feel letdown. She had wanted him to support her and yet she knew he cared little about her writing, accepting it as a matter of course. Then she waited for word from Dr. Holland. Would he want another Saxe Holm story or had the critical reviews of *Mercy* closed off that avenue of publication? She hoped he might be influenced by the unexpectedly favorable review in the *Atlantic Monthly*.

Calling the attacks upon *Mercy Philbrick's Choice* "rather foolish," the review spoke of the "greatest merit of the beautiful literary workmanship," and thought it a "style worthy of study, quiet, clear, and strong." But, to Helen's disappointment, the review noted that the poems were added, "like stucco ornaments."

Fortunately for Roberts Brothers and Helen's own self-respect, the sale of the novel was a success. A month after publication it was out of print, "the rush for it having exhausted the supply," and Roberts Brothers was ready for a new edition in October. In four months' time it had sold eight thousand copies. They had launched a bold publication in the *No Name* series and intended to advertise it fully.

Possibly the sale of this novel was the determining factor in Dr. Holland's decision. Whatever the reason, he wrote Helen that he was ready to accept another story, and Helen sent him her latest, "Farmer Bassett's Romance." Without any regret, she added the curt reminder that it was too bad he was not to have the credit for *Mercy*.

When Roberts Brothers published their second *No Name* story, Helen reviewed it and sent the review to Dr. Holland for *Scribner's*. His refusal to use it upset her, but she held her temper and sent the review to the *Independent*. Despite her annoyance, however, she capitulated and sent two more "Saxe Holm" stories to Dr. Holland, "Susan Lawton's Escape" and "Joe Hale's Red Stockings."

In the early spring, reassured by his acceptance of her Saxe Holm stories, Helen forwarded the partly finished *Hetty's Strange History*. Her request for a financial arrangement met the same fate as had that for *Mercy*. He called the demand a "prepayment" and sent back the manuscript. "Send me a long serial if you have it ready by next April," he wrote in reply.

Helen would do no such thing. She was through with *Scribner's*. She sent the story to Mr. Niles as her second *No Name* volume, the third in the series. Learning a lesson from the criticism of *Mercy*, she included only two poems.

The Colonel praised her work highly, calling the new story "as stern a tale of retribution as *Madame Bovary* or *The Scarlet Letter*."

The reviews generally were as harsh as they had been for *Mercy*. It seemed clear to Helen that her *No Name* story of Hetty was less than outstanding, and the second series of her Saxe Holm stories, published that same year, received no more cordial reception. Reviewers criticized the "excessive sentimentalism" of "My Tourmaline" and referred to it as "such stuff."

It was obvious that the Saxe Holm mine had run out of ore. Negative criticism outran praise, and Dr. Holland showed no more interest in her fiction. She would write no more of it, at least for the present, but she would keep her promise to Mr. Niles. She sent off three of her recent poems to his editor, Mr. George P. Lathrop, for the poetical anthology in process.

At last, after several days of indecision, Helen sat down at her desk and thumbed through the box of unfinished manuscripts. Time now, she thought, to work out some more of her ideas for children's books. The year before, Roberts Brothers had accepted *Nelly's Silver Mine* and she had been excited to learn that the small book was among the new juveniles published in November 1878, along with Susan Coolidge's *Eyebright*.

She reread her father's two children's books,[1] but missed in them the fantasy and imagination she wanted in hers. She put them aside and picked up her mother's letters, written to her a summer long ago in Weston, Massachusetts, when she was but six years old. The letters had been dictated by her loved cat Midge, or so she had believed even when she was old enough to know better.

For a while, as she read the letters "from your affectionate pussy," her eyes filled with tears and she suddenly wished she could tell her mother how much she had loved her all the years for her understanding of a small homesick child. Hoping that other children would gain pleasure from them, she edited them for publication, called them *Letters from a Cat*, and sent them off to Roberts Brothers.

To Sam Bowles and his wife she wrote on April 26, 1877, about her summer plans: "I shall not come to New England this summer. I have decided not to leave my husband alone here any more. He falls into the bad company of politicians when I am away and they lead him into dangerous paths of candidacy for . . . Senatorships and the like." She wished they might come West to see her.

She changed her mind when the hot days arrived, causing her discomfort. She thought of the Warners and remembered Will had said, "They are two people who must come out and make us a visit."

But Helen wanted to visit them again at Nook Farm and wrote July 1 to tell the Warners they were thinking "a little about coming East in September. . . ."

In fact, Helen was actually making plans to leave for the East—with or without Will. Though she had not wanted to go without her husband for fear he would be persuaded to run for office, he promised her he would not and told her he would join her in Boston at the Parker House in mid-October. On October 16, 1878, she was able to write the Warners of Mr. Jackson's

arrival. "Next week we are going to New York via Springfield-
Northampton-Mt. Holyoke-Amherst—and if may be Hartford?
I want to show Mr. Jackson the Connecticut Valley . . . and we
both want to see you and Mrs. Warner. . . ."

The following day they went to Concord, Massachusetts, for
Helen to take her "last look at Emerson," who was quite ill. At
Springfield they stopped for a short visit with Mrs. Bowles.
Emily had written of the death of Sam Bowles on January 16
and Helen had been saddened to think that Will had not visited
with this energetic and compassionate man, who was, he once
told Emily, "unwilling to die."

A side trip to Amherst was Helen's idea. "Emily Dickinson is
a great poet," she told Will, "and I would like to talk with her."

Since the anthology, *A Masque of Poets*, was scheduled by
the editor for November printing, Helen would call a second
time at the Mansion to urge Emily to reconsider and allow the
use of her poem "Success." On the morning of October 24, the
Jacksons knocked at the front door of the Dickinson Mansion
on Main Street. Leaving Will with Lavinia in the parlor, Helen
waited for Emily in the library across from the entryway. She
had in her hand the *Choir Invisible* by George Eliot. "Superb,"
she said of it as she shut the book and stooped to receive Emily.

For a "lovely hour," as Emily called the visit, Helen and Emily
were closeted while the Dickinson's hired man walked the Jacksons' horses along Main Street. Mattie, Emily's eleven-year-old
niece, "hopped excitedly up and down the path," thrilled at the
presence in the house of the famous Helen Hunt Jackson.

Helen had staked everything on this meeting. Yet it is undoubtedly true that Emily didn't give her the poem she wanted
during the pleasant hour together. For on the following day
Helen wrote her from the Warners' home in Hartford, Connecticut, "My dear friend—Here comes the line I promised to send—
We had a fine time on Mt. Holyoke yesterday—and I took the

5 o'clock train to Springfield—will you send me the poem? No—
will you let me send the "Success" which I know by heart to
Roberts Brothers for the *Masque of Poets*? . . . I ask it as a
personal favour to myself—Can you refuse the only thing I perhaps shall ever ask at your hand? . . ."

Emily must have finally granted permission for its use. It
hardly seems likely that Helen had any reason to falsify or pre-
tend. Whether she had already sent the poem to the publisher,
as some claim, is unknown, but it is clear that Helen's persistence
had won out.

After the *Masque* was in print, she wrote from Colorado
Springs, "I hope you have not regretted giving me that choice
bit of verse for it. . . . I was pleased to see that it had, in a manner, a special place. . . ." The poem was chosen to end the first
part of the volume. Helen, through her driving insistence, had
finally included Emily, even though anonymously, among the
poets of the day.

But much as Helen admired Emily's poetry, she couldn't resist "meddling" with the poem. The Colonel's copy bears evidence of Helen's handiwork in the insertion of "the" before
"sorest" in the fourth line, and the change of "agonizing" to
"agonized and" in the last line. Three other minor alterations
have been attributed to Mr. Niles, but Emily's protest was useless. The poem was clearly hers.

Mr. Niles sent Emily a copy of the *Masque*, noting that there
had been a slight change in phraseology. But Emily apparently
forgave both Helen and Mr. Niles. Actually, with the exception
of a valentine and a poem about a snake, both printed in the
Springfield Republican, "Success" was the only poem of Emily's
printed in a book while she lived.

Yet she continued to send poems to Helen. One that came
about mid-April 1879, was probably intended as an Easter greeting, as well as a reminder that Emily had not heard from her

recently. Helen sent it to the Colonel, adding at the bottom of the sheet of paper, "Wonderful twelve words." It read:

> "Spurn the temerity—
> Rashness of Cavalry—
> Gay were Gethsemane
> Knew we of thee."

The Colonel claimed Helen's insights were better than her count.

Another poem about a bluebird arrived sometime that spring. Impressed with it, Helen stated she was "inclined to envy" with its beauty. She learned it by heart and asked for one on the oriole. "Here is one of the ones that Midas touched," Emily answered.

And to the Colonel, Emily wrote in answer to his expression of appreciation of Mrs. H. H., "Mrs. Jackson soars to your estimate lawfully as a bird."

18

Woman with a Hobby

IN THE SPRING of 1879, Helen found it increasingly difficult to put her heart into her writing—or into her home life. For months she and Will seemed to be drifting further and further apart. It wasn't anything he actually said to her, but their interests had never been similar and now they had nothing to say to each other or do together. Will spent weeks in Denver and often stayed at the El Paso Club when he was in the Springs. He had become president of the club, elected to serve for the year 1879–1880.

When Will left in late April for New York City on business, Helen remained in Colorado. To Emily she wrote on May 12, "The 'man I live with' (I suppose you recollect designating my husband by that curiously direct phrase) is in New York—and I am living alone—which I should find very insupportable except that I am building on a bathroom and otherwise setting my home to rights." Will had finally authorized the installation of a bathroom with a tin tub upstairs, something Helen had wanted for years.

But to the Colonel she wrote during that summer, "I feel isolated in Colorado and cut off from contacts with literary friends." She was unable to conceal her feelings any longer. In the hot months she grew depressed, and even short trips to Manitou and Cheyenne Mountain were of no help.

She might have gone East with Will to see Annie and her family, but Annie would be busy with plans for daughter Ann's wedding, and Helen Fiske would be graduating from Vassar in June. The Banfields and their four daughters had moved permanently from Washington, D.C., to their home in Wolfeboro, New Hampshire. Richard, the older son, was still away at sea, a captain on a merchant ship, and Nathan had left in March for Austin, Minnesota, to accept a position with the First National Bank. At least one son had followed his father's wishes: Nathan had attended Phillips Academy for two years.

Helen wandered about listlessly, unable to relax or to settle down to writing. She had been unsuccessful in trying to make peace with Dr. Holland, though she had written him a most humble letter in April. At that time she was working on another long novel and wondered if by any chance he wanted it. "I can submit it to you whenever you like although it is only half finished."

His answer was discouraging; he was not interested. Helen put *Elspeth Dynor* aside, working on it after that infrequently. She would never completely finish it, but some of the chapters would be published posthumously.

Recalling the beauty of the fall foliage and lonesome for the lovely countryside of New Hampshire, Helen wrote her second September poem:

September

The golden-rod is yellow;
   The corn is turning brown;
The trees in apple orchards
   With fruit are bending down.

Scribner's published it and "The goldenrod is yellow . . ." would be added to the heritage of New England literature. How ironic that Helen should write in Colorado the typically Eastern "September" poem, for which she would become well-known to generations of school children.

When she heard from Monk that he was thinking of leaving England with his wife and family for America, she urged him to reconsider. "There is nothing in America to give you an equivalent for what you would give up in London. . . . America has eight tenths contempt for literary people, one tenth pity, and one tenth respect." She found little of that respect in Colorado, and pity she never could stand.

It was a letter from Sally that opened the door to her escape. Without a moment's delay she packed her bags for the trip East. "I'll be in Maine with the Woolseys at their summer home," she told Will. She asked him to forward any mail, care of Roberts Brothers. He never questioned her departure or her plans, and she couldn't have told him, for she didn't know them herself.

The visit in Maine on Mt. Desert proved successful, for there Helen found a "second Eden," and there she gained back her "flair" for writing. She described for the readers of the *Independent* the little hamlet of Bar Harbor, with its fishermen and sailors' cottages. "My desire to see the Island from the other side grew upon me like a passion of search for something hidden," she wrote of her expedition with five travelers "round the island."

In late October, Helen went to Boston and visited with her sister-in-law, Molly Hunt, on Beacon Street. She would stay only long enough to see her publishers, she told Molly, but events turned out otherwise. On October 29, she attended the reception of the Omaha Indian Committee and became caught up in the tragedy of the Ponca Indians of Nebraska. She had found Boston highly aroused over the story of their cruel eviction, and people spoke of little else, either appealing for the protection of the Poncas or discounting the stories about the "red varmints." To the disbelievers they were nothing but savages who deserved their fate.

The Poncas were originally settled by the Government at the mouth of the Niobrara River in Nebraska in 1817, but by a treaty of 1858, they gave up all but a strip of land between the river and Ponca Creek, the richest of the remaining land to be thrown open to white settlers. Soon after gold was discovered in the Black Hills, an inspector came to the tribe with a Reverend Mr. Henmale and the agent James Lawrence to order their complete removal to an Indian Territory a thousand miles south.

With the promise that the ten chiefs might go to Washington to talk with the President of the United States if they didn't like the new land, the Indian chiefs were driven down in the late fall. Of the three tracts offered them, no one place was acceptable—they were barren and untillable. But when the chiefs refused the tracts and asked to see the President, they were told there was no truth to the offer and they would have to stay on one of the three tracts.

Left without food, money, or interpreter, the chiefs left the assigned territory and made the long trek back to their home. But disaster faced them. Soldiers under order had collected all the women and children in wagons, taking everything from the farms, including reapers and mowers. They forced the men at gunpoint to leave for the territory. Only Standing Bear and his brother Big Snake refused. As a result they were thrown in jail for ten days, when they were forcibly placed in wagons and driven back to the territory.

On his arrival Standing Bear grieved to learn that there had been many deaths during the journey, including those of two of his own children. Horses and cattle had died of starvation. The chief watched and waited for months as a hundred and fifty-eight more of his people died. Unable to endure such misery longer, he ran away with thirty of the tribe—eight men, six women, and sixteen children—back to the Omaha settlement. Once more they were arrested.

The results were startling. Informed through the *Herald* of the Indians' plight, Omaha was indignant at the Government's highhanded dealings with the Poncas. General Crook enlisted the aid of the editor of the *Herald*, Thomas Henry Tibbles, and two lawyers, to test the legality of the arrest by a writ of habeas corpus. According to the decision handed down by the presiding judge, in less than a week after the arrest the Indians were declared no longer wards of the Government, but "persons and free."

The decision was one of enormous significance for the Poncas, but it meant that they could no longer go upon an Indian reservation for support or help. So they chose to settle on an island in the Niobrara River, part of their former reservation the Government had overlooked. But it was too late to plant crops; without jobs or food, they faced starvation.

An Omaha committee gave them temporary aid, but much more was needed. Mr. Tibbles came to the rescue. He formed an Indian committee, composed of the sixty-year-old Ponca chief Standing Bear, and two young Indians from the Omaha tribe, Miss Susette LaFlesche, called Bright Eyes, and her brother Frank. Mr. Tibbles would be the only white member of the group. He organized a lecture tour of the East to solicit money, leaving Omaha on October 10, 1879. The *Omaha Bee* called the tour "Tibbles' Bear Show," but his own paper labeled it "Standing Bear's Holy Crusade."

When Helen heard Standing Bear and his party give their tragic recital of the wrongs they had suffered at the hands of the white men, she was completely won over. She had found a commitment that would bring her life into balance again. Depression

days in Colorado would be a thing of the past. She sent a sum-
mary of the Ponca case to the *Independent*. "Standing Bear and
Bright Eyes" told of the Poncas' story as she herself had heard it.

She asked Mr. Warner to reprint the article in the *Hartford
Courant*, saying, "Don't be funny about the Indians. They are
right and we are wrong. . . ." She wanted to visit the Warners,
but her days were not free, she told them. Will had come East
on railroad business, but would return to Colorado on December
1. Meanwhile they roomed at the Brevoort House in New York
and Helen took the boat several times to Boston to continue her
work there.

She collected funds for the Poncas, encouraged others to take
an active part, and appealed to all who would listen. She rejoiced that the Mayor of Boston headed a committee of distinguished citizens to solicit funds. According to the poet Joaquin
Miller, Helen was the one who persuaded Wendell Phillips to
take the platform for the Indians as he had for the Negroes.

She would have gone back earlier to New York to do some
research at the Astor Library but for the invitation to Oliver
Wendell Holmes's birthday party.

The publishers of the *Atlantic Monthly* ask the pleasure of
your company at the Hotel Brunswick, Boston, on Wednesday December 3, 1879, at twelve o'clock, in honor of the
seventieth birthday of Oliver Wendell Holmes. An early answer is desired. 220 Devonshire Street, Boston, November
13, 1879.

Holmes's birthday was actually August 29, but summer was
no time for a party, since many of his friends and associates
would be out of the city at that season.

About a hundred people met at noon and spent a few hours
socializing before the luncheon. Helen was especially pleased to
meet Julia Ward Howe and to recall with her and Colonel Higginson their Newport days, but, most of all, it was an added joy

to meet the famous Mark Twain and to see Harriet Beecher Stowe, both of whom she had twice missed at Nook Farm.

She was seated at Holmes's table between the poet John Greenleaf Whittier and her good friend Charles Dudley Warner. According to Annie Fields, Whittier didn't like Helen Hunt, "poetically or personally," but he was a gentleman and made the best of the situation. Charles Dudley Warner was willing to read for the gathering the birthday poem Helen had written to the guest of honor.

"It is my pleasure," Mr. Warner began, "to be permitted to read a poem, addressed to the guest by a lady whose presence here prevents my saying what I should like to say of her. It is written by the poet who dwells in a Grand-Lama-like privacy behind the letters H. H., the author of certain works of fact and fiction...."

To Oliver Wendell Holmes on his Seventieth Birthday

> All days are birthdays in the life,
> The blessed life poets live;
> Songs keep their own sweet festivals
> And are the gifts they come to give. . . .

Helen nodded her approval of his wit, chuckling to herself. What, she wondered, might have been Mr. Warner's comments if he knew she were also Saxe Holm!

The Holmes Breakfast was a happy interlude for Helen, though she was sorry to have missed seeing Mrs. Warner, "the lady with the Brown Eyes," as she called her. She returned to New York on the twenty-eighth to stay a while with Bottanie. In order to support her stand on the Poncas and to discover the truth about the Government's dealings with them, she took an alcove in the hall of the Astor Library. She would search the records for evidence.

"A Century of Dishonor"

"I have done now, I believe," Helen told Monk in early December of 1879, "the last of the things I have said I would never do. I have become what I have said a thousand times was the most odious thing in the world, 'a woman with a hobby.' But I cannot help it. I think I feel as you must have felt in the old abolition days. . . . I believe the time is drawing near for a great change in our policy toward the Indians. . . ."

It was indeed quite unlike Helen, and even the Colonel couldn't understand the change. In the Newport days he had tried several times to interest her in the issue of slavery, but he had labored in vain. She took, he claimed, the regular army views, liked to have colored people about her as servants, but resisted any question of equality.

Nor had she any sympathy with the suffrage. In fact, she had protested the Women's Right Movement in an article, "Wanted —A Home." Except for her championship of Mrs. Anna Leonowens, she had always strongly objected to women on the lecture platform, particularly disliking Kate Field for her "desperate monologues."

Actually, nothing had given any inkling of Helen's active concern for the rights of American Indians. Although she had as a girl visited the camp of Indians in Malden, Massachusetts, she was neither disturbed nor upset by the ragged tents and the dirty children.

On her visit to California, though she spoke of her wish to use the Indian names in Yosemite, she often mentioned the Indians in terms familiar to all at that time, "loathsome and hideous." In Colorado she was never known to have found fault with her driver, who had fought Indians everywhere. Yet suddenly, for Helen, this was a crusade. She not only supported the Poncas, but also became a leader in the reform movement, helping to organize the Boston Indian Citizenship Association.

Her devotion to Bright Eyes led Helen to travel with the Omaha Indian Committee throughout New England whenever she could find the time. She threw every ounce of her influence into the case of the Poncas, and Mr. Tibbles reported that without her help they could never have won. And he turned his whole "mass of records" over to her for the report she planned to assemble on the Indians.

With Will back at the Springs, it proved hard for Helen to write him in any detail since she had no immediate plans to return—she was far too busy. In New York, she submitted articles about the Poncas to the *Tribune*, but was annoyed that the paper continued to remain neutral in its reporting. She walked, talked, wrote, and spent herself—"all in vain," she thought—and said openly to Bottanie, "The Poncas have come—New York does not care for them. . . ."

The Poncas themselves had arrived on December 6 and had taken rooms at the Fifth Avenue Hotel, their chief registering his residence as "homeless." That first evening they had visited the home of Mr. Josiah M. Fiske of No. 999 Fifth Avenue and on Friday, Standing Bear and Bright Eyes had addressed a meeting in Steinway Hall.

Helen made a direct appeal to Carl Schurz,[1] Secretary of the Interior, the department directly concerned with Indian affairs.

When Schurz remained evasive, despite her appeals, she called him in the press "that false-souled man" and flayed him in the *Tribune* on December 28, 1879, for his indifference.

She finally persuaded Bottanie to hold a reception for the Ponca Committee at her salon, Monday evening, January 19. "Wouldn't Charles Dudley Warner come?" Helen asked.

Bottanie's reception proved a festive occasion and Helen was not disappointed in the welcome. But what was most remembered, and later mentioned in Bottanie's letter to Anna Leon-owens, was the handsome appearance of this "sad, dignified old man," dressed in a scarlet blanket and a dark-blue coat worked with beads, "a very handsome eagle's feather in his hair, and a necklace of grizzly bear's claws on his neck."

It was Bottanie's invitation to Mr. Jackson to join Helen as her guest and stay at her home as long as he wished that brought Will East, though he wrote Helen he was coming to work. Perhaps he felt that he could persuade his wife to give up her "crusade" and come home.

Her further support of the Indians would, Will knew, be dangerous. Soldiers had often been called out to defend Colorado citizens from anticipated attacks by the Arapahoes and the Cheyennes. During her absence that winter a band of Utes under Chief Ouray had been responsible for the Thornberg Massacre. When the Indian agent, Nathan Meeker, had ordered the Utes to plow up their sacred dance ground for a school building, they had revolted. The agent and his eleven men were massacred, the agency pillaged and burned, and Mr. Meeker's wife and daughter Josephine and companion Mrs. Press, captured.

Helen listened to Will but went on with her "job." When Mrs. Benham invited them to dinner Friday evening, January 30, 1880, Helen accepted for both of them, saying, "Mr. J. will be very glad to come with me and see you all, but he accepts all evening invitations now conditionally for his time is not his own, while he is always ready for a 'lark' of any kind, if business does not interfere. When business does interfere, no power under Heaven can direct him from it. He is as bad as an Engineer about that." In the postscript she added, "I am at the Astor Library now all the forenoon but am usually in after five or half past."

She searched the records in the library, reading everything she could locate. The record she found was a shameful one of cruel and faithless dealings, of unfulfilled promises and broken treaties.

She firmly believed the country was on the threshold of a great revolution. But Will was unconvinced and for him there was no compromise. He finished his business and left Helen at the Brevoort Hotel, where they had taken rooms after their visit with the Bottas.

Helen continued with her research and reporting. She wrote stinging articles of protest and rebuked editors with her sharp attacks, most of which she submitted to the *Tribune*. Some went back to the *Boston Advertiser* or to the *Independent*, but it was *Scribner's Monthly* that printed her seven-page article on the "Wards of the United States Government," in which she stressed the broken treaties with the Indians. These items made, according to Bottanie, "quite a stir and called out explanations from the Secretary of the Interior."

In addition, Helen sent letters to anyone she thought might have some influence on the situation: army officers, ministers of the gospel, college presidents, congressmen. She toiled long hours into the evenings to bring the story of injustice to the attention of the public.

Unhappily, she discovered that Colorado had been as greedy and unjust in the 1860s as had Georgia in 1830. When she read of the Sand Creek Massacre of 1864, she did not hesitate to print the inhuman event for all to read. She told how Major E. W. Wynkoop of the First Colorado Cavalry, the officer in charge of Fort Lynch, had invited all the friendly Indians to come into the neighborhood of the forts for provision and safety, and how, at daylight, on the morning of November 29, Colonel J. M. Chivington marched with his men from Denver to Sand Creek. There he rode down upon a hundred and thirty-eight lodges of Cheyennes and Arapahoes, surrounded the camp, and massacred almost eight hundred Indians, including women and children. Helen could find no evidence that the Indians had provoked trouble or raided the area, and she called Chivington's men "a regiment of demons."

Through letters in the press, William N. Byers, formerly editor of the *Rocky Mountain News*, defended the Interior Department, but Helen proved immovable. She had documents to support her arguments and signed statements from the Indian Bureau, with specific names and instances. Her Washington "battle" with Mr. Byers was even more bitter than that with Mr. Schurz. It would not likely be forgotten or forgiven by Colorado citizens.

Indeed, she received no word of sympathy or agreement from her friends and neighbors in Colorado Springs. Even Mr. Carlyle C. Davis of Denver, a frequent visitor and friend of the Jacksons, failed to share her concern at the time. He was probably quite correct in stating in his 1914 *True Story of Ramona* that she was without a genuine sympathizer in the entire state.

As Helen accumulated material on the evil treatment of American Indians, she began championing not only the Poncas but all Indians. She would put her research in book form and bring into the open the Government's "wicked treatment of Indians." Determined to produce an exhaustive study, she contacted Harper and Brothers of Boston. They would publish the volume, to be titled *A Century of Dishonor*. She would quote "chapter and verse" of the treaties openly and cruelly violated. The major thesis was to show that the United States had followed an outrageous Indian policy in defiance of all principles of justice.

She agreed with Sam Bowles in his *Our New West* that "So

far as our observation exists, the greatest trouble with our Indian matters lies in Washington; the chief of cheating and the stupidity gathers there." She would expose this injustice and try to do something about it.

When the document was finished in early May, Helen was clearly exhausted from her unrelenting labors. Her good friend the Colonel promised to proofread the manuscript as soon as it came from the publishers, and she accepted the invitation of Professor Horsford and his two daughters, Mary Catherine and Cornelia, to go with them to England and Scandinavia.

The three-months' travel would give her the rest she so much needed. She wrote a detailed letter to Will, listing her itinerary and on May 29, 1880, sailed from Boston on the S.S. *Parthia.*

"Come and stay with us on your return," Colonel Higginson wrote from Cambridge, Massachusetts. He had left Newport in October of 1878 to make his home in Cambridge, and there had married Mary Thacher in February, 1879, two years after the death of his first "Mary." He had built a Queen Anne cottage and was ready for guests. "Look until you see the ugliest house on Buckingham Street," he said.

Except for her visit with the Conways for nearly a week at their London home in Bedford Park, most of the trip was disappointing. Helen's accounts of her travels lacked the old charm: her heart was with the Indians. To Bottanie, she wrote in July 30 from Bergen, Norway, to thank her for the batch of newspaper clippings "about my beloved Indians."

"Nothing puts the Indians out of my mind," she wrote. "Except that I know there is nothing to be done this summer, I could not be contented to be away, but in the autumn I will take hold again unless Mr. Jackson objects. I propose to fight it out on that line till something is accomplished. I have great hopes for Garfield."

James A. Garfield was senator-elect in 1880 when he became

the Republican nominee for president. Rutherford Hayes had not supported her cause, but a new president, especially one who had fought in the Civil War and been a member of the Ohio Senate, might. At least she was hopeful.

Helen's strong desire to resume her activity on behalf of the American Indian may have colored her reports of the trip. Even so, there were unexpected disappointments. She never saw the distinguished Norwegian violinist, Ole Bull, as she and the Horsfords had anticipated, for when he arrived with his wife in Bergen from an American trip he was so ill that he had to be carried on a bed into a small steamer for his home on the island of Lysoen. Ole Bull had made his name in Paris and had been applauded in Italy, England, Scotland, Russia, and Germany before his own country hailed him as an artist.

In Copenhagen, Helen was unduly vexed at the fuss made over Sarah Bernhardt, the renowned French actress on tour in Europe, and at the difficulty in getting decent lodgings. The Museum and the newly-erected statue of Hans Christian Andersen softened the vexation somewhat, but she left for Paris, where she learned sadly of the death of Ole Bull. She wished she might have been back in Bergen for the services, to add her flowers to his grave. Paris was "as detestable as ever," and she was grateful to reach New York, October 8, 1880.

The *Sunday Republican* reported fifteen days later, "Mrs. Helen Hunt Jackson is reading proofs of her new book on the Indian question, which will be published in a few weeks. . . ." Now settled in New York again . . . [she] will perhaps spend the winter in her western home at Colorado Springs."

During her travels abroad that summer, Helen had taken time to write for publication, mainly for children. She submitted prose articles and some of her poems to *St. Nicholas* and to the *Youth's Companion.* Writing for young people apparently gave

her a kind of relief and balance after the intensive research for
the *Century*.

Though Will arrived in November to join her and had
planned to spend two weeks with his family in Kennett Square,
the Pennsylvania visit had to be canceled. "I only wish I had
been able to do it," Helen agreed. But both were too occupied
with their own work and Will felt he should be back in Colorado by the tenth of December. After his departure, Helen left
for Boston and Cambridge, where she spent several days with
the Horsfords.

In Boston, from the Parker House, she wrote Annie Fields an
apology for not being able to dine with her. She was, she said,
"in the midst of hard work for the Indians." Then, before returning to the Brevoort, she received the "wet copy" of the
Century. Though it ran to four hundred and fifty-seven pages,
she asked Harper Brothers to send a copy to each member of
Congress—at her own expense. "I read it with some terror," she
wrote Mr. Warner. "I don't know what they'll do to me. . . ."

On January 21, Helen left for Washington, D.C., where she
interviewed each congressman individually in the hope of stir-
ring up support for the Indians. She wanted to impress upon each
of them the need to take an active part in redeeming the name of
the United States from the "stain of dishonor."

Some of her work for the Indians still consisted of answering
attacks that appeared in the press. Before leaving for Washington, she had sent a letter to the *Evening Post* correcting "mis-
statements." The editor of the "Easy Chair" column in *Harper's
Weekly*, George Curtis, charged that her letter failed to note
that the Secretary of the Interior had "later ascertained the
comment of the Poncas to their removal to be only 'alleged.' "
She had written Mr. Ward at once, asking him to follow up the
matter for her and saying, "Don't you want to give the *Weekly*
a good whack? . . . I wish you would. . . . But before the next

two months are over the truth will be known about this Ponca business."

It was actually two weeks, instead of two months, for on January 27, 1881, the President's Commission, appointed several months earlier, presented a report favorable to the Indians. Helen was jubilant. Her work had been worth the effort.

20

The City of the Angels

HELEN LOOKED AT the pile of letters she had received over the past weeks and knew she would be unable to answer all of them in as much detail as she would like. Letter after letter tried to justify the Indian massacres or prove her wrong in her accounts of atrocities. She would answer the charges somehow.

Specifically directed toward the Congress of 1880, the *Century* called attention to the need for widespread reform within the Department of Interior. But to many readers the Indians were "brutal savages" and untrustworthy. They believed that both Mrs. Jackson's book and that of George W. Manypenny, Commissioner of Indian Affairs, 1853–1857, *Our Indian Wards*, published in 1879, were abusive and untrue denunciations. The cruelties of Indians in warfare were pointed out, and Helen soon grew tired of the expression, "The only good Indian is the dead Indian."

Even the *Nation* reported in a review of the *Century*, "The influence [of this book] will work towards disunion among philanthropic people when there ought to be the utmost solidarity of effort." This was discouraging. Still, she had little time to worry about adverse criticism, even when the book was called "unreliable and hysterical." "Because we have had one century of dishonor, must we have two?" she had asked herself and others in the March 1880 issue of *Scribner's*.

To Mr. Ward, she denied that her book was history, preferring instead to call it a sketch. "I give an outline of the experiences of a tribe—broken treaties, removals, etc.,—telling the history of each tribe straight through by itself. . . . My first chapter is a lawyer's brief. . . . I have been through all the law authorities in the Astor Library on these points. . . . All the heart and soul I possess have gone into it."

The Gilders, Jeanette and Joseph, sister and brother of Richard Watson Gilder, were Helen's active allies. In their newly published *Critic*, they hoped to encourage writers to support the American Indian. Joseph Gilder, called J. B. to distinguish him from his famous brother Richard, had taken over the editing of *Ploughed Under*,[1] an Indian novel by William Justin Harsha. Helen had promised to review it, even though she thought it lacked true dramatic ability and power of characterization. It was with regret that J. B. recognized that the novel would not do for the Indians what Mrs. Stowe had been able to accomplish for the Negroes in *Uncle Tom's Cabin*.

"You are the one who should tell the story of the Indians," J. B. assured Helen.

"I haven't the time," answered Helen quickly and, hesitating briefly, she added, "nor have I the background of local color. It would take at least ten years to acquire that background."

"Take ten years then," said J. B. firmly.

Helen frowned and shook her head. "When you are as old as I am, you won't speak so lightly of ten years."

But she couldn't put the idea out of her mind. She could compromise. Even at fifty-one, she could go to California to study the missions as she had wanted to do ever since her trip West with Sally Woolsey. At the suggestion of Mr. Ward she wrote *Harper's*, and soon received an offer for a series of sketches that Harper and Brothers would publish in their monthly magazine. The offer, of course, meant staying in New York for a month or more longer to continue research and at the same time to secure letters of introduction.

Although Will had to return home first, he said he would try to meet her in Trinidad in Southern Colorado on the seventh or eighth of April, "to treat himself to the West." On Saturday, the fifth of March, she moved to the Berkeley after he had left her. This time Will was not interested in remaining in the East while she spent long hours at the Astor Library. Besides, he probably could see little reason for her staying. The Ponca business had been settled. On March 3, 1881, Congress had passed a bill that let each individual Ponca choose the land he preferred, either in the territory tract or on the Niobrara, reimbursed them for their losses, and provided funds for houses, schoolhouses, and teachers' pay. She had worked hard for months on the book, and now it was in print. Why she should want to do more research, he couldn't imagine.

As for Will, he had business for the Denver and Rio Grande he should attend to. Agreements had to be settled with the Santa Fe over the Royal Gorge rights, into which the Rio Grande had entered April 1, 1881. Both roads had valid claim to the Canyon, but the United States Supreme Court had decided in favor of the Rio Grande. The line was to agree not to build south to El Paso, Texas, while the Santa Fe promised not to extend its line to Leadville.

Leadville, a mining town near the headwaters of the Arkansas River, had grown as if by magic. By 1878, Helen had written that "in six months a tract of dense spruce forest had been converted into a bustling village. . . . It was a Monaco gambling room emptied into a Colorado spruce clearing." In fact, it was the busiest and most-talked-of town in the nation, one of the great silver camps that in the 1860s had been briefly the site of a gold boom.

All packed by April 2, the day Helen was to take the afternoon train for the West, she received, at ten in the morning, a telegraph from Will. He could not go to California with her. Too unsettled to unpack and too restless to work, she told Mr. Warner the room looked like a waiting room at the railroad depot, even to the lunch basket unopened on the sideboard.

Nor did Will's explanatory letter that arrived four days later help the situation. She telegraphed and wrote friends to go with her in his place and to use the railroad passes Will had secured for her. She asked Bertie, Jessy Bross Lloyd, Kate Horsford, but all failed her. Reluctantly, she felt compelled to decline *Harper's* offer and return home. "Perhaps I can accept your offer later..." she wrote Mr. Henry Wills Alden, editor of *Harper's Monthly*, but he canceled the deal and it went instead to a Mr. William Henry Bishop, a writer of travel articles.

Still Helen stayed on at the Berkeley, unwilling to go back to Colorado until she felt calmer. She told Mr. Warner she felt "generally demoralized," and after her signature "Helen Jackson," scribbled, "If that's my name, I'm not sure—"

To Mr. Gilder, she confessed that she had been planning to visit the Omaha reservation in Nebraska in the fall and that she had intended to describe the condition of the Omaha tribe for *Scribner's*. Actually, she had arranged to meet with Bright Eyes on a trip to the northern tribes. This would no longer be a possibility.

Finally, back in the Springs the first week of June, Helen adjusted with good grace to her disappointments. Will had already picked up the threads of his busy life without a trace of regret or apology, but she held her tongue, even when he told her about the new hotel plans for the town.

On April 7, he had attended "with almost everyone else who was anybody in town a meeting in the Courthouse Hall." Arrangements were underway for the building of a hotel. Dr. Solly had opened negotiations with General Palmer, who promised to

contribute twenty-five thousand dollars, provided a similar
amount could be raised from Colorado Springs' citizens.

The town had grown to some forty-five hundred people but
lacked adequate facilities for the tourists who still arrived in
large numbers and had to be put up at better hotels in nearby
Manitou. Even many of the finest social affairs in the region
were held in Manitou Springs. But for Helen the growth of the
Springs and the tourist hotels held slight interest. It would be
only a matter of time before she would be ready to continue
her "hobby."

Meanwhile she took occasional trips with Will, one into New
Mexico in late June and later several by herself, always finding
material for her "pencil." She also started writing up some of
the tales she had heard at the Jackson home, "The Pennsylvania
Women" and "Brother Stoltz' Beat," a history of the Moravian
Bethlehem. That same year Roberts Brothers printed her small
book for children about the hospitable Quaker home, "*Mammy
Tittleback and Her Family, a Story of Seventeen Cats.*" And
she added another Saxe Holm to her list. It might be the last one
—she would send it to *Harper's*; under no condition would it go
to *Scribner's*. She regretted the break with Dr. Holland, but she
was not willing to take the chance of another refusal.

To refresh herself and to find the solace she so often needed,
she frequently rode off to spend a night or two at the Old Log
House, three miles from the top of Gray's Peak. There she
would relax in the warm companionship of Aunty Lane. This
courageous pioneer woman had lived in the cabin each year from
June to October for more than half a century. Helen was able
to share her strains and doubts with Aunty Lane—and that summer there were many.

Yet the September days ended on a far happier note than
Helen could have foreseen. Richard Watson Gilder offered her
a commission for a series of articles on California missions and

the Indians. He added as an afterthought that *Scribner's* was no longer under the editorship of Dr. Holland—he had retired because of heart trouble and had sold his stock. As of the November issue, the name of the magazine would be the *Century*.

Helen couldn't hide her delight and answered with eager acceptance. She told Will, "It means my going back to New York this fall. I'll need to do some preliminary research and—" This time there was no question about her decision or any doubt in her mind. Will offered no objection. He had business connected with the laying of the Mexican Central rails and would himself be away from the Springs for at least a month.

If Mr. Jackson had any struggle in accepting Helen's periodic absences from Colorado, he never showed it. He must have known by now that they were to be expected. Whether he realized it or not, he had married a woman whose abilities would carry her beyond the need of him. But certainly neither one could have foreseen the result of her championing of the Poncas or the demands on her time and energies.

It was December before they met again and not in the East, but in Santa Fe, New Mexico. Two days later, while Will went south to El Paso on a railroad assignment, Helen headed west for Los Angeles, California. On December 20, 1881, she registered at the Pico House.

Built in 1869 by the ex-governor Pio Pico, the last Mexican governor of California, and his brother Andreas, Pico House was located on the site of the old Carillo adobe on the south side of the Los Angeles Plaza. At that time it was considered the finest hotel in the Southwest, the first three-story building in Los Angeles, with approximately eighty rooms, a small interior court, and quaint stairways.

The Plaza, near the original one of the first settlement, was "dusty and dismal" and still had on its east side a low adobe house. But the city itself was far more prosperous than Helen had imagined, with blocks of fine stone buildings, hotels, shops, banks, and wide thoroughfares.

The outlying regions were even more attractive, and Helen found that though they were being filled with "houses of a showy though cheap architecture," the city had not shaken off its past. In her first California article, "Echoes in the City of the Angels," she told how the "Mexican women, their heads wrapped in black shawls . . . glide about everywhere. . . . The soft Spanish accent is continually heard."

The un-American or pre-Yankee culture gave the place a quaint and foreign look that immediately charmed Helen, as did the legends she soon learned from Antonio Francisco de Coronel and his wife. "I meant to stay but a few minutes," Helen started to apologize. She had presented the letter of introduction she had received from the Roman Catholic Bishop of Monterey and Los Angeles, the Right Reverend Francis Mora.

"Please come again and stay longer," Dona Mariana Coronel insisted in "her soft Spanish-voiced broken English." Don Antonio, a gray-haired Mexican *señor*, spoke a little English and his wife served as his interpreter. He urged her to come for tea.

Helen returned on Sunday, Christmas Day, and after that spent many afternoons with the Coronels. Their home, "El Recreo," built in the typical Spanish style, was located in the western suburb of Los Angeles on what is today the northwest corner of Seventh and Alameda Streets. As often as she approached the low adobe house in the carriage, it appeared hidden, surrounded as it was by orchards, orange groves, and vineyards. Once she crossed the threshold, she felt herself "transported into the life of a half-century ago."

The rooms were decorated in the quaint gay Mexican fashion, with flowers on every window seat. In a corner room were mementos of the time Don Antonio and has father had been the leaders in the city, back, as he said, "to the lost empire of his race and people on the California shores." A lifelong friend of the Indians, Don Antonio had escaped death at the hands of the Americans a number of times through their help.

From the Coronels, Helen heard the legends and tales of the old days, from the time of the founding of California by twelve devout Spanish soldiers through the turbulent period of Spanish viceroys, Mexican governors, and United States commanders. Occasionally the *señor* strummed his guitar and sang for Helen old Spanish love songs. Each day he and his wife walked out to her carriage, presenting her on leaving with armfuls of flowers and fruit, clusters of grapes, and great boughs of oranges. As she drove away with her lap full of "bloom and golden fruit," she thought to herself, "Fables are prophecies. The Hesperides have come true."

With Don Antonio's help, Helen made out an itinerary to visit old ranches and several of the missions, for he explained that Indians still lived in and around the old deserted missions and through the hills and valleys nearby. At the time Helen started her study, not more than five thousand Indians remained out of an earlier estimate of three times that number in the counties of Tulare, Santa Barbara, Los Angeles, and San Diego. Many of these lived near their former missions. Nobody had written land grants, since such grants had formerly been ordered by decrees, first by the Spanish king, and then by the Mexican governors.

Following the Secularization Act of 1833,[2] by which the Mexican government broke the land monopoly of the mission system and freed the Indians, many of them continued to live unmolested on the farms they had been tilling. But when the white settlers began to seek homesteads after 1846, the year California became part of the United States, and acquired Mexican grants, they drove off the Indians. Indians were not considered "citizens" and therefore not landowners, even though they lived on the property. Accordingly, white men could certify to the land-office agent that the lands were "unoccupied."

Helen decided to first go north in mid-January as far as the Santa Barbara Mission, some ninety miles from Los Angeles, a mission never abandoned or abused as the others had been. Besides, Don Antonio told her that the library contained a large number of valuable old books that had been gathered from the other missions at the time of secularization. On the way she would stop at the Mission San Fernando Rey de España in the Encino Valley, a mission dedicated to Fernando III, King of Spain, and at the Camulos Rancho, situated near the present town of Piru on the Ventura Highway.

She was so cordially received by Don Antonio's good friend, General Andreas Pico, at the San Fernando Mission, that she intended to return there later with the artist she was told would soon arrive from the East to join her. Mr. Gilder would compete with *Harper's* and had assigned Reginal Birch to illustrate the series.

At Camulos Rancho, Helen was less fortunate than at San Fernando Mission. Mrs. Del Valle was not at home, so Helen only rested two hours at her house and drove on to Santa Barbara that night. "I saw some of the curious old relics," she told the Coronels, "but the greater part of them was locked up, and Mrs. Del Valle had the keys with her."

Despite the short stay, the memory of the Camulos adobe, the one remaining Spanish homestead representative of early California life, would serve Helen well in her description of the Moreno ranch in *Ramona*. The ranch was in the heart of two thousand acres, originally part of the San Fernando Mission property, and had been granted by decree to Antonio del Valle in 1839. It was on this ranch that gold was first discovered in California eight years before the great days of the forty-niners, and actually the first gold dust ever coined at the government mint in Philadelphia came from the mines on this ranch.

The ranch had passed to the son of Antonio del Valle. His wife, Señora Dona Ysabel, whom Helen never saw, was probably the prototype of Señora Moreno. It is most likely, though, that her daughter Luisa, sister of Señora Coronel, had accompanied Helen around the ranch and had told her much of its history.

In Santa Barbara, Helen stayed long enough to take a trip to the Elwood Coopers' estate at Goleta, some twelve miles from the town, "a pocket ranch," they called it, since it covered less than two thousand acres. Here she gained material for her second *Century* article on the missions, "Father Junipero and His Work."

Junipero Serra had been the founder of the Franciscan missions in California. The Santa Barbara Mission was the only one still under the charge of the fathers, who received Helen graciously and loaned her all the books she wished to use. Here she met Rebecca Ord, and with her assistance she located a daguerrotype of Junipero Serra taken from an old portrait painted more than a hundred years earlier at the College of Fernando in Mexico.

The town of Santa Barbara, where Helen stayed, was, she thought, undistinguished apart from the mission. "It is too much like any one of a dozen New England towns," she wrote Sally Woolsey; "stodgy, smug, correct, and uninteresting." Still, there was a Chinatown to fascinate her and she had arrived in time to celebrate the Chinese New Year. At night she watched the fireworks, recalling the Fourth of July as a girl in Amherst and the firecrackers being set off while the family celebrated on the lawn of their Pleasant Street home. She visited the joss house and stopped at the small mission. "Here instead of the incense and prayersticks, there were bouquets of beautiful flowers and bowls of Chinese lilies," she told her young readers in the *St. Nicholas.*

But time had run out. She left on March 3 for San Diego.

21

The Mission Indians

THE S.S. *Orizaba*, a side-wheeler and coaler of the Pacific Coast Steamship Company, landed Helen at Horton's wharf, San Diego, at the foot of Fifth Street. She registered at the Horton House, a two-story brick building on D Street between Third and Fourth, facing the bay. Rates on the American plan were a dollar and a half a day, but the special attraction of the Horton House was that transportation from trains and steamer was free to any part of the county. Considered the leading hotel in Southern California, it was headquarters for "people of means and taste in San Diego."

Without delay, Helen looked over her letters of introduction [1] and outlined her plans for the days ahead. First she would contact Father Anthony D. Ubach, the Catholic priest in charge of the San Diego parish in Old Town. Then she would make a call on Mr. Ephraim Morse, who had been identified to her as a leading citizen in business and civic affairs, and possibly on the pastor of the Unitarian Society and preacher at Horton's Hall, the Reverend David Cronyn.

She looked again at the date of Edward Everett Hale's note to Dr. Cronyn, written for her when she had originally arranged the California trip with Will. She reread the note, dated March 28, 1881: "This introduces to you my near friends, Mr. and Mrs.

Jackson. You know her long since as H. H. . . ." Some explanation would be required, she knew, but there were always Will's banking interests and the demands of the Rio Grande Railroad.

Indeed, she found the Cronyns pleasant and willing to assist her with whatever information they could offer. But with Mr. Morse and his friendly wife from Massachusetts, Mary C. Walker, Helen felt more at ease, and in her early days in San Diego they often drove her out along the shore of the bay. It was with them that she first saw Point Loma, with its distant view of the coastline. Ever afterwards she would call the drive "the most beautiful in America."

But it was Father Ubach who became her steady escort. Day after day they set out early in the morning with her faithful driver, John Hinton, to visit the missions and to locate mission Indians. She admired Father Ubach's great concern for the Indians, particularly for the children. At San Diego de Alcala, located four miles northward on a bluff overlooking the town of San Diego, the parish priest had erected a simple building for the training of the region's Indian children. The "mother" mission itself was in ruins, as was the Mission of San Luis Rey de Francia, some seven miles north of the city. It gave little indication of its original architectural beauty—a composite of Spanish, Moorish, and Mexican. Only the arches of the corridors were left standing.

Out of the San Luis Rey Mission property, after secularization, large ranches had been organized and come under private ownership. The Indians, much stirred up over the granting of the ranches they claimed as their own, caused trouble. They even formed a plot to capture the governor, but the plot was quashed and the Indians driven off the mission lands.

From San Diego, Helen traveled with Father Ubach to some of these ranches, including Santa Margarita y Las Flores to the north of San Luis Rey, where she saw livestock by the thousands

grazing on the nine thousand acres of land. She also visited
Rancho Guajome, four miles east of the mission site, with its
elegant twenty-room adobe hacienda that was the richest in
Southern California. Señor Cave Couts had designed the home,
using American frame and Mexican tile and adobe. Passing
through the open courtyard surrounded by corrals, barns, sta-
bles, and servants' quarters into the inner patio, Helen could
not help but contrast the beauty of fountain and roses and lime
trees with the ruins of the old missions and the poverty of the
Indians she had seen.

As she and Father Ubach drove farther inland, the contrast
was even greater. One morning they went east to the beautiful
valley of San Pasqual—a continuous wheat field with a small
adobe chapel, a dozen or more adobe houses, and only one Indian, old and almost blind. The whole valley, one to three miles
wide and some twelve miles long, had been taken over by the
"robber whites," Helen was to report, even though it had been
set apart by executive order of President Grant, January 31,
1870, as the San Pasqual Reservation.

The grant for the reserve had been revoked the following
year because of pressures for private ownership. Some white
men who wanted the fertile land induced the San Diego sheriff
to move the Indians out. They had been moved into the hills,
mostly on the north side of the valley, where they eked out a
bare existence. Some even went on to Mesa Grande or to other
reservations.

Helen was deeply troubled at the sight of the dirty and ragged
lone Indian in the lovely rich valley. But it was Temecula, some
fifty miles northwest of San Diego, rather than San Pasqual,
that most moved her. There all that remained of the Indians was
their graveyard.

Temecula Rancho, first used by the Spaniards as a source of
grain for the Mission of San Luis Rey, was granted by Mexican
Governor Manuel Micheltoreno to Felix Valdez, a private citi-

zen. Resentful at the loss of their beloved homeland, the Indians made a peace offering to the United States Government agents and were promised that Rancho Temecula would be removed from private ownership and placed in a vast reservation set aside for them. The Treaty of Peace and Friendship, concluded at the village of Temecula, was signed January 5, 1852, by the chiefs of many tribes "in good faith." But Congress failed to ratify this document and other treaties made that same year. According to Horace Parker, "Probably the major share of the blame can be laid at the feet of a selfish and unenlightened citizenry."

For Father Ubach, the visit to Temecula brought back sad memories of the townspeople. He told Helen how five men from San Francisco had brought legal action "to recover possession of certain real estate," namely, Temecula, and how the Indians had appealed to him for help. In a long appeal in 1869 to one of the judges in the case, he had asked, "Can you not do something to save these poor Indians from being driven out?"

But he had been unsuccessful and six years later the Indians were evicted. The white men won. Helen thought back to Don Antonio de Coronel's tales of eviction—he had not exaggerated. The fate of the Mission Indians all through Southern California was to become for Helen a familiar and sad story, not unlike that of the Temeculans.

One day in 1875, the sheriff of San Diego had arrived with a posse of men and a warrant. In three days the Indians had been moved out of their homes in Little Temecula Rancho, about twenty-two hundred acres of good rich land along the Temecula River. Though they submitted to the move, they refused to lift a hand in the packing. Instead, they sat down and looked on, "some wailing and weeping, while the sheriff and his men took out of the neat little adobe houses their small stores of furniture, clothes and food. . . ."

Left at the southern edge of the Temecula Rancho, the Indians were forced to move their goods and settle in Pechanga Canyon, three miles from their old homes. Helen felt the sting of their hardships in her visit to the canyon, a hot, dry, and barren place with low rocky buttes on either side, and not a stream of water. "Every face, except those of the very young," she said, "was sad beyond description."

From Temecula and Pechanga Valley, Father Ubach and Helen traveled to see the old Spanish Mission of San Antonio, founded in 1816 as an outpost of San Luis Rey, twenty-five miles east. Though the Indians had been moved from these lands, some had returned and still lived in huts within ten or more miles of the dilapidated little church, where they gathered for worship whenever a padre came to the valley.

Helen watched as Father Ubach talked with the Indians in their own dialects; she eagerly awaited his translations. Through the Indians at Rincon on the Potrero Creek, she had learned of an Indian school in Saboba, the first in California. Though Saboba was nearly seventy miles north of San Diego, Father Ubach willingly took Helen to this fertile village. Watered by a natural spring, it was located in the San Jacinto Valley at the foot of the mountain range. Some hundred and fifty Indians of the Serrano tribe lived there, a tribe that had claimed this section of land for more than a hundred years.

"But they are in danger of losing their lands," Miss Mary Sheriff, the schoolteacher, told Helen as they toured the village. "And I may lose my children."

In the division of the lands, the village had been allotted to Mr. M. R. Byrnes of San Bernardino, although it was within the boundaries of the Mexican grant patented to the heirs of José Guadelupe Estudillo, January 17, 1880. Mr. Byrnes had threatened to evict the Indians unless the United States Government would buy his whole tract of seven hundred acres. The Indian chief said quietly, "If the Government says we must go, we must, but we would rather die right here than move." Mary Sheriff worried lest the Indians should give in without a struggle.

Formerly a teacher of freedmen in Pennsylvania, Mary Sheriff's home state, she had learned of the need for a teacher in the Indian country of Saboba and had accepted the position eagerly. She had not regretted her decision. She had forty children in her school, whom she had come to call "her children."

On Helen's arrival with Mary at the schoolhouse the next morning, she was puzzled by the children's behavior. They scurried away from her whenever she came near, even when she offered them sweets. Finally Miss Sheriff discovered the reason as she heard a child call out "*Tutacote*" from her hiding place behind a desk. "See the owl, the bad owl," the children echoed.

"They are afraid of the head of the large owl on your bonnet, Mrs. Jackson," Mary explained. "They think it might fly over them and bring evil."

"I will not wear it," Helen said, removing her bonnet and the owl pin. Even though she had purchased the pin to match her gray traveling dress and bonnet, she surely did not wish to frighten the children.

A second incident left an equally indelible impression on Helen. Mary had taken her guest to see the interior of one of the picturesque adobe houses on the bluffs. There Helen had seen a baby lying ill in a cradle of twigs woven together, and the mother silently praying over her. When Helen asked about a doctor, the young mother said with quivering lips, "We sent for a doctor to come to the village to see if he could cure my little one, but he refused to come. He told told my husband to . . . bring her to San Bernardino, but she is too ill to bear the journey." San Bernardino was a journey of more than thirty-five miles.

That night Helen couldn't sleep and Mary thought her sick. "No," Helen said, "but when I close my eyes, I see that poor little suffering baby that might be well if the doctor had a heart."

She left Saboba the next day for Los Angeles, returning by way of San Bernardino and Riverside. Determined to fight for the Saboba School and for the Indians everywhere, she would put even more energy into working for the protection of the Mission Indians and their rights to lands in Southern California.

22

Journey to Monterey

On April 10, 1882, Helen wrote Mr. Ward from her rooms at the Kimball Mansion on New High Street in Los Angeles. There were few reputable boardinghouses in the city, but the Kimball House was the one "where comfort and decent food could be found." Helen preferred its comfort and homelike atmosphere to any hotel, even the Pico House on the Plaza. "I have had a most interesting winter," she told him, " a month in Los Angeles —one in Santa Barbara—then in San Diego—Riverside and San Bernardino, and back in Los Angeles to wait the arrival of the artist who will illustrate my articles."

The wait proved a peasant one, for Helen had time to visit the Coronels and renew her former friendship with the Carrs of Pasadena. She had first met Jeanne Carr and her husband, Professor Ezra Slocum Carr, at the 1855 meeting of the American Association for the Advancement of Science in Providence. Mr. Carr, a professor at the University of Wisconsin when Helen met him in the East, had left the Midwest in 1869 to fill the chair of Natural Science and Chemistry at the University of California.

Six years later, he accepted the office of State Superintendent of Public Instruction at Sacramento, for which position he traveled and lectured throughout the state. In his travels, he and

his wife had selected Pasadena as their future home and in 1880
they bought a tract of land a half mile long and an eighth wide,
forty-two acres extending from what is now Orange Grove on
the west to Fair Oaks on the east, northward from Colorado
Street. There at their home, Carmelita—"little grove"—Helen
visited quite often with the Carrs and their two young sons, Ned
and Allie.

It was Jeanne who drove Helen to Kinneyloa, Mr. Abbot Kinney's home of some five hundred acres in the hills of the San
Gabriel Mountains. Helen had actually met Mr. Kinney earlier
at the Kimball Mansion, where he stayed on his frequent trips to
Los Angeles.

Soon after her arrival at the boardinghouse in April, he had
come to supper one night and happened to be placed next to her
at the dining-room table. His heavy thatch of hair and sorrel-
colored beard gave him real distinction, and Helen enjoyed the
companionship of the man who had once been a globe-trotter
before settling down in the home on the hill. A friend of the
Indians, he expressed to her his sincere sympathy in her concerns.

On first sight she couldn't stand his house. "Who could put a
great staring white house on a hill like that?" she asked Jeanne.
But the location was striking and the Loa, as he called his hill
after the term he had heard on a trip to the Sandwich Islands
(Hawaii), offered a sweeping view of Pasadena and the valley
beyond.

With Jeanne, Helen made almost daily drives into the sur-
rounding country in a spring wagon with a pair of half-wild
broncos. Helen would always recall in particular the sight of a
wild mustard patch in bloom in Coyote Pass. Later, she described it in *Ramona*:

"The wild mustard in Southern California is like that spoken
of in the New Testament, in the branches of which the birds of
the air may rest. . . . The stems are so infinitesimally small, and

of so dark a green, that at a short distance they do not show, and the cloud of blossoms seems floating in the air; at times it looks like golden dust. With a clear blue sky behind it, as is often seen, it looks like a golden snow-storm. . . ."

Within a few weeks the pleasant drives ended, for Helen was to begin her travels to the south. Mr. Henry Sandham had arrived. A Canadian-born artist from Boston, he had been assigned by the *Century* to accompany her and submit illustrations for her articles. She had hoped Reginald Birch would accept the assignment, since she knew him slightly. He had illustrated one of the Pennsylvania stories for *Scribner's*, but she knew he preferred illustrating children's stories for *St. Nicholas*.

No time was to be lost. They drove to San Diego, and Helen and Mr. Sandham visited the missions, San Luis Rey and San Juan Capistrano, thirty-five miles north of San Diego, and their Indian villages. Founded in 1776, though in ruins, the Mission San Juan Capistrano still gave evidence of its original beauty. It was probably the finest of all the California missions and had one of the best mission libraries, all the books in Latin or Spanish.

With Mr. Sandham, Helen revisited Temecula, and then went to Pala, Pauma Valley, the Potrero, a mountain meadow about ten miles from Pala, high up on the mountainside, and Rincon. Mr. Sandham made sketches of Indians and Indian huts and the missions. He would later confess that Helen at times annoyed him. "She stood," he said, "at my elbow and made suggestions."

Back in Los Angeles, Sunday, May 7, 1882, after what Helen called "a most repaying ten days," she took up rooms again at the Kimball Mansion and persuaded the Coronels to let Mr. Sandham stay with them until they were ready to leave for the trip north in two weeks. She told Señora Mariana that she thought the artist would profit if he had a chance to absorb the atmosphere of their California home and hear some of Don Antonio's stories.

The next day she went out to Kinneyloa. She wanted Mr. Kinney's assistance with the Indians, since he could speak Spanish and handle several of the Indian dialects as well. Most important, he was conversant with the land laws of California and their operation. She asked him to accompany her and Henry Sandham on a journey to Monterey to see the missions north of Los Angeles.

"I just might," he said, and Helen took his answer for a promise.

To Jeanne Carr, she wrote her regrets for not having seen her before leaving for Monterey; she told her she had driven out with Mr. Sandham and had found her gone. She regretted the "seven miles in the dust." She was sorry, too, "to have seen Pasadena again—poor dust-draggled-sand-smitten cypresses," for she had boasted to Mr. Sandham that "it was a green bower from beginning to end."

Then, lamenting the lack of rain, she said, "I look forward to our three weeks' drive from Santa Barbara to Monterey with absolute horror." And well she might, for the month of May would be as hot as usual in the interior. Besides, Helen was tired from her recent trip south with Henry Sandham.

On Sunday night, May 21, they took the boat to Santa Barbara—Mr. Sandham, Mr. Kinney, and Helen. In a few days they were on their way by carriage to the missions. From the cool, moist coastal region, a two-days' journey from San Luis Obispo, they went to the dry heat of ninety-three degrees at Paso de Robles. "It was terrible," Helen said of the scorching June day at this favorite watering place.

In the valley of the San Antonio River they visited the old Franciscan Mission of San Antonio de Padua. For Helen there was a pathetic dignity about the ruins of the old mission, standing out in the fields alone and deserted. But Jolon, six miles from the mission, which they reached at noon, was drear; after a short stopover at this stage station, they continued on their way to the Mission San Juan Bautista, where they found some relief from the heat. "It has sun, valley, and seaward outlook, unsurpassed in all California," Helen recorded in her notes.

The Mission San Juan Bautista, thirty miles from Monterey, had once served a large population of Indians but was no longer active as in the old mission days; it had been partly destroyed by the earthquake of 1880. Helen attended the six-o'clock morning mass at an orphan school for girls run by the Sisters of the Sacred Heart. Comfortable as she was in the hotel on the Plaza, the party left early. Some reports say she left "in anger."

Angry or not, for a reason not quite clear, Helen apparently antagonized Father Valentine Closa, a Spanish Moor and the priest in charge of the mission. Not all felt as Helen did about the Indians and her outspoken criticism of the priests' neglect may have upset him. From evidence in the press of the time, she may even have tried to rent the long unused wing of the mission or the Castro house directly across from it. The Castro house had been built in the 1840s as General José Castro's office and to house his male secretary. At the time of Helen's visit it was owned by the Patrick Breen family, survivors of the ill-fated Donner party and was a local landmark.

It was at San Juan Bautista that General José Castro had organized forces to repel Fremont's invasion in 1846, and the humiliation that the California commander-in-chief suffered when Fremont raised the Stars and Stripes over the ex-mission had not been forgotten. Helen's interest and concern was not with the conquerors or the defeated; it was with the Indians who had been driven off their lands, Indians who had been wiped out of existence by whites settling in the region.

The three travelers reached their destination and goal, the Mission San Carlos in Carmel, about six miles from Monterey. The second mission founded in California and the headquarters of the mission project, it was the resting place of its founder, Father Junipero Serra. Henry Sandham's picture of this mission illustrates well the original "spring of the roof and curve of the walls."

On the Carmel River, a few miles from the mission, they came across, with the help of a guide, the "most picturesque of all the Mission Indian houses." The parish priest of Monterey had told Helen of their pitiful condition, saying, "They had their homes only by the patience of the thief; it may be that the patience do not last tomorrow."

By strange coincidence, Helen had missed Will's telegraph that reached Los Angeles the very day she had left for Santa Barbara. He had wired that he would meet her in San Francisco at the Palace Hotel for a trip to Oregon. Connections were finally made, but Helen overlooked his late arrival in her pleasure at meeting a Mrs. Mary Trimble, a Quaker from New York City, who reminded Helen of Charlotte Cushman.

"It was not exactly by 'heads or tails' that we won our glimpse of Oregon," she would comment in her coverage of the journey in "Chance Days in Oregon," "but it came so nearly the same thing that our recollections of the journey are still mingled with that sort of exultant sense of delight with which the human mind always regards a purely fortuitous possession."

In contrast to the Monterey journey, the trip was relaxing, despite three days and two nights of uncomfortable seasickness on the Pacific Ocean from San Francisco to the mouth of the Columbia River. Helen adored Vancouver and Portland and found Puget Sound most pleasant, but Seattle, Washington, in her opinion, was a "swarm of immigrants to test their fortunes in the new country."

From Seattle, Helen and Will headed for Tacoma and after a few days' rest, Helen agreed to return with Will to Colorado Springs and the Kiowa Street home. She couldn't deny but that she was extremely tired, and she convinced herself or was partially convinced by Will that she might be able to write out her reports on the California Indians at home more easily than back alone in Los Angeles.

She made it clear to Will, however, that she had no intention of giving up her work for the American Indian, wherever she was, or her eventual hope for a government assignment to serve their cause. Will offered no objections, satisfied that her return home with him might stop the local talk of a separation.

23

A Second Pot of Gold

THROUGHOUT THE REST of the summer, Helen wrote and submitted an astonishing number of poems and essays for publication, incredible in light of her demanding work on the California stories. Roberts Brothers put together three of her essays on the upbringing of children in a small book, *The Training of Children*. It was in these articles that Helen had expressed her strong dislike of corporal punishment and her sympathy for the punished child. "I myself was whipped . . . but I never lacked anything but the power to kill every human being that struck me," she once told Mrs. Ward, with whom she had disagreed vehemently in a Bethlehem visit two years earlier.

As soon as Helen returned to Colorado Springs with Will in mid-June, she had started her search for an appointment with the Department of Indian Affairs in Washington, D.C. She would leave no stone unturned, and she first wrote Mr. Henry M. Teller, secretary to the Commissioner. She thought he might help her, since he had been a resident of Colorado and had met her in Denver personally, though briefly, through her husband.

In letter after letter she pressed him for an appointment, "There is a grave danger of continued Indian massacres," she pleaded. "If the United States Government does not take steps to avert this danger, the chapter of the Mission Indians will be the blackest one in the record of our dealings with the Indian race."

If she could secure a position, she would return to the West, no matter what Will or anyone in the Springs thought. She waited impatiently while Mr. Teller promised to do all he could to prevent any further injustices to the Indians. He would take her request under consideration.

With all her other writings and correspondence, Helen never for a moment forgot the Indians. Finally she wrote the Commissioner himself, the Honorable Hiram Price; he might give her a more direct answer. She told him in her letter, "My own expense I will rate, as I told Mr. Teller, at twelve hundred dollars." She urged his concern. Perhaps this figure, fifty dollars less than she had received for her *Century* papers, would encourage him to plead her case with the President. "If it takes longer and costs more, I will defray the remainder myself."

This letter, outlining the work she wished to perform, made its point, and on July 7, 1882, she was instructed by the Indian Department that her appointment as Special Commissioner of Indian Affairs in Southern California had been approved by President Chester Arthur. She was to visit, and report on the conditions of, the Mission Indians, to find out whether suitable lands could be made available for them as permanent homes for Indians not on reservations.

Without delay Helen wrote out her acceptance, but with one proviso, namely that Mr. Abbot Kinney be appointed her co-agent and interpreter. Although Mr. Price gave little indication of approval at once, she held to her request, writing Mr. Teller again for his support. Again she waited. She would have gone East to see her publishers but decided instead to join Will on another trip to Mexico in the fall; he had to inspect the proposed extension for the Mexican Central Line and she might collect items for some articles. Whatever their differences, they both liked to travel, especially on the new trains.

The road had been projected and partly built across country connecting Tampico on the Gulf of Mexico with San Blas, an old shipping port. San Blas had been originally the point for supplies from Mexico to California as far back as the days when California was a province of Spain; the heroic men who founded the Jesuit and Franciscan missions had all sailed from this port.

On September 27, they left Colorado Springs at six in the evening on a crack new train of the Atchison, Topeka, and Santa Fe, the Thunderbolt, for La Punta, where a connection would be made at ten thirty with a train for Mexico. On the morning of the second day, they reached El Paso at dawn in time for breakfast. From the train on the banks of the Rio Grande River, they could see the Mexican town of Paso de Norte opposite," an almost unbroken line of mud houses."

In her notebook Helen recorded for a future magazine article, "A few years ago, to have spoken of running down from Colorado to the Mexican boundary for a few days' trip would have been preposterous, yet to do it today is only a matter of thirty-six hours." From El Paso it was necessary to cross the river by stage, and they went by "hack," a remnant of the old Butterfield Stage Line that formerly went from Tipton, Missouri, to San Francisco by way of Arizona, a long and tedious haul of more than twenty-five hundred miles. The stagecoach was "antiquated, ragged . . . with seats of bare boards," but Helen was content. "To be there on Sunday is to escape from America and the nineteenth century," she declared.

On their return, however, a row of trim gay-colored horse-cars at El Paso brought a new way of crossing, and Helen suggested waiting a few days for the sole purpose of crossing on these cars. But Will was ready to leave and Helen had to be satisfied to watch as two horses were being patiently trained on the tracks to draw an open platform car up and down and across the newly erected bridge.

During all her busy schedule that summer and fall, Helen had taken time to encourage and assist new authors as she had Sarah Woolsey ten years before in New Hampshire. There had been a time earlier in New York that she had said she was being "bothered to death by these aspiring daughters of rhyme," but that was during the winter that she was exhausted with researching *A Century of Dishonor* and time was of the essence. Afterward she was grateful she had taken time to look through Edith Thomas's scrapbook, even though she had at first refused her and had actually sent her away discouraged. Once she had read Miss Thomas's sonnet "Frost," she changed her mind, telegraphed her so, and sent for Mr. Gilder, the editor of *Century*, to read the poem to him. "Indeed," she told him with vivacity, "you and I would give our eyes if we could ever write so well as that." He published her poetry.

Later, Helen asked Ellen Hutchinson, "Do you know . . . Edith Thomas's work?" In her letter to Ellen on October 29, 1882, she had praised Miss Hutchinson's own poems, saying, "The original two poems of yours seem fully as remarkable, fine and original. . . ." She helped Aurelia Barr as well, stating in answer to the receipt of a poem of hers on apples, "I would give anything—anything—if I had written that myself."

Soon she packed to go East to New York City. "Six inches of snow fell night before last," she wrote Mr. Warner, "and that means banishment for me." She said Mr. Jackson would possibly follow in December and stay a month or so, but she would later go alone to Southern California as an authorized agent for the Interior Department. Will had his own plans.

On November 15, 1882, Helen boarded the Denver train eastward for what was to be an absence of more than six months from the Springs. Only Effie, her housemaid, would really miss her cheery presence, but this time Helen went strictly on business.

The California articles were as ready as she could make them. She would deliver them in person to Mr. Gilder, but not until the Colonel had put his stamp of approval on them. She would have gone to Boston in early December for that approval had she not been ill and in bed at the New York Infirmary for Women. She stayed with Mary Trimble to convalesce for a few days, "an oasis in a New York Sahara," and by the end of the month was well enough to go to Boston.

From the Parker House there, she went at once to Cambridge to the "Queen Anne cottage" of the Higginsons, where she not only enjoyed the company of the Colonel and his wife but also delighted in Margaret Waldo, their bright and attractive two-year-old daughter.

The Colonel was "moderately satisfied, but suggested several changes," and Helen went back to Boston to edit further. A note to Annie Fields on January 5, 1883, asked if she and Sarah Orne Jewett would listen to the reading of her two papers on Junipero Serra. Since Mr. Fields' death in 1881, his wife Annie had gone to live with Miss Jewett and together they became acquainted with most of the Boston circle of writers. Miss Jewett was herself an established New England author, famous for *Deephaven*, sketches about a Maine village. Helen had first met her through Horace Scudder, editor of the *Riverside* magazine.

"I am going to do a most audacious thing, may I?" Helen asked in her note. "I want to come and read you my two papers on the Franciscan Missions. . . . It will take nearly two hours."

Helen announced to Annie Fields her uneasiness about the articles, since she felt hampered by Mr. Gilder's "demand for a popular treatment," and wanted to test the judgment of "minds comparatively uninformed about the subject."

Grateful to Annie and Sarah for their reassurances, Helen left the manuscript with Mr. Gilder, who thankfully was satisfied with it. A few days later, to her great pleasure and satisfaction, she received word of the acceptance by the Interior Department of Mr. Kinney's appointment as her co-agent. She had known in a letter she had received on November 28 of the possibility of authorization, but the January twelfth letter was explicit, giving full and final instructions for a California tour that would take five weeks and produce a government report. She thought of Will and the Springs but could see no reason to stop off for even a short visit. He had no need of her now and was far too busy to interfere with her arrangements to go West alone.

She would join Mr. Kinney by March for the tour of the Indian settlements in the three southernmost counties in the state, and she arranged with Henry Sandham to travel with them with "pencil, paint and brushes." Then she packed and took the earliest train possible for Los Angeles.

Partly to give Will some idea of her travels on the railroad, she wrote a record of the trip from New York to Los Angeles, calling it a "Pot of Gold." In late February, California was indeed for her "a miraculous sight." After having left "snow, sleet, hail, and icy rain" only seven days before, she had found a pot of gold—"fields green, lambs skipping, . . . sycamores, willows, flowers, square miles of orange orchards, everyone outdoors as though it were midsummer." She knew Will would share the article with railroad men of his acquaintance, and for herself, she sent a copy to the *Independent*—for a price.

Almost on arrival in the sunny city, Helen had word from Ephraim Morse of San Diego on March 9, encouraging her further in her undertaking. "I am glad," he wrote, "you have not forgotten our Mission Indians. I am ashamed of my government when I think of the heartless cruelty with which their kindness of the whites has been treated." In answer to her question about a proper boardinghouse, he indicated she would have no difficulty in getting rooms at Mrs. E. W. Whipple's and described it as "most excellent, the best in town and patronized by nice people." Otherwise, he told her, they could stay with a Mrs. Bowers on Tenth Street.

Quite soon she heard from Mary Sheriff, telling her that the Indians in the village of Saboba had been ordered to move or be evicted. Mr. Byrnes, a shopkeeper in San Bernardino, had decided to push his claim to the property and had demanded a payment from the government of thirty thousand dollars if the Indians were to remain on his land. The claim seemed unbelievable, and it was obvious to Helen that the government would never pay the sum he asked. The Indians had no written title, nothing beyond the "protecting" clause in the old Mexican grant.

She and Mr. Kinney would leave at once for Saboba. On March 14, she sent a hurried note to Jeanne Carr of Pasadena: "We may be back on Saturday but probably not till next week...." Strange, she thought, that her chief help should come from a man who only twelve months before she had told Jeanne not to mention: "Don't say anything to me about that man ... who could put a ... white house on a hill like that."

She realized now how "silly" she had sounded. She undoubtedly realized as well "gossip" that might be bruited about in her lone travels with Mr. Kinney, a bachelor. Still, she had an assignment from the government and no amount of suspicion or social disapproval could stop her. Without waiting for Henry Sandham, she and Mr. Kinney headed for Saboba to talk first with Mary Sheriff; then they would go to San Bernardino to interview the mission agent, Mr. S. S. Lawson.

It was a sad meeting with Mary. Mary saw no recourse to the action for removal and Helen felt helpless. "Can you get from the Estudillo heirs [1] any details of the original grant?" Helen asked Mary, suggesting that she find out if there was anything in the grant about a promise that the Indians would not be disturbed. The Estudillo family had lived for years in the Casa de Estudillo in Old Town, San Diego. Mary shook her head, but she would try.

Helen sent off a special statement to the Interior Department asking that no more patents be granted without finding out first if there were Indians on the property. But for Saboba, even this might be too late. Aware that immediate steps would have to be taken to prevent the eviction, Helen and Mr. Kinney left for San Jacinto, the trading center for the area.

Perhaps they could find out something about the situation there. But though they boarded with a Mrs. C. C. Jordan for several days, contacting local people, they obtained very little additional information. The townspeople hesitated to discuss any matters relating either to Mr. Byrnes or to the Indian Territory. In San Bernardino they had no more success. Mr. Lawson listened to their questions but showed no indication that he could, or would, prevent action. Agent Lawson had no intention of siding with the Indians or with Mrs. Jackson.

If Mr. Kinney and Helen were to bring about any change in the planned eviction, some legal action was required. They would return to Los Angeles for the assistance of the firm of Brunson and Wells. "We shall get the best legal counsel possible," Mr. Kinney promised. "But until we make our final plans, let's not say anything to anyone—not even to Miss Sheriff."

24

Bird of Passage

"THE LADY IS a comparative stranger and what she possesses in the way of qualifications for this responsible position will have to be shown by such action as she may see fit to take in this important matter," reported the *Los Angeles Express* on April 6, 1883. California apparently offered Helen no "pot of gold" in her capacity as an agent of the United States Government. She would have to prove her worth.

Even though Helen knew Southern California quite well, California knew little of her, either as a writer or as a person, and doubted that she would be effective in her job of protecting the Indians in their property rights. Many of the old Spanish and Mexican families looked at her with distrust—to them, she represented, in her official role, the Americans who were despoilers and had cut into their vast estates. But she was most disliked by the Californians. They were angry at, and fearful of, her efforts to secure homes for the Indians at their expense, and criticized her as a "junketing female commissioner."

A happier note came from Emily in early April: "To be remembered what? Worthy to be forgot, is their renown—"; she enclosed bluebells in the letter. It had been almost four years since Helen had written Emily, four years during which she had been, she said, "a bird of passage." For this she felt somewhat guilty and promised she would write her friend as soon as she returned from her tour of the Mission Indian country.

In preparation for the trip, Mr. Kinney engaged a Mr. Newell Harris Mitchell, proprietor of a livery stable and manager of the Planter's Hotel in Anaheim, as their driver.

As final plans were being firmed down, Helen drove out one day with Henry Sandham at his wish to visit the Baldwin ranch at La Puente, twenty-five miles east of the city. While at the ranch, they watched a sheep shearing,[1] an event Helen would not easily forget. She witnessed the entire process without a comment. Later she wrote, "A sheep being grasped, dragged in, and thrown down, seized by the shearer's knees until it was set free, clean shorn, and its three-pound fleece tossed on a table outside the shed."

"Are you tired?" Henry Sandham asked when he noticed she had remained silent for what seemed to him an unusually long time for Helen.

She shook her head and answered quietly, "No, but for the first time in my life I appreciate the text, 'As a sheep before her shearers is dumb.' "

According to Mr. Sandham in his recollections of this experience, "The helpless protest of the Mission Indians had a new meaning for her from this moment."

On April 12, ready for the month's trip through the reservations of Southern California, the party of four set out in a "two-horsed, double-seated carriage" for San Juan Capistrano, where they arranged to stay for two days. Mr. Kinney, as interpreter, would try to adjust any difficulties as they arose while Helen was to take notes and record the names and important details. She was considered the leader—Mr. Kinney called her "General" because, he said, "She was the directing spirit in all our work." She called him Comrade, or Co, for short; Mr. Sandham was always Henry.

As they journeyed from San Juan Capistrano south to San Diego, they stopped at ranches along the way, Rancho Santa Rosa, Santa Margarita y Las Flores, Rancho Guajome, and Rancho Buena Vista. Twelve days later they reached Mrs. Whipple's boardinghouse on the corner of Tenth and G Streets. Helen took rooms on the second floor facing south, and, according to Margaret Allan,[2] "made a most delightful addition to the family." The family consisted of several railway officials, army officers and their families, professional men, and some eastern tourists and a few teachers.

From San Diego as their base, they went to places in Indian country now familiar to Helen. From Pala to Rincon Valley the Indian women and children swarmed around her, greeting the "lady" warmly and touching her face and dress with affection. Though she could not speak their language, she understood their words of welcome.

At Temecula she prevailed upon Co and Henry to stay overnight in the Wolf Tavern. The adobe tavern was indeed the community trading center on the Pauba Ranch, owned by Louis Wolf. During the Civil War it had been a station on the main military road between Los Angeles and Arizona, and prior to the coming of the railroad in 1882, it was a much-heralded stopping place on the Southern Immigrant Trail. It was here that Helen met Ramona, wife of the owner of the store and tavern, with whom she formed a close friendship. And it was here, too, that Helen found the source for her Indian novel.

The following morning they were on their way again, this time, at Helen's wish, to rocky Pechanga Canyon. To her great surprise she saw that the canyon, formerly dry and dusty, had become an almost fertile valley within a year's time. The patient efforts of the Temeculan exiles had wrought a miracle. Helen marveled at the sight.

Traveling north into Riverside County, they spent days with

the Indians on the San Gorgonio Reservation in the pass, some six miles east of San Jacinto Valley. From there they went on to Cahuilla Valley, high up among the peaks and spurs of the San Jacinto Mountains. While ten miles from the nearest white settlement, Helen was amazed to find a school paid for by the United States Government and a teacher—one of the two white women there—living alone with her daughter. The Cahuillas, Helen thought, were the most interesting Indians they had visited—and the most intelligent. She would have liked to have stayed longer than the few days they had planned.

Their travels proved at times very difficult, especially in reaching isolated places and mountain passes. Occasionally they had to change to unshod ponies, the only animals that could keep their footing over the rough trails. When Henry once suggested that the traveling might be too arduous for Helen, she answered sharply, "I'll go if it kills me." She found it hard to accept Henry's constant concern for her welfare, however well-intentioned. She thought his solicitousness unwarranted, since he was the one who tired easily and complained the most.

Following some of the old stage routes, they went to the Mesa Grande reservation by way of Warner's Springs and into Julian. Sometimes their visits to the villages were of immediate help to the Indians, as was the case when they reached the home of the San Ysidro Indians just in time to prevent two illegal seizures by white squatters trying to preempt the land. From the San Ysidros they went on to Los Coyotes, five miles up from the head of the San Ysidro Canyon, reached only by a steep and narrow trail on the desert side of the valley.

The only really dangerous experience came on their drive out of Santa Ysabel, seven miles from Julian. Santa Ysabel was located in a pleasant valley, but on the climb up toward Julian they were suddenly caught in a severe snowstorm and were compelled to take shelter in an old shack. Though it was spring, nights were cold, and, according to Mr. Kinney, "It was impossible to travel in such a storm." For three days they were "imprisoned there . . . with the storm beating upon them through the cracks in the wall."

At last Mr. Mitchell took matters into his own hands and decided he couldn't stand Helen's or his discomfort any longer. He harnessed the horses and drove with the party "right into the teeth of the gale." In less than an hour they reached the valley and sunshine. "The gods have been kind to us," Helen commented.

Although she had originally anticipated visiting all the Indian reservations in Southern California, she had to be content with seeing all but two: the desert Indians and the Conejos. The desert Indians of Agua Caliente were too distant to reach in the remaining time—Helen would have to use a report by Mr. J. G. Stanley,[3] which strongly described the advantages the whites had taken of these desert Indians. She saw no need of softening his statements. She would report him exactly, word for word.

The Conejos of the Dieguino tribe could be reached only by a nine-mile horseback ride up a steep trail on the Capitan Grande Reservation. Despite Helen's encouragement, neither Co nor Henry could be prevailed upon to make the climb. Helen had to be satisfied with a secondhand report from a Mrs. Mariette Gregory, who had spent eleven summers in the vicinity and was welcomed and respected by the tribe.

It was just a month to the day when Mr. Mitchell left the party, tired and weary, at the Kimball Mansion in Los Angeles. Henry departed almost at once for the East while Helen and Co stayed long enough to arrange at the office of Brunson and Wells for a statement on the rights of the Saboba Indians to remain on their lands. "Now we can notify Miss Sheriff, General," Mr. Kinney said, with obvious satisfaction that a solution had been reached. "Urge her though on the necessity of secrecy—at least until our report has been submitted."

Helen nodded her approval. "I plan to tell her that if the Government will not pay the lawyers, not to worry. I will guarantee payment, even if I have to pay for some of it."

On Sunday, May 20, soon after an early breakfast, Helen wrote Mary to tell her of the chance for saving Saboba, but asked her not to tell anyone. She also sent off a note to Jeanne Carr, saying she was sorry not to see here again, but that she was "delayed by packing."

Then Helen took the evening train for Colorado Springs, where she could work quietly on the report. Despite her friendship with the Coronels and the Carrs, who supported her efforts for the Indians, Californians in general were undoubtedly glad to see her leave the state. Mr. Morse sent her clippings that attacked her in the *San Luis Rey Star* and in the *San Diego Union*. Aroused to a high pitch of anger, she tried to find out who the authors of the articles were, but without success. Mr. Morse could only conjecture that the "scurrilous letter" in the *Union* was written by Major Utt, brother of the editor and anti-Indian, but he had no direct proof.

On June 1, everyone in the Springs except Helen flocked to see the opening of the Antlers Hotel, a "noble structure" on four acres at the head of Pikes Peak Avenue. Will had been a partner in the scheme that resulted in a hundred-thousand-dollar hotel, the finest in the West, which everyone agreed was "magnificent." But Helen's interest was in the poor Indians, not in beautiful carpeting, central heating, or gas lights.

She went to work on the report. Before the month was out, she had the pleasure of welcoming her comrade, Mr. Kinney, who stopped off for a few days to talk over the final editing of the manuscript. She had already finished the document, written out in pencil from her thick pages of notes, and there was little more to do but change or add a few words. "I am not the writer you are, General," he said. "I trust your judgment completely."

On July 13, 1883, the manuscript went off to the Government

Press in Washington, titled "Report on the Conditions and Needs of the Mission Indians." It was signed by Mrs. Helen Jackson and Abbot Kinney.

Although it was mainly an account of the Mission Indians— the Serranos, the Cahuillas, the San Diegenos, and the Luisenos —the report included a legal brief and comments on the wretched condition of tribes—"gypsies in brush huts"—near Riverside, San Bernardino, and the San Gabriel Valley. It closed with eleven specific recommendations, one of which was that all white settlers now on reservations be removed. Many items recommended improvements for the Indians: more schools, better distribution of agricultural implements, and more farm equipment. A small sum should, she added, be set aside for the purchase of food and clothing for the old and sick.

Well-satisfied with the report, Helen asked Commissioner Price to send copies to more than two hundred people, including, of course, every member of Congress. If she had expected more response or reaction to this report than to the *Century of Dishonor*, she was at first headed for disappointment. However, in a letter to the Coronels four months later, she would be able to say, "Our report has been favorably received and its recommendations incorporated in a bill before Congress this winter." She wasn't too hopeful of its passage, but even so she thought her work had not been in vain, since it had secured the appointment of Brunson and Wells as United States attorneys to protect Indian rights on their lands.

The *Century*, along with Manypenny's *Our Indian Wards*, may have shocked its readers, but it failed to stir a "Christian nation to action." It soon became apparent that the second report would also have little lasting impact. Sarah Woolsey claimed it was promptly "pigeon-holed and forgotten," which she said was a natural condition with reports "which conflict with the greed and self-interest of the settlers."

The summer dragged by. Shortly after the report was in print, Helen heard from Mary Sheriff that her salary had been reduced. She threatened to resign. To Helen it seemed no less than an act of retaliation against her, and she sent her own money to Mary to make up the difference and urged her not to leave the Saboba School that so needed her. Within a short time the lawyers notified Helen that the Saboba tract had been rented but the Indians could continue to pasture their stock in Indian Canyon. In her letters to Mary, she insisted that if anything came up to trouble the Indians, the Sabobans should go directly to Brunson and Wells.

She then waited for an answer to her letter to Brunson and Wells concerning the legal aspects of Mary Sheriff's salary reduction. She wanted also to have more information about the suit by which the Temecula Indians had been evicted. If only she were there to help in person! Suddenly Colorado Springs seemed not only isolated but depressing. She felt her absence from the Indians of Southern California almost unbearable.

Even though the mail brought laces, baskets, rugs, and handicraft of every kind that she had purchased on her California tour, Helen chafed at having to be in the Springs. And Will was away—in Denver for weeks at a time. "To be here in the summer without Mr. Jackson is intolerable," she said. But more than Will's absence, her own ill health worried her. She blamed her illness on the climate, and in her despair sent *Scribner's* her first negative article on Colorado, "A State without a Debt." A week in Salt Lake City gave her no comfort. She said she nearly died of the dust! "If only Will would move to some country" where she could stay the year around. She even thought of going to Cuba.

Relief of a kind came in the fall with cooler weather, and she gained back some of her energy, enough to welcome the Elwood Coopers from Pasadena for a three weeks' visit. While they discussed the problems faced by the Mission Indians, she began to consider the slow effect of her work on their behalf. Neither her reports nor articles had made much of an impact on the nation.

When free to check newspapers and magazine articles in more detail, Helen became convinced she should try another approach. Papers from Washington, D.C. clearly showed that the white men had the right to deprive any Indian of the land of his forefathers. It was obvious to her that to support the Indians was more than any man's political head was worth.

Perhaps with the background she had accumulated in her travels west, she should try writing the novel J. B. Gilder had once suggested. Perhaps, like Mrs. Stowe's *Uncle Tom's Cabin*, that would move a nation and help right a wrong.

"Still I did not see my way clear; got no plot 'til one morning, late . . . October," she later told the Colonel, "before I was wide awake, the whole plot flashed into my mind . . . in less than five minutes, as if someone spoke it. I sprang up, went to my husband's room and told him. I was half frightened."

She would need privacy and she knew the social life in the Springs would be distracting. For by the 1880s, the Springs had grown to a population of some five thousand and it was considered a modern city, with a telephone system, two banks, gas works, the El Paso County Library, a School for the Deaf and Blind. Interested in the theater and music, the leading people of the city heard from thirty-four to thirty-six excellent professional offerings a year. The Opera House, which cost eighty thousand dollars, was opened in 1880, with Maude Grange's appearance in *Camille*. The week of April 12, 1882, Oscar Wilde had lectured on Art Decoration.

"I can't write here," she told Will. "I must go to New York if I am going to get the story down on paper."

For a while neither said a word. Then Helen remembered

they had invited her niece Helen Banfield [4] to spend the winter months with them. Twenty-four and unmarried, Helen Banfield had accepted the invitation with great pleasure. She had graduated from Vassar in the class of 1879, but had been ill much of the time since then. Her mother had written to ask if she might spend the winter in the Springs, thinking it hight help her as it had previously helped Helen.

"What about Helen?" she asked Will. "Do you think you can manage with one maid, my good Effie? And Helen can take care of the house for you?"

"Yes, we can manage. You will probably be back by the time she comes, or perhaps you could come back with her."

The last statement was all but a question, and Helen hardly listened to his explanation. She knew that Will did not attach much importance to her writings. Besides, he was concerned with the financial weakness of the Denver and Rio Grande and the stock manipulations by the wily fiancier Jay Gould. Gould had forced Palmer out of the railroad that summer and construction westward had stalled at Red Cliff, just over the Tennessee Pass twenty-five miles beyond Leadville.

The idea of an Indian novel absorbed Helen's energies. She had much to do before she could leave for the East. That evening she wrote out a brief outline for the story that she would later say was "at her fingertips." But some of the details were lacking in her notes, and she sent off urgent messages to Father Ubach and Mr. Morse. Of Mr. Morse, she asked for an accurate account of two things in San Diego County: "the ejection of the Temecula Indians; the taking of a lot of sheep from some of the Pala or San Luis Rey Indians by Major Couts. . . ." She explained that she planned to write a book but urged him "not to speak of this." She intended to keep it a secret from all except her more intimate literary friends. She was able to notify him that the agent Lawson, whom she called "a bad man," had been removed. She trusted that the new agent, Mr. J. B. McCallum, appointed October 1, 1883, would be a better one. Even so, she received several copies of the *San Luis Rey Star* from Mr. Morse that contained "slurring and contemptuous references" to her in connection with Lawson's removal from office.

To the Coronels, she wrote five days later, on November 8, 1883, in great haste, "I am going to write a novel, in which will be set forth some Indian experiences in a way to move people's hearts. . . . People will read a novel when they will not read serious books. I wish I had this plan in my mind last year in Los Angeles. . . . I would have taken notes of many interesting things you told me. . . . Mr. Jackson is well and would send his regards if he were home."

Ramona and Alessandro

HELEN SAT AT HER DESK, where she could look out at the heavy fall of snow. The rooms she had taken in New York City at the Berkeley House on Fifth Avenue and Ninth Street were crowded but comfortable. Around her were the Indian blankets she had brought with her, "things from Marsh's store," and on the floor were antique rugs. She had found room for all her "traps," as Will called her Indian articles from Southern California. The place looked as though she had lived there all her life.

On the writing table beside the portrait of Rennie she had placed an unframed photograph "after Rossetti"—two heads, a man's and a woman's, set in a halo of clouds. They were, Sarah Woolsey recalled later, "strangely beautiful, exactly her idea of what Ramona and Alessandro might have looked like."

Within ten days after her arrival, Helen was writing "at lightning speed," she told the Colonel. "I wrote the first words on the 1st of December," she was to tell her many friends.

"It was sheep-shearing time in Southern California, but sheep-shearing was late at the Señora Moreno's." Thus she opened the first chapter of the novel that, when finished, would run as a serial in the *Christian Union*. Thinking of herself as the Indian Mrs. Stowe, she wrote to Mr. Ward on January 1, "If I can do one-hundredth part for the Indians as Mrs. Stowe did for the Negroes, I will be thankful...."

Only occasionally did she take time out to write a personal letter. To Mary Sheriff she actually wrote one the very day she had begun the novel, asking for more details on the shooting of a Cahuilla Indian, Domingo, on the charge of horse-stealing. The *San Diego Union* had carried the story in the April 1, 1883, issue under the San Bernardino items, stating that the Indian Domingo of Cahuilla Valley had taken Sam Temple's horse from the corral of E. T. Hewitt and, when Temple caught up with him, he refused to give up the horse and made for Temple with a knife. She understood that no one felt any remorse, since killing a horse thief was considered justifiable homicide. Besides, an Indian had no chance against a white man, and to betray sympathy for the Indian was tantamount to guilt. A bit hazy about the steps in the legal procedures, she urged Mary to get all the specifics she could from Will Webster, the young rancher mentioned in the government report.

A letter started to Abbot Kinney on January 17 wasn't completed until February 2. For as the novel progressed at some two or three thousand words a day, she found letter-writing next to impossible, even to Will.

Whether from the "horrible weather," or from overwork, she didn't know, but she collapsed for a week. The days had been raw and cloudy and it had snowed incessantly. But no sore throat could keep her long from her writing, and she was back at her table with such energy that by February 2, she had one-third of the book done. "I hope it is good," she told "Dear Co." "Am pretty sure the 1st of March will see it done. Then I will play...."

Three days later she sent a line to Colonel Higginson: "It racks me like a struggle with an outside power.... Twice, since beginning it I have broken down utterly for a week. What I have to endure in holding myself away from it, no words can tell. It is like keeping away from a lover, whose hand I can reach. . . ."

She scribbled away on long sheets of yellow paper, certain that only a lead pencil could keep pace with the swiftness of her thoughts. By late February she had completed twenty chapters. Though loath to stop, she pushed herself to do other things, shopped for her niece Helen Banfield as she had promised, and visited her friend of San Francisco days, Mrs. Merritt Trimble of 59 East 25th Street, whose opinion she grew to trust. Other than that she had a lonely existence, with no social engagements. She was never out after 5:00 P.M.

She resumed her correspondence on behalf of the Saboba Indians and was delighted to know she had been able to get Mary's salary restored. Every now and then she forced herself to write a short story or a bit of verse to avoid the strain of the novel.

Spring was in the air when Helen finished the last chapter. It was March of 1884. She often "sighed" for Southern California and, in particular, for the San Gabriel sunshine. She was glad indeed to see the end of a New York winter—and, she hoped, the end of her sore throats.

On April 12, the "cat was out of the bag." J. B. Gilder announced in the *Critic* that Mrs. Helen Jackson would soon publish a long novel. She sent the manuscript to Sarah for her opinion, and Sarah returned it with high praise, agreeing with Mary Trimble, who had called it "tremendous." Helen had read most of the chapters aloud to Mrs. Trimble. Yet she worried for fear she had done some harm in departing from the factual chronological sequence of events. For dramatic effect, she had placed the eviction of the Temeculan Indians before the first troubles in San Pasqual.

"Will anybody be idiot enough to make a point of that? . . ." she asked Co, adding, "I am not writing history."

* * *

The scene of *Ramona* is laid in Southern California and the heroine gives her name to the book. Ramona is a beautiful, half-breed Indian girl, brought up in a Mexican family in complete ignorance of her parentage. She falls in love with an Indian, Alessandro. Their love story is one of the most tender and touching ever written about Indians.

The first half of the book is largely a series of picturesque descriptions of life on a ranch, while the second half points out, through the love story, the wrongs and cruelties the Indians suffered at the hands of the white race—ending in the hero's death. The whole book is a plea for justice for the Indians of Southern California. The tale is wonderfully graphic and filled with pictures of ranch and Indian life, as well as sharp character sketches of the Catholic missionary fathers.

According to a review in the *Nation*, in June of 1885, "Mrs. Jackson . . . arranged her groups to present all the striking contrasts the situation can furnish. Spaniards, Mexicans, and Indians all play their parts, with the old rancho, the Franciscan mission, the Indian village, and the mountain canyons for background. . . ."

Helen could not have imagined in her wildest thoughts the attempts that would be made for many years after *Ramona* was in print to locate scenes, incidents, and characters she had used. The charges and countercharges would have dismayed her, as would the countless Ramonas and Alessandros identified as the originals, from Cahuilla to Temecula.[1] But she would have been more than repaid to know *Ramona* would become a classic.

In her own lifetime, Helen would know of the sale of more than fifteen thousand copies. Fifty years after her death, it would go into forty-one printings and survive three motion pictures, a stage play, and a pageant. Even now, each spring in Hemet, California, the book is immortalized with an outdoor pageant of the tragic love story.

The *Christian Union* told its readers on the first of May that the serial would begin in two weeks' time, serialized weekly rather than monthly as originally planned. On May 15, chapter one appeared. It was an instant success. Thousands read *Ramona* in serial form, a form Helen called "the pill." "I have sugared the pill," she wrote the Coronels. She hoped above all else that if the pill went down, her readers would be moved to action for the American Indian.

Ramona carried her own signature, though with H. H. added. In fact, the government report with Mr. Kinney was her first publication that carried her name as a signature, Mrs. Helen Jackson. She might never acknowledge the Saxe Holm stories publicly, but she would never disavow her Indian writings. To Colonel Higginson she had once tried to explain her dedication to the Indians. "You have never fully realized how for the past four years my whole life has been full of the Indian cause. Nor how I felt, as the Quakers say, 'a concern to work for it'. . . ."

Unfortunately, Helen became ill on her Cambridge visit in mid-May, so ill that she had to call a doctor to attend her. This time it wasn't a sore throat, she told Dr. C. L. Nichols, a homeopathic physician, but a general feeling of weakness and exhaustion. However, she couldn't accept his prescription: to stay out of Colorado for two years and refrain from "brain work." It was absolutely absurd. "I would rather die," she declared, "than leave Mr. Jackson for so long a time."

Although Dr. Nichols told her that a general nervous breakdown could well be worse than dying, she packed her bags and went to Boston. But her nine days at the Parker House were of such "ignominious prostration" that she was unable to see friends she had planned to visit. It particularly distressed her that she had "lost the Boston visits," and wrote Annie Fields on Sunday, May 25, to thank her for the lovely white roses, regretting that she could not see her and Miss Jewett. She urged them to come instead to Colorado, a ride of "only four days and but one

change of cars from New York and Denver." Helen never tired
of the trip across country.

Meanwhile she had a decision to make concerning William H.
Rideing's request to include her in the list of "American Augus-
tans" in the *Youth's Companion*. This magazine had been a good
source for her articles for young people and she had even submitted to it two years earlier a Saxe Holm story, "Tommy Bill-
ings' Misadventure."

She offered Mr. Rideing, now the magazine's assistant editor,
instead of her name and biography, two or three stories, saying
she disliked lists of any kind. And added, "I do not care to give
out anything about my private life, but I could send you in three
or four months two stories, an Indian story, and one about the
underground railroad."

But Mr. Rideing objected strongly to the underground railroad tale as offensive to his Southern readers. "So might the
Indian story be offensive to some of your California and Western readers," she answered. "Had you thought of that?"

Then she offered to submit stories for two hundred dollars,
even though she should have held out for five hundred, her
present price, she told him. "The desire of a woman with a
hobby, to gain for having the widest audience possible," was her
explanation for the lower fee. She sent him a copy of her report
on the Mission Indians, saying, "You can see from this what material I have for Indian stories and whether you would be willing
to run the risk of their being offensive to some white men."

Mr. Rideing pressed Helen no further and the episode ended
there. On June 8, she stepped off the Denver and Rio Grande
train back in Colorado Springs. She was returning to the home
she had left in November, to discover that "young Helen" had
stayed all winter, from late November to March, serving as
mistress of the house. Helen learned from Effie about Mr. Jackson's and Helen Banfield's activities, the trips they had taken, the

picnics and the horseback rides into the mountains. It had obviously been a pleasure for Mr. Jackson to show her Colorado territory and to introduce her as well at various social functions.

That winter, while Helen was in New York City, Will had been appointed receiver for the Denver and Rio Grande railroad for a period of two years. The railroad had gone bankrupt and Will had been given the responsibility of reorganization. Tracks, roadbeds, rolling stock, and equipment would have to be investigated, and he would have to get permission from the English bondholders to build from Red Cliff to Aspen. If Helen wondered how Will had had time to escort her niece, she said nothing about it.

Clearly, Helen could not have imagined that her niece would be eager to return to the Springs five years later to take her place in the empty house— After all, Will was old enough to be her father.

Refusing to accept Dr. Nichols's medical advice to spend months in bed, Helen was soon up and around. With the help of Effie, she worked "like a Trojan," redecorating the house with new shades, curtains, furniture covers, and rugs. For furnishings, she added many of her "traps" and adorned the living room with animal skins and Indian ornaments, a water bottle once carried by a Mission Indian girl, and some of her vases, gold and silver Aztec jars from New Mexico, and Chinese and African carvings. In her own rooms at the top of the stairs she laid a rug woven by an old Saboba Indian woman.

Finally, she had a tiny lift put in to carry coal, water, and heavy burdens to the second floor. "Never did I have such a sense of delight in prospect of the summer," she wrote Co. But she didn't tell him that she had already sent to the publishers a book about him and Kinneyloa.

During her visits at his hilltop home in San Gabriel, California, she had gained material for a book for children that she would call *The Hunter Cats of Connorloa*. Her descriptions were realistic, even to the Chinese servants and the seventeen cats he kept for hunting gophers, and the snow-white building she had grown to accept and appreciate.

Helen had planned to sit down to work the first of July on a new story, a child's story about the Indian question. She hoped that with it a few thousand children would grow up ready to be just. But on Saturday evening, June 28, probably "going too fast," she caught her heel on the upper step and fell the whole length of the flight of stairs. "I could recall nothing, after the first tripping of my foot," she wrote Co, "and a vain clutch at the balustrade. If we had a free hand rail as we ought I should not have fallen."

It was a wonder, she said later, that she hadn't broken her neck. She bruised herself badly and broke her left leg. "Two inches of the big bone smashed in and the little one snapped, as compound a fracture as is often compounded," she later wrote Emily.

For weeks she suffered intensely from her leg set in plaster, although she was as comfortable as possible with her bed in the dining room and three splendid local Scottish women to take care of her. Effie, her housemaid, proved a born genius for nursing, and Helen found her a constant delight and tireless. The weather was "mercifully cool and moist."

Will was away most of the time, "never home except for a Sunday or overnight, but in Denver all the time." This time his absence did not trouble her. "I dread having people know I am an invalid," she said to Effie, "and most of all Mr. Jackson."

On July 21, she wrote Mr. Warner to thank him for the best laugh she had had in twenty-one days. "I went to sleep chuckling . . . to think of frescoing it. . . ." She decided to follow his suggestion and print L.E.G. on the plaster cast for the doctor to see the next time he called.

She spent her time reading "silly novels," seeing her friends, and looking out at the top of Cheyenne Mountain. By August she was able to slide into a chair twice a day, a blessed relief from lying in bed constantly. Her leg had healed sufficiently to have the cast removed and crutches provided. She thought it "a most remarkable success for an old woman past fifty and weighing a hundred and seventy pounds." It had taken four men to lift her from the floor onto the bed after the accident, but hopefully she would soon be on her own feet again.

Although she had wanted the news of her accident kept out of the press, editors differed with her. It was considered news. Emily Dickinson saw the notice in the *Republican* and wrote Helen a small note of sympathy, hoping it was not quite a "massacre." Helen's answer showed Emily that she had "taken Captivity captive," for her letter was bright and cheery. "I trust you are well and that life is going pleasantly with you." She added as well her deep feeling in Emily's greatness as a poet and said, "It is a cruel wrong to your day and generation that you will not give them light. If such a thing should happen that I should outlive you, I wish you make me your literary legatee and executor."

Whatever Emily's reaction, she failed to acknowledge Helen's wish, writing instead, "I shall watch your passage from Crutch to Cane with jealous affection. From there to your wings is but a stride— ..." She signed it, "Loyally, E. Dickinson."

The one event that most cheered Helen through the days of adjustment to crutches and to the strain of moving about the house was the receipt of copies of *The Hunter Cats*. Though she still waited for *Ramona* in final book form, the plate proofs of *The Hunter Cats* had reached her in mid-July and she thought it a "jolly story," although she did not like Marble's pictures. "Poor fellow, he can't draw," she forewarned Co. She ordered a copy sent to him as soon as it was out in hard cover and this time with "delightful illustrations by Addie Ledyard." "You will laugh to see yourself saddled with an orphaned niece and nephew," she told him. "I hope you don't dislike the story. . . ."

The book was an accurate picture of Kinneyloa. But Helen had introduced the two children as a way of telling the story of an actual case of the eviction of an aged Indian and his wife from their home in San Gabriel Valley. Helen hoped the "scalawag C— of Los Angeles" would come across the tale and see himself in it, as well as recognizing Fernando, the Indian he had turned out of his land. Co could find no fault with the "General's motives."

Helen was also heartened considerably by the advance reviews of *Ramona* in the *Critic* before the novel appeared. In April, the magazine stated briefly that "Mrs. Wm. S. Jackson (H. H.) has completed the first long story she has ever written over her own name. The scene is laid in Southern California and the heroine gives her name to the book—'Ramona.' The incidents are largely historical and the peculiar conditions of the early settlement of the country by Americans furnish elements of great pathetic and dramatic interest."

In May, after publication had begun in the *Christian Union*, the *Critic* praised *Ramona* again as being worth reading in serial form, calling it "an exceptional work" and a "novel with a very exciting purpose."

As the cooler days arrived in late September and Helen's leg failed to mend as completely as the doctor had expected, she began to worry about the winter months ahead. She couldn't risk the heavy snows or could she bear the thought of being "cooped up in Colorado." Remembering how she had been "deluded" the fall before into staying on until the twentieth of October and the heavy snowstorm that kept her in bed with bronchitis for three weeks, she decided she would leave "as soon as she could hobble." Two or three months of "sunshine and outdoors in Southern California" should make the difference.

She wrote at once to Mrs. Whipple's to engage rooms in San Diego, "the only place . . . in all California where there was real comfort. . . ." She liked the climate there the best. But, to her disappointment, she discovered that Mrs. Whipple had left "the best of all towns" and had opened up a boardinghouse in Los Angeles. Helen could not bring herself to take rooms in a hotel, even a recommended one in San Diego—she had a "mortal dread" of hotels. Instead, she sent word to Mrs. Whipple for a description of her Los Angeles house, expressing her need for a place that was "high, sunny, and airy."

By October, Helen knew without doubt that her junketing days were over. Ten months earlier she had suggested jokingly to Co that the Government send them somewhere and had finally answered her own suggestion by saying, "They never will. I've had my last trip as a Junketing Female Commissioner." After the accident she no longer joked about going; but neither did she give in to self-pity, writing merrily about her shortened leg and crutches.

A letter to Co on October 5 expressed in full her joy in learning that Mr. Kinney had fallen in love and would be married within the month. She would have liked putting him and his bride up in the "blue room," but she was about to leave for the West and Mr. Jackson was never at home. "There are but two things in life which could have pleased me more than the news in the last letter of yours . . . first, to have a whole leg in place of this broken one. . . . Second, to have Mr. Jackson tell me that he would give up Colorado and go to live at some Christian altitude, and before settling down, travel for a few years. . . ." Helen would not have either of these wishes fulfilled—and she knew it.

On October 12, she sent a letter to Mrs. Whipple with her appreciation of the floor plan of the house at 439 Pearl Street, and told her that the "two first-floor rooms—back—with the south windows would suit . . . admirably if the verandah did not shut off the sun." She suggested that the owner might let her "unroof the verandah opposite her rooms" if she put it back all right on leaving. "I have done that in two different places in the course of my life," she explained further.

Reserving the two ground-floor rooms at the back of the house, Helen said, "I would be glad of that little side entrance, while I am so helpless—one hates to be a spectacle. . . . I can't start before the first of November, anyway—I am not gaining in matter of walking as I hoped to. . . . My weight is a sad hindrance," she complained. Getting around with one crutch was difficult. If she had weighed less, she was assured she could eventually walk with a cane and no lameness. But despite the lameness that even a daily massage could not relieve, the doctor thought she could travel if her maid went with her. With Effie's help, Helen packed her trunks and several valises. On November 12, 1884, they left for Los Angeles. It is very possible that Will wondered if and when he would see his wife again. But Helen had no regrets about leaving Colorado Springs and her home at 228 East Kiowa Street for California sunshine.

26

Russian Hill

"THERE CAN BE nothing in this world nearer perfection than this South California climate for winter," Helen claimed as she settled in with Effie at the large residence on the hill at Sixth and Pearl Streets (later to be known as Figueroa) in Los Angeles. But her progress was slow, even though she tried to walk without her crutches, managing a few steps with a cane for a short time and "prancing about on the verandah."

She half regretted not having gone to San Diego and risking the new hotel, for she found the ground-floor rooms had "an icy chill" about them—too close to the earth, she imagined. The Coronels would have liked to have had her stay with them at El Recreo, but she felt too helpless and troublesome to be comfortable anywhere except in a boardinghouse. She compromised by spending many mornings with them, sitting on the long verandah listening to stories of early California days or writing out some of her magazine articles.

Since it was necessary for Helen to write in a reclining position, Don Antonio had a little mahogany table made for her with two lower shelves for notes. There she finished "From Icicles to Oranges," a piece about travel from the Springs to Los Angeles that Will could circulate among his railroad associates. Whenever she had a manuscript ready to send back East,

Señora Mariana would go with her to the post office. While there one day in late November, a package came for Helen from Roberts Brothers. "It must be *Ramona*!" she exclaimed with excitement. "Let's open it at once."

She had long anticipated this moment. At the time of her departure from Colorado Springs, though she knew the book had been ready for the Christmas sale, for Roberts Brothers had listed it in the November eighth *Publishers' Weekly*, she had not yet been mailed a bound copy. But there it was in her hands, the first copy of *Ramona*. To her delight, it was bound in very light green with gold decoration and maroon lettering, and on the cover were three seed vessels of artichokes.[1] In the book she had described them in some detail as "great soft-round disks of fine straight threads like silk, with a kind of saint's halo around them of sharp, stiff points."

Her signature, Helen Jackson, appeared as though handwritten, with the initials H. H. below in parentheses. Without a minute's hesitation she handed the copy to the *señora*, saying simply, "Mariana, here is the first copy of my book,[2] and I give it to you." Then, taking a pencil out of her handbag, she wrote on the flyleaf, "With the compliments of the author."

It was with regret that she had to refuse in December an invitation from Abbot Kinney and his new bride to spend a few days at Kinneyloa. But she promised that if she got on her feet she would come and stay a day or two before leaving for New York. She would have liked to have seen Margaret Thompson Kinney, whom he called "young H. H.," but she sent her love instead, saying, "I liked your calling her 'young H. H.' There is no doubt she looks as I did at twenty."

But prospects were not good, either for going to Kinneyloa or being well enough soon to "encounter the Atlantic seaboard winter." Effie had fallen and wrenched her knee badly, and Helen had an inflammatory condition in her good right leg from the long strain of its doing "double duty." "The broken leg is gaining," she wrote the Kinneys, "and except for my whole leg I could walk with a cane now. Is not that maddening? . . . Do drive up here some morning. I am dying to have an Indian talk with you."

When, two days after Christmas, Co still hadn't come to see her, she wrote again, telling him she had his gift for the holidays —the *Rubaiyat* with Vedder's drawings—worth his climbing the hill if he came for no other reason. "I am walking better," she said, "—can take a few steps with canes, instead of crutches—and do most of my hobbling in my room with only one crutch." She anticipated that in about six months she would be able to walk fairly well.

Before the New Year of 1885 came around. Helen had already received some personal congratulations for *Ramona* from her friends. They had read the book in serial form and sent words of praise to her. The Colonel had been the first; he had written that it was "the best novel written by a woman since George Eliot" and quoted in his letter a remark by an unknown lady reader, "To me it is the most distinctive piece of work we have had in this country since *Uncle Tom's Cabin* and its exquisite style is beyond that classic." And Charles Dudley Warner stated, "*Ramona* is one of the most charming creations of modern fiction."

Pleased as she was with the friendly letters of commendation, she read the reviews in the press with some misgivings. The *New York Times*, in its review of December 7, had asked questions she had often asked herself: "In sustained fiction, will she remain equal to her average? . . . Essayist and verse-maker that she is, will her hand be equally cunning and her brain equally fertile under the strain of a romance of the approved length?"

The major difference in the questioning was that she never thought of *Ramona* as a romance, although the *Times* did. She agreed with the statement that "her efforts to mitigate the hard lot of our Indians has caused her to study very seriously that race, both historically and on their reservations . . ." but she bemoaned the closing suggestion that it was a romance, even though the article praised it as "of the finest type."

But the *New York Daily Tribune* revived her hopes that her true story in the form of a novel would call the attention of the readers to the sorrowful and shameful catalogue of the wrongs and cruelties of the white settlers dealing with the Mission Indians of California. "It is told with dramatic force . . . and still better than any literary excellence is the generous indignation which glows in the impressive pages," Helen read with obvious pleasure. "We do not mean that Mrs. Jackson scolds. Her measured words make us think of the majesty of a prophetess and dread the curse of heaven upon the spoilers of the helpless."

But most of the reviews disturbed Helen and, after reading the January issues of the *Atlantic* and the *Nation*, she wrote Mr. Warner, "Not one word for the Indians; I put my heart and soul in the book for them. It is a dead failure." Only the *Tribune*— and Mr. Warner—seemed to her to care "a strand for the Indian history in it." It was a disheartening thought.

She had so wanted the story, as she had written Roberts Brothers for the item in the *Publishers' Weekly*, "to depict the injustices the Indians suffer at the hands of our government and the terrible persecutions they encounter from the white race." And she had expected more from her readers than they could give. She could never accept the fact that for many the story would appeal only as a romance, another Virginia and Paul, as the *Times* had indicated, a tender love story of Ramona and Alessandro in early Spanish-Mexican California.

Helen felt quite sure that California critics would have even stronger negative reactions. Nor was she mistaken, though even she was amazed at the angry tone of many, especially of the San

Diegans, who thought the account of the half-breed Indian completely one-sided. Perhaps in time the real meaning of her novel would work for the good of the Indians; for the present she would have to wait. But she would continue her writing for them.

During late January, the winter rains aggravated her condition but she managed to drive out every day in spite of rain and wind. Almost every sunny afternoon she went in an open carriage with Effie. Often they drove to Santa Monica "on roads where larks sing and flowers are in bloom." It was a drive of eighteen miles to the seaside, a long stretch of bluffs.

People in Los Angeles in the 1880s made buggy excursions to this beach for swimming, for beach bonfires at night, and on Saturdays for dances in the big tent. But for Helen it was a place of beauty, a place to sun herself and enjoy the breezes off the ocean front. In a letter to Emily that February, written at "Santa Monica By the Sea," she told of her joy in the seaside spot, "green to the edge of the cliffs, flowers blooming and choruses of birds, all winter.

From her bed at the Whipples, Helen imagined she was looking straight toward Japan—over a silver sea, even though in the foreground she saw only a strip of grass and mallows and a row of eucalyptus trees. Emily took up the fantasy, in her answer, "That you glance at Japan as you breakfast, not in the least surprises me, thronged only with Music, like the Decks of Birds."

She praised Helen's book with the telling force of simplicity, "Pity me, however, I have finished *Ramona*. Would that like Shakespeare, it were just published." It is not difficult to imagine Helen's pleasure in this letter from Emily. The reviews in the press might bother her and still nag at her, but she would consider Emily's "pity me" her highest praise always.

In March, Los Angeles had several dreary and rainy days that not only prevented Helen's sunning, but also made her rooms seem even more chill and damp. A slight fever, similar to the one she had had in Rome, added to her fear of an atttack of malaria. At last, certain that she had "malarial poisoning," she grew restive and increasingly disturbed. She finally decided to try the warmer coast climate of Long Beach, some thirty miles south. Perhaps the location in San Pedro Bay would bring improvement.

She stayed there a week, but when she grew no better, returned disheartened to Mrs. Whipple's. Day after day she lost weight, unable to keep food on her stomach. She lost forty pounds, and her face became yellow and wan. "Nothing ever before so utterly upset me," she wrote Mr. Kinney, but her letters to Will gave no indication of the seriousness of her condition. If he realized it at all, he was far too busy with his own life and the receivership of the Rio Grande to leave the Springs. His absence, he had told Helen earlier, would mean risking the fortunes of hundreds of common people. As receiver, he was administering an important trust.

Unwilling to stay longer in Los Angeles, Helen learned through her doctor there of another homeopathic physician in San Francisco and arranged to make the trip up by train. She went, she said, "for the benefit of better medical advice and more comfort, if possible." Her faith in homeopathy was as absolute as ever. Miss Sara Thibault of San Francisco, a friend of Sarah Woolsey's, was able to locate rooms for her at the corner of Sutter and Leavenworth Streets—801 Leavenworth.

It was a sad parting for everyone. Everybody cried as the good-bys were said at the Los Angeles station. The Coronels embraced Helen in the Spanish fashion and, with a half sob, Don Antonio put his arms around her, sighing, "Excuse me, I must." Even her driver stood speechless, his eyes full of tears. Only Helen didn't cry. Knowing that none of them expected to see her alive again, she put forth her "last shred of nerve energy" to prove them wrong.

A slight improvement gratified her San Francisco doctor, Dr. A. T. Boericke,[3] a young European-trained homeopath. Helen liked him at once and felt certain that, with his pills, he could bring her back to health. She even started writing again, and he had a writing table made for her similar to the one she had had at the Coronels. One morning when she called, she handed him a poem, "A Rose Leaf on a Snowy Deck," as though it had been a rose she had just picked for him. He bowed graciously as he took it and they both laughed gaily.

She continued to write regularly to Will and may have wondered why he couldn't make the trip West to see her if only for a few days. He had been in New York in December. She blamed herself at times when she thought of the angry words they had written to each other in January. Will had sent her a copy of the January third issue of the *Journalist*, pointing out an article about her titled, "A Famous Literary Woman," and had accused her of talking too freely to a newspaper correspondent. He was upset that she had made biting criticisms of several outstanding writers, including William Henry Bishop, whom she called "a most slovenly workman." But she imagined he was most annoyed that he himself was mentioned in the article.

For the first time in a letter, Helen upbraided him for having supposed she would open her mouth to anyone she knew was a journalist. Actually, Helen had considered Miss Helen Bartlett merely an eager audience and a young aspirant who had chatted with her several times as Helen took her daily sun bath on the porch. She didn't find out until after the article appeared that Miss Bartlett was indeed a full-fledged correspondent for the *Milwaukee Sentinel*. Helen never forgave her and wrote an attack about her "bad faith," both to the *Sentinel* and the *Milwaukee Sunday Telegraph*.

In early April, Helen had a relapse. The writing table had to be put aside. Though the malarial symptoms and fever soon disappeared, she was exhausted and had what she called "nervous prostration." She could sit up only long enough to have her bed made, and nothing would stay on her stomach but heated milk and gruel.

At last, in mid-April, realizing she might not recover and that if she did she would have to remain in bed for a very long time, she asked to be moved to a higher location where she could see beyond the trees to the ocean. Fortunately, a Mrs. Helena Chevers at 1600 Taylor Street on Russian Hill had rooms for her and Effie. Though the house was at the foot of the street on the southeastern slope of the hill, the ground fell away behind it so that Helen said, "I was on the ground floor and yet in the second story."

Tall windows faced the south and west, overlooking Telegraph Hill, the waterfront, and the broad and beautiful bay. On first seeing the rooms—the large parlors, dressing rooms and adjoining bath, and a balcony off the bedroom, all tastefully furnished—Helen commented, "I did not imagine it was so pleasant! What a beautiful place to die in." From her rosewood bed she could see past Goat Island, with its rocky outlines to "where Oakland and Berkeley nestle at the base of the purple Contra Costa hills."

"But no reading or writing," prescribed Dr. Boericke.

"I shall not read if you insist," Helen acquiesced, "but I must write. I can't just lie here in bed and have my friends and Mr. Jackson think I have forgotten them."

She sat up for short periods of time, feeling somewhat better again. She started an Indian story for children and continued her correspondence with Mr. Kinney and Mary Sheriff on matters concerning the Saboba Indians. She even persuaded the doctor to permit her to interview Charles Painter, an agent of the Indian Rights Association: She thought she might influence him to work for the appointment and support of competent Indian agents for California.

A correspondence with J. B. Gilder drained her energies more than she liked to admit. Contrary to her wishes, J. B. had printed in the April *Critic*, under the heading "Authors at Home," an article titled, "Mrs. Jackson (H. H.) at Colorado Springs," by Alice W. Rollins.

"The cruel and idiotic hurt of this picture of me and my life there without my husband," Helen complained angrily. For Mrs. Rollins had not once mentioned Mr. Jackson, and Helen knew that if it hadn't been for her husband, Mrs. Rollins would not have set foot inside their home. "I tried to prevent her from visiting me, but Mr. Jackson would not hear of it," she told J. B. It was his hospitality, not hers, that Mrs. Rollins had enjoyed.

"You can make reparation," she demanded, "by omitting the Rollins article from appearing in her book." When he hedged, she begged him, using her illness to move him. In May he gave a firm promise. "I can die in peace," she wrote in gratitude.

Often, as Helen lay looking out across San Francisco Bay, she recalled her first California trip with Sally and thought back to the pleasures of Yosemite and the High Sierras. Would a trip to the mountains, sleeping out at night under the stars and breathing the pure air of the forests, cure her? Hadn't Dr. Boericke said that in six weeks she might be strong enough to be laid on a bed in a wagon and drawn about?

"If the experiment doesn't kill me," she told him, "I believe it will cure me. I shall go as a gamester throws his last card."

And who better to help her arrange an itinerary but John Muir,[4] who lived nearby in Martinez? On June 8, Helen wrote both Mr. Muir and Jeanne Carr. She asked Jeanne if she would give her a letter of introduction to Mr. Muir. Though she didn't know John Muir personally, she had heard of him from the Carrs, who had sponsored him in his undergraduate years at the University of Wisconsin.

Instead, Jeanne proposed camping in San Gabriel Valley, but

Helen's reply was completely negative: "I can't eat corned beef. . . . I can't abide dirt, disorder, irregularities of hours, discomfort. . . ." She told how she had spent many a day camping in Colorado but had always "abhorred it." All she wanted was hints as to regions "where moisture and shade could be got." And that wasn't the San Gabriel Valley. She'd as soon go to the Sahara.

The correspondence with Mr. Muir proved more satisfying. She believed she had read every word he had written. "I never wished myself a man but once," she wrote him about his "A Wind Storm in the Forest of Yuba, "and that was when I read how it seemed to be rocked in the top of a pine tree in a gale."

At the time Helen wrote, she couldn't sit up more than ten minutes at a time and took "teaspoonfuls of food," mainly frozen custard. She felt so hot that on occasion she longed for the sound of rain and thought of the joy it would be to lie for days in the fine spray of a waterfall. "I know with certainty of instinct," she said, "that nothing except three months out of doors day and night will get this poison out of my veins." And she listed what was needed: eight horses, a wagon for herself, two camp wagons for tents and supplies, a phaeton for her maid Effie, a doctor, and four servants.

"What an outfit you are to have," Mr. Muir noted. "Terrible as an army with banners. I scarce dare think of it. What will my poor Douglas squirrels say at the sight?"

Then he replied with kindness, listing possible routes they could take—to Northern Sierra, King's River, Yosemite, Truckee or Tahoe; "But go to the mountains . . . and God's sky will bend down about you as if made for you alone, and the pines will spread their healing arms about you and bless you and make you well again, and so delight the heart of John Muir."

His letter gave Helen courage, and she made a valiant effort to sit up in the wheelchair. But complete prostration followed.

She was forced to give up her "camping air-castle." Dr. Boericke was forced to tell her there was no chance of her being
strong enough to go by the first of August and it would be too
cold in September.

She wrote John Muir, "If only you could see me, you would
wonder that I have the courage to even dream of such an expedition. . . . They tell me Martinez is only twenty miles away. Do
you ever come to town? The regret I should weakly feel at
having you see the 'remains' of me would, I think, be small in
comparison with the pleasure . . . in seeing you."

By strange coincidence, John Muir was ringing her doorbell
at the very hour of Helen's death of cancer on August 12, 1885.
The shades were drawn and no one answered the bell. "Mrs.
Jackson may have gone somewhere," Muir told his wife Louisa.

Ten days before, Will had finally arrived from Colorado, but
only at the request of the doctor. It was Helen's wish that this
be the arrangement, and she made the doctor promise not to send
for her husband until it was absolutely necessary. When he told
her that he had sent the telegraph, she finished her letter to Sally:
"My work is done. I believe that I have now got everything
written out that I can possibly arrange for anybody."

Finale

DURING THE LAST OF JULY, Helen had come to terms with the full reality of her condition. She ordered most of her library sent to Sarah Woolsey, and, to her sister Annie and family, some boxes of personal belongings. Special gifts were mailed off to her niece Helen Banfield, to Jennie Abbott Johnson, and to Mary Sheriff. For Effie, she had written out cards with directions for the distribution of her various articles at home in the Springs, and, last of all, she requested Sara Thibault to burn all her manuscripts and letters in her room.

To Thomas Niles of Roberts Brothers she had sent on August 7 her unfinished manuscript of *Zeph*, a story of humble life in the West. She closed her note by saying, "I shall look in on you in your new rooms, be sure—but you won't see me."

Not long before her death, according to Mr. Hamilton W. Mabie, she had written, "As I lie here, nothing looks to me of any value except the words I have spoken for the Indians."

She had already written her final words to Colonel Higginson, telling him again of her faith in her work for the Indians. "My *Century of Dishonor* and *Ramona* are the only things I have done for which I am glad now. The rest is of no moment. They will live on and they will bear fruit. They already have."

To Mary Sheriff she had said in her letter of July 17, "Hope has not yet died in my heart, though the time is very long, and bad men are in greater numbers in the Grand Council at Washington."

Her last letter went to Grover Cleveland, President of the United States, on August 8, spelling out the meaning of her long crusade waged for the American Indian. "I ask you to read my *Century of Dishonor*. I am dying happier in the belief I have that it is your hand that is destined to strike the first steady blow toward lifting the burden of infamy from our country and righting the wrongs of the Indian race. . . ."

In keeping with her request in a letter to Will, Helen Hunt Jackson was buried in her "private park" [1] beneath a cairn of stones on the northern slope of Cheyenne Mountain within the sound of Seven Falls. When she was laid to rest on the last day of October, the ground was covered with a soft carpet of pine needles and trailing kinnikinnick.

In the late summer, Mr. Jackson had received an unexpected message from Emily Dickinson of Amherst, Massachusetts: "Helen of Troy will die, but Helen of Colorado, never. 'Dear friend, can you walk' were the last words I wrote her—'Dear friend, I can fly'—her immortal reply."

APPENDIX

Notes

Chapter One

1 A letter written by Helen's father, Nathan Welby Fiske, to Aunt Martha Vinal, dated October 15, 1830, sets as the birth date of Helen Maria Fiske October 14, a little before midnight. The letter was located in the Jackson collection by Jay Leyda.

Chapter Two

1 Originally a boys' academy, chartered in 1816, Amherst became coeducational in 1839, and remained so for several years.
2 Incorporated in 1821, chiefly for boys, Hopkins Academy, Hadley, Mass., was coeducational in the 1840s.
3 The Pittsfield Seminary was known as the Female Seminary for Young Ladies. It was run by the Reverend Mr. Wellington Tyler, whose brother William Seymour Tyler was Professor of Latin and Greek on the Amherst College faculty.
4 The name of this coeducational academy was changed from Falmouth to Lawrence on January 17, 1847, as the result of Shubael Lawrence's legacy of ten thousand dollars.
5 According to Emily Dickinson's sister Lavinia, Emily called Helen "prodigal H.," for her failure to correspond regularly.

Chapter Four

1 The American Association for the Advancement of Science held its sixth meeting in Albany, N.Y., August 19–24. The Governor of New York State, the Honorable Washington Hunt, brother of

Edward Bissell Hunt, entertained the Association at his Mansion, Monday, August 19.

2 Authority for the meeting of Edward Hunt and Helen Fiske at the "Governor's Ball" came from Ruth Davenport, daughter of Helen's niece, Ann Fiske Banfield (Mrs. William Church Davenport), according to Ruth Odell.

3 Lucy was the oldest daughter of the Reverend and Mrs. Julius Palmer of Boston, and niece of the Reverend Ray Palmer of Albany.

Chapter Six

1 A letter written by Edward Hunt to Mrs. Ray Palmer on December 2, 1885, places the birth of Warren Horsford Hunt (Rennie) on December 2, not December 1, as recorded in the Bureau of Vital Statistics in Providence, R.I. By error, his tombstone at West Point reads December 2, *1857*.

Chapter Nine

1 Thomas Wentworth Higginson knew Emily Dickinson only through correspondence, which began in April 15, 1862, until he finally met her when he called at the Main Street home in Amherst, Mass., August 19, 1870.

2 The Northampton meeting Helen attended as a reporter was that of the National Academy of Sciences, not the American Association for the Advancement of Science. This Academy was entered by an act of Congress, August 25, 1868, originally approved in 1863 by President Lincoln.

Chapter Ten

1 Charlotte Cushman (July 23, 1816-February 17, 1876) was born in Boston, Mass., but lived much of her life abroad. She was one of the most powerful actresses of the nineteenth century, excelling in melodramatic and tragic roles.

2 Dr. Holland, in charge of the *Republican*'s Cultural Department, persuaded Emily to give him three of her poems in all, but altered them so to the point of rhyme and metrical exactness that Emily could not be blamed if she failed to accept them as her own.

Chapter Eleven

1 Sarah Woolsey's younger sister Jane had already written stories under the pen name of Margaret Coolidge, and in 1870 she had printed anonymously *Hospital Days* for private use.

2 Of the letters Helen sent home from Europe, one set, to a Circle of Friends (also referred to as Letters from Abroad) was not included in the encyclicals, in *Bits of Travel*. These letters, which Colonel Higginson identified as written for Helen's friends Miss Sarah Woolsey, Colonel G. E. Waring, and others, include a good deal more familiar material than the *Encyclicals*. They are in the Aldis collection of Yale University Library.

3 Charles Dudley Warner (September 12, 1829-October 20, 1900), editor and author, joined the *Hartford Evening Press* (later the *Courant*) in 1860 and became its editor. He collaborated with Mark Twain in the *Gilded Age*, published in 1873. Helen's friendship through correspondence led to two visits of the Jacksons to Nook Farm, the Warners' home in Hartford, Connecticut.

4 Kate Field (October 1, 1838-May 19, 1896) wrote for the *Boston Post* as "Straw Junior" and published under the pen name of Fanny Fern. A lecturer, a faddist, and a "cause" woman, she had offended Helen by charging she had been a "spendthrift of brains" in writing her encyclicals.

Chapter Twelve

1 The Hunts first met the Benhams in Washington, D.C., where Captain Henry W. Benham was the assistant in charge of the U.S. Coast Survey Office, 1853–1856. Mrs. Elizabeth Benham renewed the friendship in Boston after the Captain was placed in command of Boston Harbor, June, 1865.

2 According to Colonel Higginson, Mrs. Guild was the wife of the Reverend *Edward* Guild of Boston. By error, the *Springfield Republican* called her Mrs. *Charles* Guild.

Chapter Thirteen

1 Mrs. Sara Jane (Clarke) Lippincott (September 23, 1825-April 20, 1904) wrote under the pseudonym of Grace Greenwood. In

1871 she traveled west to visit her relatives, the Mellens, at Glen Eyrie and, falling in love with Colorado, had a small cottage built for her in Manitou.

Chapter Fourteen

1 Gerald and Marcellin de Coursey, twins, both Springs pioneers, were members of General Palmer's famous Fifteenth Pennsylvania during the Civil War. According to Marshall Sprague, Helen Hunt took buggy rides to Cheyenne Mountain with Gerald, who had a wife at that time.

2 R. W. Grannis and William S. Stratton were partners in the Grannis and Stratton firm, Contractors, Carpenters and Builders, located on Pikes Peak near Nevada Avenue. Grannis, who had purchased the "red lot" on the northeast corner of Weber and Kiowa Streets, built a house there that Mr. Jackson bought two years later "to live in with his bride," according to Frank Waters in the *Midas of the Rockies*.

Chapter Fifteen

1 Search for the marriage announcement of Helen Hunt to William Sharpless Jackson in New Hampshire and Wolfeboro records was unsuccessful. The placement of the wedding service at Helen's sister's home in Wolfeboro was made in *Portrait and Biographical Record of the State of Colorado, 1899*. It was personally verified by Helen Jackson, the grandniece of Helen Hunt Jackson and daughter of Helen Banfield Jackson.

Chapter Sixteen

1 The widow of Prof. Aaron Warner, Mary had been ill for some time. She had recently had a serious operation, probably for cancer. She died in 1877.

2 The kinnikinnick is an Indian name for the vine often called the "bearberry." Green and glossy all year, it grows in long trailing wreaths or in tangled mats, with berries in scarlet clusters.

Chapter Seventeen

1   The authority for ascribing the authorship of two children's
books published by a bookseller of Amherst, Mass., John S.
Adams, is the *Amherst Imprints* by Newton S. McKeon and Kath-
erine C. Cowles, 1946, of the Robert Frost Library, Amherst
College. Roorbach's *Bibliotheca americana, 1820–1861*, lists Prof.
A. Fiske as the author of *Alec*, but Newton changed the A. to
Nathan and states that Nathan Fiske's authorship is explicitly
stated in an anonymous volume, *Annals of Amherst College . . .*
Northampton, 1860, p. 20.

Chapter Nineteen

1   Helen's controversy over the case of the Poncas with Carl Schurz
was a bitter one, appearing in the press, partly in the *Tribune* and
partly in the *Boston Advertiser*. Afterwards the entire correspondence was published in the 1883 version of *A Century of Dishonor*,
together with that of Mr. Byers'.

Chapter Twenty

1   *Ploughed Under* was written by the son of J. J. Harsha, a member of the Omaha Ponca Committee, with an introduction by
Bright Eyes. Helen hesitated to say anything to offend the author,
whom she admired for his courageous writings.
2   Secularization meant the freedom of the church from the control
or help of the state. A Secularization Act, passed on August 17,
1833, gave the Indians freedom from Mission supervision. It also
made possible the division of property to provide for the services
of the church, the support of the padres, and the colonization of
California. The result was unexpected disaster, and, under Governor Alvarado's rule from 1836–1842, one of plunder and ruin
for the missions. The Mission establishment became the object of
legalized pillage.

Chapter Twenty-one

1   In March of 1881, Helen secured letters of introduction for herself and her husband to persons who might assist in her California

trip. Although she used these letters, there is no evidence that Jackson ever went to Los Angeles or San Diego with her.

Chapter Twenty-three

1 Señor José Antonio Estudillo protected the rights of Indians on his property, but after his death, his many heirs began selling unlocated claims whenever they needed money. The Surveyor General in San Francisco, however, said there was no clause protecting the Indians on the land. Some individuals bought from the Estudillo heirs and evicted Indians on the site.

Chapter Twenty-four

1 There is considerable difference of opinion about the date and place of the sheep-shearing incident. This reference is taken from Helen Hunt's own account in "Outdoor Industries in California," in which she describes the large sheep ranch at Baldwin's in La Puenta.

2 Margaret V. Allan, in a small booklet published in 1914, *Ramona's Homeland*, describes Mrs. Whipple's boardinghouse, but misdates the time by two years. Helen was first there in the spring of 1883, not the fall of 1881.

3 Captain J. G. Stanley was a former Indian agent in Southern California and had made many friendly contacts with the desert Indians around Agua Caliente.

4 Helen Fiske Banfield, niece of Helen Hunt Jackson, graduated from Vassar in June, 1879. Never really well after that time, she finally went to Colorado for her health in 1883–1884, November to March, the winter her aunt was in New York writing *Ramona*. Though Marshall Sprague places her in Colorado Springs the following winter while Helen was in California, no evidence of this visit could be located in letters, journals, or other documents, including her obituary in the *Gazette*.

Chapter Twenty-five

1 Many claims were made by the people of California saying they knew the original Ramona and Alessandro. Though the characters suggest certain living persons, all evidence points to the statement

in James's *Through Ramona's Country* that Ramona was "a structure composed of fact and fiction; there was no real Ramona."

Chapter Twenty-six

1 Spaniards and Mexicans, besides using the artichoke for food,
often made wreaths of them for the statues of saints.
2 The first copy of *Ramona* was presented to the Coronels. Although many have claimed that Helen carefully marked in one
copy all the passages contributed by Mrs. Carr, this copy has
never been located. The possibility of Mrs. Carr's having written
any of Helen's book is most unlikely and highly improbable.
None of Mrs. Carr's writings gives any indication of the same
style or form.
3 Dr. A. T. Boericke of San Francisco was at that time an outstanding physician trained in Germany.
4 John Muir (April 12, 1838-December 24, 1914), American natu-
ralist and explorer, came to America with his father from Scotland
in 1849. After a special course of four years at the University of
Wisconsin, he began his journeys to Canada and Western United
States, and for six years made his main camp at Yosemite. To support himself, he wrote for newspapers and magazines, many of
which caught Helen's attention.

Finale

1 The private park above South Cheyenne Falls was on land owned
by the James Hull family. When, in 1891, Mrs. Hull began charging tourists ten cents to visit the grave with its huge pile of stones,
Jackson tried to buy the plot but was unable to come to terms
with the owners. The following year, he had the remains removed
to Evergreen Cemetery in the Springs. The grave, a raised vault-
length slab of dark stone, is in the old part of the cemetery in the
large Jackson plot. It is marked simply, "Helen, wife of Wm. S.
Jackson, died August 12, 1885."

Selected Books About

HELEN HUNT JACKSON

And Her Times

Allen, Margaret V., *Ramona's Homeland*. San Diego, privately published, 1914.

Bade, William Frederic, *Life and Letters of John Muir*. Boston and New York: Houghton, Mifflin and Co., 1924.

Bishop, Isabelle Lucy (Bird), *A Lady's Life in the Rocky Mountains*. New York: G. P. Putnam's Sons, 1879.

Bolles, Rev. Simeon, *The Early History of the Town of Bethlehem, New Hampshire*. Woodsville, N.H.: Enterprise Printing House, 1883.

Botta, Vicenzo, Ed., *Memoirs of Anne C. L. Botta*, written by her friends with selections from her correspondence and from her writings in prose and poetry. New York: Selwin Tait and Sons, 1893.

Bowles, Samuel, *Our New West*: Records of travel between the Mississippi River and the Pacific Ocean. Hartford: Hartford Publishing Co., 1869.

Bradley, Glen Danford, *The Story of the Santa Fe*. Boston: The Gorham Press, 1920.

Buckman, George Rex, *Colorado Springs, Colorado and Its Famous Scenic Environs*. New York: Trow Prin, 1893.

Carpenter, Edward Wilton and Morehouse, Charles Frederick, *The History of the Town of Amherst, 1731–1896*. Amherst: Press of Carpenter and Morehouse, 1896.

Conway, Moncure Daniel, *Autobiography, Memories and Experiences*. Riverside Press, Cambridge, Mass.: Houghton, Mifflin and Co., 1904.

Cullum, George W., *Biographical Register of the Officers and Graduates of the U.S. Military Academy at West Point, New York*; from its establishment, March 16, 1802 to the army reorganization of 1866–67, vol. 2. New York: D. Van Nostrand Co., Inc., 1868.

Dana, Arnold G., Ed., *Pictorial New Haven, Old and New*: its homes, institutions, activities, etc. New Haven: New Haven Colony Historical Society, 1883.

Davis, Carlyle Channing and Alderson, William A., *The True Story of Ramona*: its facts and fictions, inspiration and purpose. New York: Dodge Publishing Co., 1914.

Davis, William Heath, *Seventy-Five Years in California*. San Francisco: John Howell, 1929.

Davis, Francis S., *Town of Roxbury*: its memorable persons and places, its history and antiquities with numerous illustrations of its old landmarks and noted personages. Boston: Municipal Printing Office, 1905.

Dupuy, Richard Ernest, *Men of West Point*: the first hundred and fifty years of the U.S. Military Academy. New York: Sloane, 1951.

Elliott, Maude Howe, *This Was My Newport*. A. Marshall Jones, Cambridge, Mass., Mythology Co., 1944.

Ellis, Amanda M., *The Colorado Springs Story*. (pamphlet) Colorado Springs: The Dentan Printing Co., 1954.

Elphick, Robert, Ed., *Falmouth Past and Present*. (pamphlet) Falmouth: Kendall Printing Co., n.d.

Encyclopedia of Biography of Colorado, vol. 1. Chicago: Century Publishing and Engraving Co., 1901.

Hafen, Leroy R., *Colorado: The Story of a Western Commonwealth*. Denver: Peerless Publishing Co., 1933.

Higginson, Thomas W., *Carlyle's Laugh and Other Surprises*. Boston: Houghton, Mifflin and Co., 1909.

Higginson, Thomas W., *Contemporaries*. Boston: Houghton, Mifflin and Co., 1899.

Higginson, Thomas W., *Oldport Days*. Boston: James R. Osgood and Co., 1873.

Higginson, Mary Thacher, *Thomas Wentworth Higginson; The Story of His Life*. Boston: Houghton, Mifflin and Co., 1914.

Hill, John J., *Reminiscences of Albany*. New York: Medole and Son, 1884.

Humphrey, Heman, *Memoirs of Rev. Nathan W. Fiske, Professor of Intellectual and Moral Philosophy in Amherst College*: together with selections from his sermons and other writings. Amherst: J. S. and C. Adams, 1850.

Hunnewell, James F., *A Century of Town Life, A History of Charlestown, Massachusetts, 1775–1887*, with surveys, records, and twenty-eight pages of places and views. Boston: Little, Brown and Co., 1888.

James, George Wharton, *In and Out of the Old Missions of California*; an historical and pictorial account of the Franciscan Missions. Boston: Little, Brown and Co., 1912.

James, George Wharton, *Through Ramona's Country*. Boston: Little, Brown and Co., 1909.

Johnson, Frances Ann, *Mount Washington Carriage Road since 1861*. Littleton, N.H.: The Courier Printing Co., 1961.

Johnson, Thomas H., *Emily Dickinson: An Interpretive Biography*. The Belknap Press, Cambridge, Mass., Harvard University, 1955.

Kingsley, Rose Georgina, *South by West, or Winter in the Rocky Mountains and Spring in Mexico*. London: W. Isbister and Co., 1874.

Ladd, Horatio Oliver, *A Memorial of John S. C. Abbott, D.D. . . .* Boston: A. William and Co., 1878.

Leonowens, Anna Harriette (Crawford), *The English Governess at the Siamese Court*. Boston: Fields, Osgood and Co., 1873.

Leyda, Jay, *The Years and Hours of Emily Dickinson*. New Haven: Yale University Press, 1960.

Madison, Charles A., *Book Publishing in America*. New York: McGraw-Hill Co., 1966.

Manypenny, George W., *Our Indian Wards*. Cincinnati: Robert Clarke Co., 1880.

A Masque of Poets, No Name Series, vol. 13. Boston: Roberts Brothers, 1878.

Merriam, George Spring, *The Life and Times of Samuel Bowles*. New York: The Century Co., 1885.

National Academy of Sciences, Annuals. Cambridge, Mass.: Welch, Bigelow and Co., 1865.

National Academy of Sciences, Biographical Memoirs, vol. 3. Washington, published by the Academy, 1895.

Odell, Ruth, *Helen Hunt Jackson ("H. H.")*. New York: D. Appleton-Century, 1939.

Ormes, Manly Dayton and Eleanor R., *The Book of Colorado Springs*. Colorado Springs: The Dentan Printing Co., 1933.

Osterweis, Rollins C., *Three Centuries of New Haven, 1638–1938*. New Haven: Yale University Press, 1953.

Parker, Benjamin Franklin, *History of Wolfeborough, New Hampshire*. Wolfeboro, N.H., published by the town, 1901.

Pierce, Frederick Clifton, *Fiske and Fisk Family*. Chicago: W. B. Conkey Co., 1896.

Portrait and Biographical Record of the State of Colorado: containing portraits and biographies of many well-known citizens of the past and present. Chicago: Chapman Publishing Co., 1899.

Proceedings of the American Association for the Advancement of Science, vols. 6–15. Published in places where the meeting is held, 1851–1860.

Riegel, Robert Edgar, *The Story of the Western Railroads.* New York: MacMillan Co., 1926.

Saunders, Charles Francis, *The Story of Carmelita: Its Associations and Its Trees.* (pamphlet) Pasadena: A. C. Vroman, Inc., 1928.

Semi-Centennial History of the State of Colorado. Chicago: The Lewis Publishing Co., 1913.

Shepard, Odell, Ed., *The Journals of Bronson Alcott.* Port Washington, New York: Kennikat Press, Inc., 1966.

Sprague, Marshall, *Newport in the Rockies: The Life and Good Times of Colorado Springs.* Chicago: The Swallow Press, 1961.

Stebbins, Emma, Ed., *Charlotte Cushman: Her Letters and Memories of Her Life.* Boston: Houghton, Mifflin and Co., 1878.

Taylor, Hattie Whitcomb, *Early History of the Town of Bethlehem, N.H.* (pamphlet) Bethlehem, N.H. private publication, 1960.

Thompson, A. C., *Rev. Henry B. Hooker, D.D.: A Memorial Sketch.* (pamphlet) Boston: Congregational Publishing Society, 1881.

Tibbles, Thomas Henry, *Buckskin and Blankets Days:* Memoirs of a Friend of the Indians. Lincoln, Nebraska: University of Nebraska Press, 1905.

Ticknor, Caroline, *May Alcott, A Memoir.* Boston: Little, Brown and Co., 1928.

Tyler, William Seymour, *History of Amherst College during the First Five Presidents from 1821–1891.* New York: Frederick H. Hitchcock, 1895.

Vroman, Adam Clark and Barnes, T. F., *The Genesis of the Story of Ramona, Why the Book was Written, Explanatory Text of Points of Interest Mentioned in the Story,* with thirty illustrations from original photographs by A. C. Vroman and T. F. Barnes. Los Angeles: Press of Kingsley-Barnes and Neuner Co., 1899.

Waters, Frank, *Midas of the Rockies: the Story of Stratton and Cripple Creek.* New York: Covici Friede Publishers, 1937.

Wilson, Rufus Rockwell, *New York, Old and New;* its story, streets, and landmarks. Philadelphia and London: J. B. Lippincott Co., 1902.

Selected Books by
HELEN HUNT JACKSON

MANY OF Helen Hunt Jackson's poetry and prose articles appeared originally in newspapers and magazines, the *New York Evening Post*, the *New York Independent*, *Atlantic Monthly*, *Scribner's*, *St. Nicholas* and *Youth's Companion* among them. For many of these she wrote extensively, and, except for a few items, mostly anonymous book reviews, the author located the references to gain background for her biography. Several collections, mainly of her travels, however, were made of her writings and published in book form, both during her lifetime and afterwards. Of the books she published, the following, in the editions listed, were particularly useful in the preparation of this book.

Bits of Talk about Home Matters. Boston: Roberts Brothers, 1889.
Bits of Talk in Verse and Prose for Young Folks. Boston: Roberts Brothers, 1876.
Bits of Travel. Boston: Roberts Brothers, 1876.
Bits of Travel at Home. Boston: Roberts Brothers, 1887.
A Century of Dishonor: A Sketch of the United States Government's Dealings with Some of the Indian Tribes. New York: Harper and Brothers, 1881.
Glimpses of Three Coasts. Boston: Roberts Brothers, 1887.
Hetty's Strange History. No Name Series, 1, no. 8. Boston: Roberts Brothers, 1877.
Hunter Cats of Connorloa. Boston: Roberts Brothers, 1884.
Letters from a Cat. Boston: Roberts Brothers, 1879.

Mercy Philbrick's Choice. No Name Series, 1, no. 1. Boston: Roberts Brothers, 1876.

Nelly's Silver Mine: A Story of Colorado Life. Boston: Roberts Brothers, 1893.

Poems. Boston: Roberts Brothers, 1892.

Report on the Conditions and Needs of Mission Indians, joint report with Abbott Kinney. Boston: Roberts Brothers, 1886.

Ramona; A Story. Boston: Roberts Brothers, 1885.

Saxe Holm's Stories, First Series. New York: Charles Scribner's Sons, 1901.

Saxe Holm's Stories, Second Series. New York: Charles Scribner's Sons, 1890.

Verses. Boston: Fields, Osgood and Co., 1870.

Selected List of

HELEN HUNT JACKSON'S

Publications in Periodicals

Title	Date	Periodical
Mountain Life: the New Hampshire Town of Bethlehem	October 20, 1865	Post
In the White Mountains	September 13, 1866	Independent
A Protest Against the Spread of Civilization	August 29, 1867	Post
The Great Bore in Nova Scotia: A Chase after a Norman Kirtle	November 4, 1867	Post
A Morning in a Vermont Graveyard	November 14, 1867	Post
A Christmas Tree for Cats	January, 1868	Riverside
A New Sleepy Hollow	January 13, 1868	Post
The Basin of Minas and Evangeline's Home	July 2, 1868	Independent
An Out-of-the-Way Place: from Sleepy Hollow to Block Island	August 18, 1868	Post
In and Out of Boston	August 27, 1868	Post
A Bethlehem of Today	June 23, 1870	Independent
A Second Celestial Railway	October 13, 1870	Independent
The Miracle Play of 1870 in Bethlehem, N.H.	December, 1870	Atlantic

A Glimpse of a Country Winter in New Hampshire	January, 1871	Atlantic
A Winter Morning at Colorado Springs	June 25, 1874	Independent
The Grand Canyon of the Arkansas	July 1, 1875	Independent
A Colorado Woman's Museum	October, 1876	St. Nicholas
The Kansas and Colorado Building at the Centennial Exposition	October 12, 1876	Independent
A Dream about Fairies	August, 1877	St. Nicholas
Eden, formerly at the Euphrates	October 9, 16, 23, 1879	Independent
Standing Bear and Bright Eyes	November 20, 1879	Independent
Wards of the U.S. Government	March, 1880	Scribner's
The Naughtiest Day in My Life	September, October, 1880	St. Nicholas
The End of a Century of Dishonor	January 13, 1881	Independent
A Trip into the Gunnison Country	December 29, 1881	Independent
A Mid-Summer's Fete in the Pueblo of San Juan	January, 1882	Atlantic
Estes Park	June 29, July 6, 13, 1882	Christian Union
A Chinese New Year's Day in Santa Barbara	January, 1883	St. Nicholas
By Horse-Cars into Mexico	March, 1883	Atlantic
A Chance Afternoon in California	April 5, 1883	Independent
The Pot of Gold	July 26, 1883	Independent
Christmas in the Pink Boarding House	January, 1884	St. Nicholas
A Short Cut from Icicles to Oranges	February 19, 1885	Christian Union

Index